BLOOD, SWEAT AND TREASON

HENRY OLONGA

MY STORY

To all the peace-loving Zimbabweans who yearn for a better life.

BLOOD, SWEAT AND TREASON

HENRY OLONGA

MY STORY

VSP

Published by Vision Sports Publishing in 2010

Reprinted 2010

Vision Sports Publishing
19–23 High Street
Kingston upon Thames
Surrey
KT1 1LL

www.visionsp.co.uk

ISBN 13: 978-1905326-81-5

A CIP record for this book is available from the British library

Editor: Jim Drewett
Design: Neal Cobourne
Copy editing: Ian Turner
Cover photography: Getty Images
Back cover photography: Reuters

Typeset by Palimpsest Book Production Limited, Falkirk, Stirlingshire

Printed in the UK by CPI William Clowes Beccles NR34 7TL

CONTENTS

FOREWORD BY HENRY BLOFELD ix

ACKNOWLEDGEMENTS

My first thanks go to my God as I have been sustained in great times of trouble.

My thanks go to my wife, Tara, who has had to endured living with a man with so much baggage. Your support is invaluable and thank you for your patience, love and understanding.

Thanks especially go to my parents who made amazing sacrifices to enrich my life and the lives of my brothers and sisters, to my siblings and innumerable relatives scattered across the globe who have been a tremendous support through my life's ups and downs and to the numerous friends, old and new, that I have made over this brief lifetime – thank you for being there. You are all too numerous to mention, especially those on Facebook. Thank you, particularly to those that have been kind enough to forgive me for the times when I have needed grace.

Thanks to all in the Zimbabwe cricket fraternity who continued to take a chance on me even after my disastrous start. Although things ended up somewhat acrimoniously I will always be grateful that so many people gave of their time and resources for my development.

Thanks to the teammates who I played with over the years with whom I had tremendous success and also shared bitter disappointment. As we all came to know, professional sport can be exceedingly cruel but also tremendously rewarding and I am grateful that many of you were willing to share both sides of the coin with me. We bled, sweat and cried with each other, and it was great.

Thanks also must go to all my teachers in the various schools I attended for they have truly shaped me into the man I am. Thanks also to all the former schoolmates who, to this day, I still keep in touch with. I will soldier on in the words of Plumtree School's motto, *Ad definitum finem* (To a definite end).

Thankyou to everyone who has ever shown me any form of kindness whether it be accommodation, a kind word, sharing a meal or buying me an air ticket. I will always remember and endeavour to 'pass it along'.

I would also like to thank the many people who have made this book a possibility. The publishers VSP for taking a chance on me and Derek Clements who worked tirelessly to help me tell my story. There are so many other nameless and faceless individuals to whom I am indebted and if I fail to mention any person or group of people please accept this general thankyou.

Finally to the many passionate and patriotic Zimbabweans out there, thankyou for your love and support and I pray that one day, when the dust has cleared, all Zimbabweans irrespective of colour, creed or tribe will truly be able to call this land 'Our Zimbabwe'. This book is dedicated to anyone who loves the fabulous country that made me who I am.

Thank you the reader for picking this book up, God bless you and I hope you enjoy the story of my life.

Henry Olonga, June 2010

FOREWORD

BY HENRY BLOFELD

In the grasping age in which we live where money and naked power are everything, it is rare to come across a man who is driven by principle alone and even in the most unenviable of circumstances of life and death. This is why it is such a joy for me to be asked to write a foreword to Henry Olonga's autobiography. It must and should be stated in the baldest terms that Henry is a black man who was born and reared under Robert Mugabe's murderous and despicable regime in Zimbabwe and had the guts to stand up and be counted in his opposition to all that goes on in that country.

He was a young man with great talents. The most obvious were an ability to play cricket and to bowl fast which is not given to that many and a singing voice which, when you catch a snatch or two, will have you wondering whether it is Luciano Pavarotti or Placido Domingo who is lurking round the next corner. Even in Mugabe's Zimbabwe, the world was at Henry Olonga's feet.

As a young man he was playing cricket for Zimbabwe with a cricketing future which beckoned with impressive certainty. But Olonga was unable to stomach the atrocities which were being carried out on a daily basis by Mugabe's henchman in his own beloved country. Many of his fellow countrymen disapproved, but were content to stand by and watch. Not Olonga. In 2003 he showed his hand when in Zimbabwe's first World Cup match, against Namibia, he took the field wearing a black armband in protest at the murders, the pillaging, the raping, the stealing of property which was going on all around him and all the other atrocities. He stood admirably with Andy Flower who would later become England's highly successful cricket coach.

This was a shot across the bows for Mugabe and Olonga was forced to leave the country within a few weeks and was almost certainly lucky to escape with his life. The stakes were that high. With a little bit of help from his friends he found his way to England.

My own involvement with Olonga began shortly afterwards when he joined the *Test Match Special* commentary team for the series against Zimbabwe. I immediately found out that Olonga was not only a man of great and unchanging principle, but also a man with a splendid sense of humour – and does anything do more to help you through moments of severe personal crisis more than a sense of humour? – huge common sense, a beguiling and attractive way with words and a great knowledge of the game of cricket. He was that rare thing: a balanced human being,

His progress since then has been remarkable. He would be the first to admit that he has been helped considerably by David Folb who had the genius to found the Lashings World XI which plays cricket all round the country and also in other parts of the world where former and some current Test cricketers are unlikely ever to be seen. Olonga has been important to Folb too, not least in his magnificent singing of Nessun Dorma and other songs during the lunch interval or protracted breaks for rain.

This is a book which must be read. It tells an extraordinary story about one man's beliefs and how he has acted upon them in a way which should be an inspiration to all of us.

We must not forget, too, the huge help and inspiration that Henry himself has been given by his beautiful Australian wife, Tara. Theirs has truly been a team effort.

Henry Blofeld, June 2010

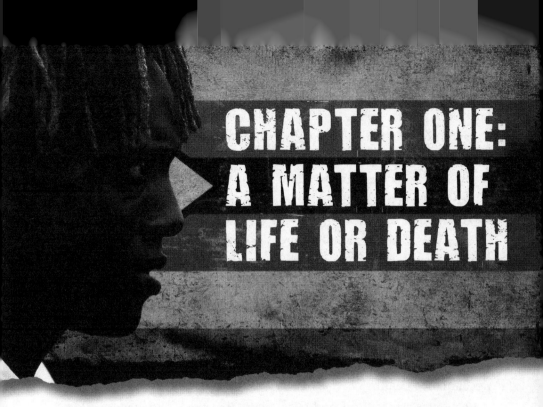

CHAPTER ONE:
A MATTER OF
LIFE OR DEATH

All that is necessary for the triumph of evil is that good men do nothing.
Edmund Burke

"Tell your son that he needs to get out of Zimbabwe before the World Cup ends."

With these words my life in my homeland came to an end. I already knew that the secret police were bugging my phone and I was pretty sure they were following me too. I'd been dropped from the Zimbabwean team and banned from taking to the field even to distribute drinks. I had received death threats by e-mail; I'd been intimidated by members of Mugabe's infamous youth militia and warned that members of the government were seriously displeased. Now my father had received this urgent message from a contact within the central intelligence organisation. It was a warning based on concrete information.

When Andy Flower and I had made our black armband protest a few days earlier at the 2003 World Cup cricket match between Zimbabwe and

Namibia, mourning the death of democracy in our country, I'd been really energised. Over a number of years I had come to know the full extent of Mugabe's atrocities against the Zimbabwean people and to finally take a stand against him had been the biggest challenge of my life. But now I was really concerned, even a little scared.

I knew what could happen to people who crossed Mugabe. I knew that he and his henchmen were alleged to be responsible for the torture, rape and murder of hundreds and thousands of my countrymen. I felt I could be carted away at any minute and never be seen again. I knew there were rumours that people had quite literally disappeared by being thrown into baths of sulphuric acid. Maybe I would just be imprisoned. But Zimbabwean prisons are amongst the worst in the world. They are brutal, disease-ridden places where beatings and rape are part of the daily routine. In a country where one in four people has AIDS, as far as I was concerned prison meant death.

Of course Andy and I had been aware that the consequences of our actions could potentially be life-changing. I had hoped they would not be, but now it was clear to me that my life was in danger. In fact probably the only thing keeping me alive was the presence of foreign journalists covering the World Cup here in Zimbabwe and a watching world. Allowing the presence of the world's press had been a stipulation in awarding Zimbabwe the World Cup, and many of the world's top news reporters had taken the opportunity to gain access to the country and get an insight into what was really going on in our increasingly troubled and controversial nation. But what would happen when they left? I had to get out. But how? Unless I made a run for the border, my only chance was Zimbabwe qualifying for the Super Sixes of the World Cup which were to be held in South Africa. Mugabe's people would never be able to stop me leaving then, it would be too obvious if I didn't turn up for the second round of matches.

OK, so that was all great in theory: there was only one problem. Between me and that flight to Johannesburg and freedom was the small matter of the mighty Pakistan, one of the great teams of the tournament, boasting a host of world-class cricketers including Wasim Akram, Waqar Younis, Saeed Anwar and others. To get to the Super Sixes we needed at least a draw against Pakistan but who draws one day matches? Since they themselves needed a win to stay in the World Cup, to say it wasn't going to be easy would be a massive understatement.

To be honest, in the run-up to the game, cricket was the last thing on my mind. I had been dropped from the team after the black armband protest anyway by the furious officials of the Zimbabwean Cricket Union, as it was called then. I had also received an e-mail from a well-wisher who said a woman who worked in a government minister's office had a warning for me. In it she warned me that the minister had been overheard in his office saying, "This Olonga guy thinks he is so clever. Just wait until after the World Cup is over. He won't be so clever then. We will sort him out." And a few days after the protest I had been speaking on the phone when I'd heard a third voice on the line: they were clearly tapping my calls. I started seeing secret police everywhere. "How long has that car been following us?" "Who's that man lurking in that doorway?" One day in practice in the nets I joked about something and Heath Streak said, "You won't be laughing when they're putting electric shocks through your balls!" Then in the end my father got the message that I needed to get out.

I was in a daze. All sorts of different people were saying all sorts of different things to us – we were going to be charged with treason, warrants were going to be issued for our arrest. Treason? They could call me anything they wanted other than a traitor. We were making a stand for our country's future: how could we be traitors? To this day I don't know if I was ever formally charged with treason, but I do know that the penalty for treason in Zimbabwe is death and that there is no right of appeal. Mugabe has charged many an opponent with treason and very often it is a gruelling process to receive justice.

So why did I do it and how did I get here? The famous quote from Edmund Burke, "All that is necessary for the triumph of evil is that good men do nothing" rang through my mind. I would never call myself a good man but people had to stand up against this evil regime.

During all this time I never once doubted that what we had done was the right thing. I never once regretted the decision to make a stand. In the years leading up to our protest I had read dossiers that told of unspeakable atrocities being carried out in the name of Mugabe and I had spent hundreds, if not thousands, of hours on the Internet trying to get a feel for how the outside world viewed my homeland. I had been brought up to believe that my president was a hero, but the rest of the world viewed him very differently and it had become clear to me that the foreign view was most accurate. That is a pretty dreadful thing to realise about your country and its politicians.

It was this journey of discovery that had led me to the place where I was now, fearing for my life and the lives of my family. On the eve of the Pakistan match I really didn't know what I was going to do, and then I had an encounter in the foyer of the team hotel in Bulawayo that was final confirmation for me that if I didn't get out of the country I really was finished.

As I was preparing to leave for the match, I was chatting to an old friend when a man called Ozias Bvute, a big noise in Zimbabwean cricket, came over and butted in. He was an administrator and had played a key role in the integration taskforce employed to make sure more black players made it into the Zimbabwean team. He was a powerful man in the game. My friend looked him in the eye and said, "Ozias, I know you ZANU-PF guys, and Henry is my friend and I don't want you to mess with him."

ZANU-PF is an extreme political party in much of its ideology. If someone not a member of the party was accused of being one they would surely protest. But Bvute didn't deny he was a member: all he did was laugh. There was something about his laugh: it was cold and heartless. His mouth laughed but his eyes held no humour. He was saying, "Oh no, Henry's a part of our plans for a very long time into the future," but I sensed that he wasn't being honest. If he was ZANU-PF then perhaps he knew that the minister had it in for me as soon as the World Cup was over. The second I heard him laugh I knew my time was up. If there had been the slightest doubt in my mind up to that point, now it was gone. If there was a single defining moment for me, that was probably it. I find it almost impossible to describe how unsettled I was by his insincerity. I knew that I simply had to get out and that I might never be able to come back.

So it came down to our match against Pakistan: my life-or-death game, a game in which I wasn't even going to be playing so I wouldn't even have the opportunity to play the match of a lifetime to save my skin.

The night before the match I was in my hotel room in Bulawayo and I got down on my knees and prayed. "God, I think I heard you on this," I said. "I think this was the right thing to do, to take a stance against this tyrant. I need your help to get out of Zimbabwe." It was a short prayer, simple and to the point. He had helped me before and I believed that if He thought it was right to do so again then He would step in one more time.

Then I went out for dinner with some friends and when I returned to the hotel one of my teammates, Craig Wishart, asked if I had seen the weather forecast. I didn't pay too much attention. Instead I went upstairs to my room and went to sleep. But when I woke up the next morning and turned on the TV weather report, lo and behold a cyclone had built up off the coast of Mozambique.

We got to the ground and although I was not playing I spent my time geeing up the players, telling them they could win this game. *Please win this game!* We bowled 14 overs and had Pakistan 73 for 3, and then it started to rain. From the Queens Ground in Bulawayo it is usually possible to see far into the distance towards a place called Ascot, famous for its racecourse just like the place of the same name in England. There is a huge building at the course that stands out for many miles, but when it rains heavily you can't see it from the cricket ground so it's a good barometer for how likely it is that play will resume soon. I had been keeping my eye on Ascot and it had disappeared. The rain was still falling in Bulawayo. Not too heavy, but enough to stop play. It kept coming in sheets. Wave after wave after wave of this rain kept coming. I kept glancing over in the direction of Ascot, hoping of course that it would not reappear.

As the rain continued and continued, my sense of fear and trepidation lessened and lessened. Mid-afternoon arrived and the umpires announced that they were abandoning the game. The match was a draw. Sensationally, Pakistan were out of the World Cup and we had got the point we needed and were through to the Super Sixes. Within a short time of play being called off for the day, the clouds disappeared and the sun peaked through briefly. Pakistan may have felt they had been undone, but not me. I believed my prayers had been answered. I had been given the chance to get out of Zimbabwe and preserve my life.

I had been running all sorts of ideas through my head about how I was going to smuggle myself out of the country, usually involving a late-night dash to some remote border post, to Botswana or Zambia. Had we been ejected on that day, who knows whether they wouldn't have sent someone to pick me up straight away. Maybe the police would have come for me in the changing rooms, I don't know. This is Zimbabwe: there's a news blackout, so there's no story. There would have been no foreign journalists in Zimbabwe any more with the World Cup switching completely to South Africa. Even if there had been anyone to ask the questions, what would the answer have been? "What happened to Olonga?" "Oh, we don't know?" End of story.

But that hadn't happened, because the rain had come. You can make of this what you will. It might have been coincidence but at the time I was convinced that it was divine intervention and I still believe that to this day. God decided that He had plans for me, and they did not include being thrown in a rotten, stinking prison cell, being beaten to within an inch of my life, or worse. I'm sure there are a lot of people who will read this and think, "This guy's nuts: what's he on about with divine intervention and isn't he exaggerating the consequences?" But as coincidental as it may appear to a lot of people, for me that was an answer to prayer. Whether it was an act of nature or an act of God I will not endeavour to explain, because I cannot adequately give an answer that will appease everyone. But what I know is that I was in trouble, I needed something extraordinary to happen, I prayed and it happened. That enabled me to get out of the country and may well have saved my life.

Now we were still in the World Cup and on our way to South Africa, the authorities couldn't touch me. I knew it and they knew it. I went home to Harare. Days later I got on a plane to Johannesburg with the rest of my teammates, knowing that I had my ticket out. Beyond that I hadn't a clue what was to become of me, but at least I had escaped the clutches of Mugabe's murderous regime for now.

CHAPTER TWO: COMPLICATED BEGINNINGS

When a young man asked, "Henry, do you know who I am?" I assumed he was a distant relation. "No," I said and smiled politely. He said, "I am your brother." I said, "Pardon?"

I was born in Lusaka, Zambia on 3rd July 1976. We lived on Cheetah Road in an area called Kabulonga for a couple of years. I have an older brother called Victor, who is two years older than me, and he was born on 30th June 1974. My dad, Dr John Olonga, was born and raised in Kenya and informed me that he went to school with the father of Barack Obama. To be honest, because of my Kenyan roots, I suspect that he always wanted me to be an athlete and dreamt of me running for Kenya at the Olympic Games. It's not often you see Kenyans in a race they lose. Even Obama won! Mum, who started life as Sabina Guchutu, is from Chilimanzi, in the Mvuma region of Zimbabwe. She had relatives in Zambia, the

Mwanzas, and I believe that she stayed with them and worked in the hospital as a nurse where she met my dad.

Until I married my wife, Tara, in 2004, I believed that this was my complete family unit – my dad, my mother Sabina, stepmother Judith, half brother Lionel who is ten years younger than me, stepsister Yolande, half sister Veronica and of course Victor. But then a quick and unexpected conversation in Kenya changed all that. It was at my uncle's house in Nairobi during one of the meetings we had before our wedding that a young man named Japheth came and introduced himself to me. We had met a lot of people we didn't know but who were apparently related. Lots of uncles and aunties, and lots of cousins as it were. My dad is one of 13 children so the extended family is pretty large and colourful so when this young man asked, "Henry, do you know who I am?" I assumed he was a distant relation. "No," I said and smiled politely. He said, "I am your brother." I said, "*Pardon?*"

It turned out that Dad had been married before and had had ten children with his first wife – there had actually been 12, but two had died young. Discovering this at the tender age of 28 was a shock to say the least. So I ended up having a half brother whom I'd only just met, Daniel, as my best man at our Kenyan wedding celebration. (We had previously had a ceremony in Australia.)

It had never been discussed, but I'd always felt that there was some family secret that had always been kept from us. I didn't know what it was, but I just had a sense that there was something hidden away in the background. And, of course, not knowing only makes you think the worst. Even now, my mum still finds it hard to talk about because it is ultimately what led to my parents splitting up. When she married my dad she didn't have a clue about his other family. To this day many issues around this still lie unresolved.

Dad had contracted polio at a very young age, but he did his best to overcome it and has always had to wear specially made heavy orthotic shoes. It is to his eternal credit that he didn't let his condition get in his way and he went on to become a very fine paediatrician. I believe that part of his motivation for wanting to work as a doctor was because of his own personal infirmity and he felt that this was his way to help others. Thankfully, with vaccination programmes worldwide polio has almost been completely wiped out today.

When my dad was growing up, I think there was a stigma attached to polio and its victims. Indeed, his first marriage was more or less arranged because his parents felt that his condition might prevent him from forming a relationship with a woman. Not that they needed to worry on this account. He has always walked with a limp but it wasn't until much later in his life that he required a walking stick to help him get around, and he has always had a twinkle in his eye that women have found difficult to resist. Oh, and a great smile as well. So, in the classic way, he swept my mum off her feet and they got married, Mum blissfully unaware of the complicated life she was about to enter into.

While we were in Zambia and I was about two years old, my father was treating a boy for what I believe was a foot infection. Dad would sort it out but every time he went home the condition would flare up again until eventually his father turned round to Dad and said, "If you keep sending him home with me he is going to die, so why don't you have him?" It sounds cold and uncaring, but it was actually anything but, and so it was that I ended up with a foster brother called Benedicto, who was around five years older than me.

When I was three years old my parents moved to Kenya, ending up in Nairobi, the capital city. It was while they were there that Mum came across a number of children running around who bore more than a passing resemblance to Victor and I. Francis Masakhalia, my dad's elder brother and a Kenyan politician, was married to my Auntie Florence, who decided that my mother had a right to know and came clean about my dad's past. That's when she discovered that her husband had another family, that his relationship with his first wife had ended but there was a healthy brood as a result.

Naturally, the news of Dad's previous family came as a bolt from the blue to my mum. I don't know if it would have made any difference if he had told her everything at the outset but once she discovered the truth the marriage sadly came to an end and Mum, Victor and I went back to the land of my mother's birth, Zimbabwe, when I was four years old.

Initially Mum took us to Harare, the capital, but Victor and I were soon shipped off to stay with a distant aunt. My memory of all this is sketchy but I do know that the conditions in which we lived were deplorable. One vivid memory concerning the woman we stayed with was that she used to catch field mice to eat. She would put bait, usually peanut butter, in the bottom of milk bottles and the mice would squeeze into the bottle, take the bait and then find that they couldn't get back out again. She would then cook and eat them. She also used to cook locusts, flying ants, insects called *nswabandas* and probably anything that moved. However, before you get queasy, remember that in Africa poor people will eat just about anything to survive. None the less our health did suffer.

Bear in mind, too, that we had lived a reasonably comfortable life up to that point. To be fair to Mum she had no choice other than to send us away because there was simply no way that she could deal with the emotional trauma, facilitate the move, look after us and hold down a job all at the same time

Nothing had been explained to Victor and I as we were so young, so we had no clue what was going on. All we knew is that in a matter of months the family had been split. Even now, all these years later, when I think about it, it still seems very messy and it is so sad because it could all have been avoided by open and honest dialogue. To this day my mum and dad do seem to struggle to talk about it and I can understand why. As an adult who has had his fair share of heartbreak and mistakes, I can now truly walk in both their shoes.

Before long we had contracted ringworm and we had also lost a good deal of weight so Dad left Nairobi, came to live in Bulawayo and took us in. Soon after independence in 1980 there was a great need for doctors in the optimistic country and so with that opportunity he joined us and helped to nurse us back to full health.

Bulawayo is the second largest city in Zimbabwe and we found ourselves in a middle-class area called Southwold in the west of the city. My school was called Greenfield, and I was there for perhaps a year. It was a day school but Victor, meanwhile, had been sent to a small boarding school called Rhodes Estate Preparatory School (REPS). It had about 150 pupils, all boys, and it was named after Sir Cecil Rhodes, the staunch imperialist, politician and businessman and one of the few people in history who have had a country named after them.

With the passage of time Dad ended up moving to a better middle-class area called Ilanda. The area we lived in there was like an athletics stadium with the houses in an island and the road going round in an oval, exactly like a running track. Next to us were open fields where we used to ride our bikes, although Dad would always be telling us not to take our bikes into the bush. This was because there were these incredible things called devil thorns growing everywhere, which were like a ball with needles coming out in all directions. Whenever we ran over one of these we ended up with a puncture so we were forever coming home with flat tyres. What is it with children when their parents tell them not to do something? It used to drive the old man crazy, as well as Benedicto, who had to fix the holes. Eventually we learnt how to do it ourselves and then we finally got some tubeless tyres.

We also used to make catapults made with the old tubes and would go out trying to shoot birds, but those African sparrows move like lightning. There were no rules. All of this was stuff that we could do for free, without anybody bothering us or telling us that we couldn't do it. I look back on it now and I am not proud of the fact that we used to kill defenceless birds for fun, but I was young and I didn't know any better. We used to set traps and snares as well, although we very rarely caught anything. We did most of our hunting on bush land, but most people felt that you had the freedom to just roam about and be a kid so there was never any question of us being chased off the land or being accused of trespassing.

Next to our house there was a home for old people and beside that was a school called Tennyson, all within 400 yards. I went to Tennyson for a year or two. I remember the uniform was grey with a blue and yellow tie. Before I went to Tennyson I attended a nursery school which was also only a short walk from home.

This was where I got my first taste of how fickle people can be. I was the only black child in the whole place – my father was a doctor so he had enough money to be able to afford to send us to what he considered to be the best nursery school in the area. When I first went there at the age of six I was a complete stranger; I didn't know a soul. I remember on my first day I was playing on my own on a climbing frame when a boy walked up to me and asked if I wanted him to be my friend. I told him that would be great. Then we went into the building.

As it was my first day there I hadn't known that I was supposed to have brought my own lunch. So when it came to lunchtime I was asked where my lunch box was. I explained that I didn't have one, so the teacher said that she would take a bit from this child, another bit from another child and so on, so I wouldn't go hungry. I was aware of all these children staring at me, thinking, "Why haven't you brought your own food?" It was bad enough that I was already standing out because I was the only black child but now I had to contend with this too.

We were then told to sit in groups. There were about 20 children so I gravitated towards the group containing the boy who had said he wanted to be my friend. As I went to sit down, one of them asked what I was doing. I pointed to the boy and said, "He's my friend." He looked around and replied, "No, no, no, you're not my friend." So I had to clear off and sit with another group. I was six years old and it was like receiving a slap on the face. It was my first taste of rejection.

When I was seven I was sent to Tennyson. I believe that I was a good student, and that I worked hard while I was there. I certainly got decent reports during my time at the school. Partly because of my nursery school experience I became a slightly introspective kid. I was shy and I kept myself to myself. Maybe I just didn't want to let that happen again. I had an in-built sense that people could not be trusted. Remember, too, that I had been moved from pillar to post and had had very little stability in my life. During this period of time, around about 1983, my dad met another woman, Judith, who effectively became the stepmother I mentioned earlier.

Benedicto walked me to school every day before continuing his journey on to the senior school he attended. He was a big influence on my life at this stage, both good and bad. He had a bad left arm as a result of the sickness he had contracted in Zambia and would eventually go to a school called Milton, which become a rival of mine in later life. He was given a golden opportunity by my father but he didn't make the most of it and he flunked his exams.

Some years later, worse was to come. Dad loved tinkering with and repairing old cars and sent Benedicto to South Africa to collect some spare parts. He gave him a large sum of money to cover the cost of the spares and that was the last we saw of him for a number of years until he was picked up by the police and deported back to Zimbabwe. Having lived rough for some time my father felt it was too dangerous to keep him around the family and so sent him home to Livingstone in Zambia, back to his original family, where he contracted malaria and sadly passed away. We were all quietly devastated as a major part of our lives was no more. My older brother was dead after he had just disappeared from our lives. It took my father a long time to get over Benedicto's betrayal and death.

Tennyson was a small school and I don't remember much about it. There was a girl called Jane who was the child that nobody wanted to sit next to. She didn't bathe and so had bad body odour. She often had ringworm and would regularly wet herself. Nowadays I guess I would say that she had special needs but of course kids don't understand any of that and nobody wanted to sit next to her or spend any time in her company, but I did without prejudice – well, until the first time she peed in her seat.

We all had small desks and they were tightly packed, so if somebody smelt there was no way of avoiding it. I remember, even at that young age, feeling a sense of compassion for Jane and, again, it may have had something to do with the way I had been treated myself. Kids can be cruel.

One of the teachers asked me to befriend Jane during the year or so I was at Tennyson and that was fine by me. Perhaps I just never knew what it was to be judgmental. Sadly, the inevitable hardening of heart a lot of us experience was still to come as I grew older. But as a seven-year-old I did not have a bone of prejudice in me. There are two things I wish I still had: young knees and that childlike innocence.

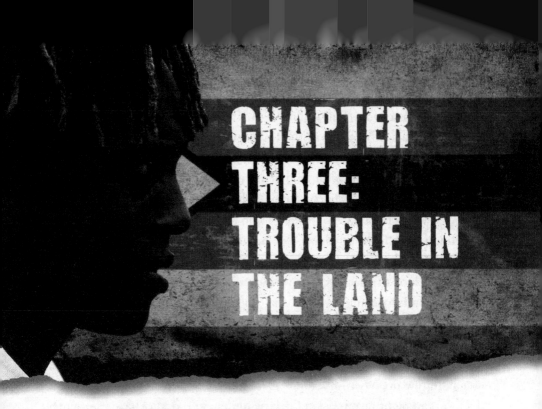

CHAPTER THREE: TROUBLE IN THE LAND

I caught my first ever glimpse of Mugabe when I was eight years old, at the 1984 Bulawayo trade fair, an annual show for farmers and other traders. He was surrounded by mean–looking bodyguards.

After I left Tennyson, I joined Victor at the boarding school REPS. Just as it was at Tennyson, the split between black and white kids was about 50/50, although by the time I left the school nine years after independence there was just one white pupil. The school was about 30 minutes from our house although if you were my dad, who was always running late, the journey when he would take us back to school after weekends took about 20 minutes – it was quite hair-raising.

Dad loved cars and he loved driving. He usually had three or four on the go at the same time. I remember him having two Mazdas and an Audi, his prized possession. The Audi was the smoothest ride and fastest car we had and in fact he drove it all the way from Kenya to Zimbabwe when he moved, taking days to complete the trip. We loved arriving at school in the Audi. We always felt important. The little white Mazda was more economical so we used it more often but we always sat a little lower as the car went through the school gates. It could be much worse, though. One of the meeting places for returning school children was the bus terminus in the middle of Bulawayo. It was right opposite the City Hall and arriving there on the back of my dad's scooter wearing a dreadful oversized helmet was the most embarrassing thing I ever experienced.

I got used to flying very early in my life because we used to go by plane from Bulawayo to Harare when we went to visit my mum for part of the school holidays. It was a means of transport that became second nature to me as I grew up. My first flight was on a propeller-driven Viscount when I was about eight or nine and I remember the pressure building up in my ears and being absolutely petrified. I hadn't the first idea what was going on until a very kind white man sitting next to me told me to swallow and the feeling disappeared. Then there was the horrible roar of the engines as the pilot descended and, once again, this gentleman gently told me that it was perfectly normal and that everything was OK. It calmed me down and from that day until this I have been absolutely fine on planes.

In the middle of each term we would have special holiday weekends when we would go home to see our parents – you would leave the school on Thursday night and return on Sunday evening. Return times were to be strictly adhered to and we had to be back by 6 pm. Parents could also come to the school after church on ordinary Sundays and take their children out for the day – the favourite place to go was the nearby game reserve. Another favourite trip was to the burial place of Cecil Rhodes. The hills where Rhodes was buried lay in the distance and one could just make them out from the school. Another kopje, as we called these little rocky hills, was called Baby's Bum because it looked like… a baby's bum. The surrounding scenery was stunning and there was also a dam nearby that provided the school with water.

Life at REPS was a whole new experience. It was a boarding school, away from Mum and Dad, and with only teachers to instil discipline in us. I was on my own now and basically had to fend for myself. It made me fiercely independent. Even though Victor was also at the school, I didn't often hang out with him. Being older than me he had made his own friends, so why would he want to spend time with me? And it worked both ways. In saying that, it was always good to know that he was there. Just in case.

It was also at about this time that I first started to become aware of the politics of my country. After the war of independence, which was fought from 1964 until 1980, there was a period of calm in Zimbabwe. Unbeknown to me, there was this guy called Robert Mugabe. He was elected prime minister in 1980 and went on to become the only premier Zimbabwe has known.

I caught my first ever glimpse of Mugabe when I was eight years old, at the 1984 Bulawayo trade fair, an annual show for farmers and other traders. He was surrounded by mean-looking bodyguards. I only saw him briefly but it intrigued me that a man could be so important. I discovered that he was essentially a socialist and Marxist in his political outlook and others, such as his former ally Joshua Nkomo, disagreed with many of his policies, in particular the fact that Mugabe wanted a one-party state. This being Africa, the disagreements were solved by violence.

So who is Robert Mugabe?

After his secondary schooling he trained and became a qualified teacher. Mugabe then left Rhodesia for South Africa and furthered his studying at the University of Fort Hare, eventually graduating in 1951. This was a key institution in the creation of a black African elite from 1916 to 1959 before the apartheid system was introduced. Other notable alumni include Nelson Mandela, Seretse Khama, the first president of Botswana, Archbishop Desmond Tutu and Julius Nyerere, the president of Tanzania. So at that time there was a group of revolutionaries with similar ideologies rubbing shoulders at such educational institutions and many went on to become prominent African politicians.

Returning to Rhodesia, he began his political career by joining the Nkomo-led National Democratic Party (NDP) in 1960.

The NDP were fighting a strengthening campaign against white minority rule in the country. For years the status quo had been that white people had about 95 per cent of the vote even though they represented only about five per cent of the population. The constitution was biased towards whites in that voters had to possess a certain amount of property or meet a minimum standard of qualifications to take part in the vote. Over time, simmering resentment over the patently unfair system saw a more militant nationalist black movement emerge.

A seasoned politician since 1948, Ian Smith was elected to power as prime minister of Rhodesia in 1964. He began demanding independence from Britain but they insisted that Smith introduce majority rule, something which Smith and his Rhodesia Front Party were unwilling to accept. The NDP were banned under the new regime and Mugabe joined a new party called the Zimbabwe African National Union (ZANU).

Mugabe was imprisoned for using 'subversive speech' in 1964 and would remain in Salisbury Prison for 11 years, during which time he attained three degrees. He has eight degrees to his name. Before being jailed he had married Sally, a Ghanaian, and they had had a son. One of the most devastating and life-shaping experiences for Mugabe was when Ian Smith refused to allow him to attend the funeral of his four year-old son.

Unwilling to introduce majority rule, Smith, with the cabinet behind him, declared unilateral independence from Great Britain in November of 1965. So unpopular was this move abroad that widespread international condemnation was followed by the issuing of the first ever economic sanctions by the United Nations. Several countries, including South Africa, did not comply with the sanctions.

At this time various segregation laws were in place in Rhodesia and only a few prominent whites wanted them repealed. Whites and blacks did not generally use the same public toilets, attend the same schools, live in the same suburbs or play in the same sports teams. Other disparities revolved around employment, land ownership and the key voting structures. It was effectively a system very similar to apartheid.

When he was released in the mid-1970s, Mugabe took the reins of ZANU. Many opposition leaders mysteriously died around this time as Mugabe consolidated his grip on power. And as the opposition to white rule intensified, the Ian Smith government ended up conceding to the British demands for change.

However, the warfare continued unabated until, in 1979, Britain gathered all the major stakeholders together at Lancaster House in London where an agreement was reached which would allow for a fresh constitution and fresh elections based on a one man, one vote system. The end of white minority rule was in sight only four years after Ian Smith had said, "I don't believe in black majority rule in Rhodesia, not in a thousand years."

Multiracial elections occurred in 1980 and Mugabe surprisingly swept to victory amidst widespread allegations of voter intimidation and violence, although international observers declared them free and fair. Many had thought the popular Nkomo, who was the leader of the Zimbabwe African People's Union (ZAPU) party would win. Rhodesia came to an end and, on 18th April 1980, Zimbabwe was born and Robert Mugabe was sworn in as its first prime minister.

After the election, many white people wanted to leave, fearing persecution, but most remained when Mugabe gave many reassuring speeches. In one of these he said, "Ladies and gentlemen, we will ensure that there is a place for everybody in this country and those who have talked about the possibility of personal and other properties being nationalised, being seized, well, have not read us correctly: we will not do any such thing." Many stayed with these words of comfort. But within a couple of years the political landscape of Zimbabwe was to become very tumultuous when the rivalry between the two leading parties came to a head.

At the heart of this was the fierce personal rivalry between Mugabe and Nkomo. Universally known as the father of black nationalism in Zimbabwe, Joshua Nkomo was born in Semokwe Reserve in 1917, one of eight children fathered by preacher and rancher Thomas Nkomo. He grew up in Matabeleland South and tried a few careers before becoming a carpentry teacher in his mid-20s.

He married his wife, Johanna MaFuyana, in late 1949 and decided to further his education in South Africa. He went on to acquire a BA in Social Science in 1952 at the Jan H Hofmeyr School of Social Work, the first institution of its kind to train black social workers in apartheid South Africa. While there he became increasingly politically aware and had meetings with nationalist leaders like Nelson Mandela and others with similar political aspirations, including Mugabe.

On returning to Rhodesia he became involved in the trade union move-ment and later entered the world of politics as president of the National Democratic Party. Nkomo's sharp mind and business skills made him a wealthy man even in a segregated Rhodesia.

As one of the most forceful of the new generation of black politicians and a possible threat to Ian Smith, in 1964 Nkomo was detained at the internment camp called Gonakudzingwa (which means 'where the banished ones sleep') where he was held for ten years. After pressure from the South African premier, BJ Vorster, all political prisoners were released in 1974 and Nkomo made his way to Zambia to spearhead a military faction of ZAPU which was now waging a guerrilla war in the Rhodesian countryside. However, he was hoping to use negotiation as well as military strategy to bring about independence.

Nkomo survived several assassination attempts and on one occasion the rather rotund leader was found stuck in the window of his bathroom having tried to escape when he thought he was under attack. I can imagine the ineffable leader's debrief, "Not a word of this to anyone, you hear."

In the course of the civil war, Nkomo's military wing committed numer-ous atrocities including the shooting down of a couple of civilian planes, killing 107 people. Apparently in one of the cases some survivors were murdered when his forces went to inspect the wreckage but miraculously a few managed to get to safety and report what had happened. Amnesty laws passed later meant that no one was brought to trial over the killings. In his memoirs, however, Nkomo claimed that he regretted shooting down the planes although at the time of the incidents he had joked about it.

From his very early days as prime minister, Mugabe had a distrust of Nkomo, and after the discovery of weapons on a ZAPU farm in 1982 he was accused of attempting to overthrow the government and booted out of the cabinet. It was later alleged that some South African double agents who wanted to cause dissension between the two parties had planted these weapons and tipped off Mugabe. Mugabe even publicly said, "ZAPU and its leader, Dr Joshua Nkomo, are like a cobra in a house. The only way to deal effectively with a snake is to strike and destroy its head."

With distrust high surrounding the alleged stash of weapons, members of the Zimbabwe National Army who supported Nkomo deserted and –

after a few fully fledged gun battles on a number of bases – fled into the countryside with their weapons. One of these ex-soldiers was a notorious guy called Richard Gwesela and he led a reign of terror in Matabeleland, the region which included our school. Tourists, farmers and civilians were murdered in growing unrest. Mugabe was never going to stand for this so he sent in his elite wing, a militia called the Fifth Brigade who had been trained by the North Koreans and who were given the task of flushing out the dissidents and destroying them.

The consequence of this was the Matabeleland massacres, one of the darkest episodes in Zimbabwean history, when the Fifth Brigade went on the rampage through the region – a traditional heartland of support for Nkomo – on the premise of flushing out the dissident soldiers. Trained in advanced forms of combat, torture, cruelty and merciless murdering techniques, the Fifth Brigade descended on Matabeleland and enforced Mugabe's will. I was too young to know what was really going on but the facts we know today are that perhaps up to 30,000 innocent civilians were brutally murdered at the hands of the militia.

Members of my stepmother's family were victims of the atrocities in the operation which was code-named Gukurahundi. This is a Shona word which means 'the early rain which washes away the chaff before the spring rains'.

At the beginning of the troubles Nkomo's chauffeur and two others were killed and his home was ransacked during a Fifth Brigade raid. He was forced to flee abroad to the UK in fear of his life. He would give some telling interviews including one with Jeremy Paxman, and later in his memoirs he would write, "… nothing in my life had prepared me for persecution at the hands of a government led by black Africans". He did later return to Zimbabwe.

I would not for one minute defend the dissidents – they were committing atrocities too. But, compared with the Fifth Brigade, they were pussycats. The troops were committing even more heinous crimes, such as beating up and whipping villagers for hours on end, trying to force them to reveal where the rebels were hiding. Most of the villagers didn't know, but that didn't stop the punishments being meted out and, in hundreds of cases, it would result in death because the Fifth Brigade didn't know when to stop.

Raping young girls was fair game and lining a family up to kill them with one bullet was regarded as sport. They burnt people alive for fun. Hospitals were full of villagers bearing the marks of astonishing cruelty and human rights abuses.

The Fifth Brigade fenced off entire villages and starved the occupants to death. To this day mass graves dot the landscape in Zimbabwe, known only to the perpetrators of these gross violations. In recent years bodies have been found down mine shafts and few people have been brought to justice. Few ever will, because in 1987 Robert Mugabe signed the Unity Accord with Joshua Nkomo sealing an end to the disturbances and combining the two leading parties ZANU and ZAPU to form ZANU-PF. ('PF' stands for 'Patriotic Front', which was an alliance between the two parties prior to independence.) An amnesty was pledged to all dissidents and also for all security forces involved, effectively pardoning them for any human rights violations.

After the Unity deal was struck, Nkomo became one of two vice-presidents. He was called a sell-out and other unsavoury things by some within his own party who maintained that the government had always used the dissident problem to crush them and create Mugabe's one-party state. When asked, later on in his life, why he had done it he said that he had given in because he wanted to stop the slaughter of those who supported his party. Nkomo died of prostate cancer in Harare in 1999, aged 82.

With the massacres still only relatively recent history, it is hardly surprising that there is a lot of ill feeling in Matebeleland towards the Mashonaland people, the most prominent of whom is of course Robert Mugabe. It spills over from politics into sport, so whenever I was playing cricket for my province against Mashonaland there was always a 'them and us' attitude. We used to call them 'shifties'. It is very similar to the rivalry between the Scots and English, but with far more of an edge.

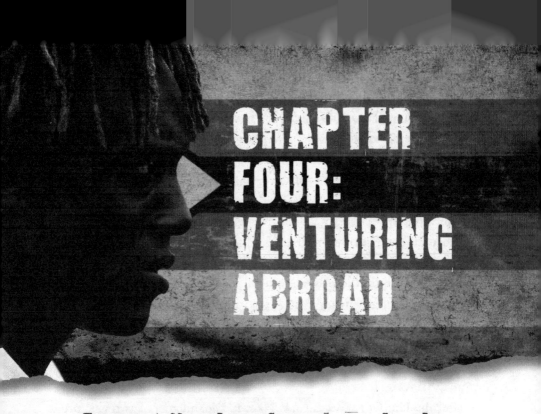

CHAPTER FOUR: VENTURING ABROAD

Eventually they found me in the company of a white woman. She was holding my hand and I was happily following her. The police were called and when they arrived she refused to give me up, insisting that I was her child.

My school was in the heart of Matabeleland so of course all this upheaval affected my daily life as a schoolboy. The main thing that happened was the curfews. Whenever we played sport at other schools we had to be back by a certain time. This was because the teachers were afraid that we might be rounded up by the militia or dissidents or be caught in the crossfire.

I remember Bray Mudavanhu, who was one of my first teachers, walking around with a gun after dark, and he was not the only one. As kids we were all fascinated by being up close to these weapons and it was explained to us that there were some bad men (the dissidents) roaming the countryside and we had to be careful, and that our teachers had guns in case they needed to protect us. I remember one teacher telling us that if we heard a shot it meant that we were still alive, that we would never hear the bullet that killed us. It was pretty chilling, but it was also very exciting. We also had grenade screens on the dormitory windows.

Of course it was different from anything I had experienced before and I became aware that there were serious problems in the rural areas of Zimbabwe. The government's propaganda machine was in full swing, making it clear that the rebels were the bad guys and that they were the saviours. At the time of course we had no idea that the soldiers of Mugabe's regime were also committing dreadful atrocities.

So, did our teachers support Mugabe? We never had those sort of discussions with them but I guess that they knew that failing to toe the line could have fatal consequences. And I think that probably, after all the years of disruption, they all just wanted a period of calm and hoped that Mugabe would sort things out. At this stage, most people still thought he was the right man to lead Zimbabwe although increasing numbers of white people were packing up and fleeing the country, which accounted for the dwindling number of white pupils at the school.

Eventually we heard that Gwesela had been caught and killed, and the guy who fired the fatal shot was rewarded. This was the beginning of the end for the dissidents, but it all truly ended when the Unity deal was clinched.

Bray Mudavanhu was a very colourful character who had fought for independence. I remember that he had dreadlocks and there was a rumour that he had had a baby with the school secretary. The headmaster also supposedly made one of the matrons pregnant. I guess this underpins that the school was essentially in the middle of nowhere and there wasn't much else to do for the adults once the boys were put to bed.

Throughout this time, Benedicto was still attending Milton school and we would see him when he accompanied my father to REPS on Sundays, or when we went home for long weekends and holidays. Whenever we went home we would always marvel at the new flowers as my dad and stepmum went through their romantic streak. My dad loved flowers more than Judith, which was weird, but it gave me a healthy appreciation for nature. I also picked up my dad's habit of not liking alcohol and up until my late teens I never touched the stuff. It is only now that I enjoy the odd glass of wine with a meal but that's usually all I can tolerate. To my young mind my dad knew everything. How far is the sun, how do we hear, why does a plane fly? He had an answer to every question.

By 1984, Victor had built a large circle of friends at the school. I was somewhat slower to make friends and the teachers noticed this. After the first term, I was assigned to a teacher called Derby Sher who was asked to keep a special eye out for me and would play a huge part in my development. I wasn't aware of it, but the teachers noticed that I never smiled. Who knows why? I was a very serious person. I knew that I wasn't happy but, as a child, how do you explain it? It's hard enough for adults to address their feelings. I guess that the reason they were on my case was that even at that early age I was a decent athlete and I used to win a lot of races, so they were aware of me.

Our sense of adventure was growing with every holiday spent with Mum, and now we had a younger half sister called Veronica to really annoy. We would also play with my older cousin, Jacob, who unlike us was a very upright young man. I remember we had a fence that was made out of elephant grass and Victor and I would make bows and arrows and make targets on the fence to shoot at. On one occasion we were firing our arrows and an elderly neighbour came out to admonish us for damaging the fence. Jacob had painted a black moustache on his face, presumably to make him look older, and it obviously worked because the neighbour thought he was our father and started talking to him, asking him if he was happy that we were destroying the fence? She was quite surprised when he told her it was absolutely fine.

In the heat of the day when cold-blooded creatures came out to sunbathe our naughty streak would surface again and we would shoot lizards with our catapults for fun. Then there were the dogs that would crawl through holes in the fence and knock over our bins and litter our garden. One day Victor and I decided that we were going to teach them a lesson so we got lots of pieces of broken glass and put them where the hole in the fence was. Anybody else would have fixed the hole, but we were typical boys. Lo and behold, the dogs came back and, surprise, surprise, they shredded their paws on the glass. There were trails of blood all over the garden. "Yes, we got 'em!" They never returned, although I later realised just how cruel this was. Considering that my mother was pretty devout and we had been taught the difference between right and wrong it is surprising looking back now how easily corrupted our young minds had become. There was always prayer going on in the house – before meals, at bedtime and suchlike – more so with my mother than in Bulawayo. So there was always a spiritual influence, both at home and at school.

Even before I went to REPS I knew that I was a good athlete. One day Victor and I were digging in the garden and I saw something glint in the sunlight. It turned out to be a Zimbabwe dollar coin. To me at that time it was a fortune, enough to buy a couple of ice creams at least. The trouble was, on this particular day the ice-cream man had been and gone. But I'd found this coin and we knew where he'd be, so I raced Victor to the ice-cream man who was about a mile or so away and beat him hands down. This feat was all the more impressive because I was wearing a pair of flip flops, called 'patter-patters' in Zimbabwe.

I had never run so hard, and it was the first time I heard the roar of the wind going past my ears so loud. It was a big moment for me, and even Victor was impressed. "Boy, you are fast, and you were wearing patter-patters," he said. It was a story that he told a lot of people so I recognised that it was pretty significant.

By accident, I also found that I had an aptitude for throwing things. I had developed a strong arm because my brother and I used to love throwing stones. At Dad's house in Bulawayo we were surrounded by lush bush that had tons of rough stones lying around. If you searched hard enough you could find one that had the perfect aerodynamics to travel a great distance in the air. They came in two versions: the flat disc-shaped stones that cut through the air horizontally and could fly perhaps 50 metres and the long, thin spearhead-shaped variety that you would try to spin as much as possible so they fizzed through the air. We also loved skimming flat stones off the surface of water and attempting to get more than five bounces. My strong arm was to prove useful in sport.

At school I enjoyed the high jump, triple jump and all the sprints. I tried it all and loved it all, apart, that is, from any race that made you really tired – like cross country or anything over 200 metres. I didn't see the point in punishing yourself in that way. Running over a long distance was painful so I stuck to the races that were over and done with quickly. When we had to do cross country we were woken up and forced to run before breakfast. What was that all about?

I was soon winning sprint races at school and I wasn't bad at tennis either. Sport looked like it could be my thing.

There was a teacher at REPS called Alistair Lowe, who was an interesting character. He was a very lively man who brought a huge amount of life and joy to the school. He was mixed race, or 'coloured' as we used to say in Zimbabwe. He was a good singer and actor and was a funny man. Mr Lowe saw some potential in me and made me work hard, telling me that I had the ability to become another Carl Lewis if I wanted it badly enough. I remember watching the 1984 Olympic Games on an old black-and-white TV and seeing Lewis win all those medals, and it really inspired me.

Passionate teachers drive schools and I came across a few in my time. Lowe was the first. He tried to teach me to do the Fosbury flop high jump technique that I had seen athletes doing on TV. During one training session I had so much spring in my step that not only did I clear the bar, but also the mat. Consequently I landed on my head, my back and my shoulders and ended up seeing stars. He kept making me do it again and again, telling me to jump from further back. On one occasion I was bawling my eyes out because I'd landed on my head and it hurt like hell but he drove me on. I was late for dinner and just wanted to get away but I learnt that anything worth pursuing in life needs commitment. Eventually I mastered it and started breaking school high-jump and sprint records.

Because of my success in races at REPS, when I was eight years old I was sent to an inter-schools meeting, where I won the 60 metres race but ducked under the tape because I didn't realise you had to hit it with your chest. I was crying my eyes out because I thought I'd done something wrong. Derby Sher couldn't understand why I was crying when I'd just won a race – not only that, but I'd set a new inter-schools record. She sat me on her lap and I calmed down. This was my first experience of affection from anybody in the school. It was a boarding school after all, with almost a military approach, but here I was feeling loved and appreciated.

Every time I won a race, she would sit me on her lap and say, "I am not going to let you go until you smile for me." I look back on it and think how odd it all was, but that is the way they dealt with me. If she saw me walking alone, she'd call me aside and ask me how I was doing. I had a huge affinity with her and she became a mother figure for me. Whenever I saw her, my heart would leap. I was definitely a teacher's pet and the teacher's pet rarely ends up being friendly with other students. She had a profound impact on me in that she gave me confidence: if ever I had insecurities about being likeable and loveable, she helped me to overcome them.

I remember once falling off the jungle gym (a bit like a climbing frame), landing awkwardly and cutting my knee. I was hobbling around when Miss Sher wandered up and asked what had happened. I told her and she took me to her class and rubbed ointment on the cut. For me, it was the sort of thing my mum would do. Derby left after a year. She had an impact on me for a short moment in time and her departure devastated me. I have always responded well to mentors but I have also been mindful, subconsciously, that they always leave. They come for a time into my life and then they are gone.

My first class teacher in grade 3 was Mrs Geary, who did something wonderful for me. She asked the class one day to write down the name of somebody they liked, somebody they thought deserved something nice to happen to them. I don't know if it was contrived or if it was genuine but she announced that most of kids had voted for me. Maybe the children genuinely felt sorry for me. I was called to the front of the class and given a box of chocolates and I had to kiss the teacher on each cheek – now this was a real shock to me because it wasn't something that my family did, and certainly not with people who weren't members of the family. It just wasn't the thing to do. There were no great shows of emotion in the Olonga household and it was something that would cause me difficulties later in life in my relationships with women because I just wasn't very demonstrative. I found it difficult to show my true feelings.

By now I had acquired my first proper friend at REPS, a boy called

Lotshe Moyo, who approached me and asked me if I wanted him to be my friend, only this kid was genuine and we became close. His father was a war veteran, a hero. And I had other friends in the class, so I guess that maybe they all really did vote for me. I began to feel comfortable and started to regard school as home.

Evans Mleso was an older boy who enjoyed acting and inspired me too. He took the lead role in a school production of *The King and I* and it had a huge impact on me. Afterwards, I thought, "Wow, I want to act too."

But for now I was focused only on sport. There was a boy in Victor's class called Ronald Chiwerera and my brother always came second to him in races, he could never beat him. He was really fast, set a host of school and district records and should have eventually gone to the Olympic Games. His dad worked at the school for a while and that's when I got to witness my first ever real-life fight. It was during break time and Chiwerera Senior got involved in a heated argument with another man who worked at the school, who grabbed a hoe and began to bludgeon Ronald's father with it. The police were called and we saw Mr Chiwerera walking around later with both arms in slings. It was farcical. Amazingly, instead of the guy being sacked, they patched up their differences and carried on as if nothing had happened.

In the same year as Victor was another pupil called Justin Adams and he also used to win a lot of events in track and field, and there was Ndabezinhle Mdlongwa, who became a world-class triple jumper, and he did represent Zimbabwe at the Olympics. He was an inspiration to all the boys.

It was also at REPS that I had my first encounter with one of Africa's most feared predators, the king cobra. One bite from the fangs of this guy and you're toast. I was walking around the corner of the school quadrangle and heard a hissing sound to my left, just past a dustbin. I looked down and there was the biggest snake I had ever seen about two feet from my legs, reared up, hood expanded and ready to strike. Seconds later I was 50 metres away. If you think Usain Bolt is fast you should have seen me that day! I reported that I had seen a huge snake but my claim was dismissed as nonsense – until, that is, the cobra decided to enter staff quarters later that week and Mr Mudhavanhu and some other teachers had to stone the life out of it. Bray came down dangling his huge prize from a stick.

In 1985 the teachers announced that there was going to be a tour to Europe and if anybody would like to go they should ask their parents. Victor and I were desperate to go so we told Dad at the first available opportunity. Like most parents would, he rolled his eyes heavenwards. He worked out that it was going to cost the equivalent of about £2,000 to send us on this tour, which was a lot of money in 1985.

My dad was not lavish with his earnings and although he could have given us a superlative lifestyle he chose instead to instil in us the value of hard work. Put another way, he was tight. So much so that we nicknamed him 'Expensive', as that was his standard answer for any money requests: "It's too expensive." But when it came to things that he believed would enrich our lives he was kind and forthcoming. So we made the trip.

We went to 14 European countries, which was incredible for a nine-year-old, as I was at the time. In fact, I was the youngest in the party. Dad had to get special permission from the school to allow me to go. We visited England, France, Germany (East and West), Italy and the Vatican, Austria, Switzerland, Belgium, Holland and others, all on board an orange double-decker bus supplied by the tour company – Budget Tours – with whom the school had booked the holiday.

On Friday nights in school we used to watch a film, and one of the favourites was *The Sound of Music*, which we fell in love with. While we were on holiday we went to Salzburg, where we saw the glass house that had been featured in the film, the one where Rolfe sings to Liesl, "You are sixteen going on seventeen." That was a special day for me as I realised that films were actually made in real places. We went to the Swiss Alps and took a cable car, and we all saw snow for the first time. I felt a little let down and cheated when I realised that I had come all the way to Switzerland in search of snow only to discover that I had just needed to open the freezer door and *voila*! But what an experience for a little African kid. The teachers had heard all sorts of horror stories about injuries being caused by snowballs containing stones so we weren't allowed to throw snowballs. Can you imagine? It was the first time we had ever seen this wonderful white stuff and we couldn't throw snowballs.

While we were in Italy a woman tried to kidnap me, believe it or not, although I should say that I have no strong memory of this. We were in a market square and they only found I was missing when they did a head count. As you can imagine, everybody got themselves into a state of panic and started flying around looking for me. Eventually they found me in the company of a white woman. She was holding my hand and I was happily following her. The police were called and when they arrived she refused to give me up, insisting that I was her child. At this point, Mr Lowe asked her how I, a black child, could possibly be her son and also why I was dressed the same as the other 30 or so kids that were with him.

The guy who was running the party had told us to call him 'Steward'. That wasn't his name, but because he was the holiday company steward he just felt it would be the easiest way for all of us to remember what to call him. He also had a young woman assistant. Towards the end of the tour Victor and I ran out of pocket money. We didn't have anything to spend on extras here and there or on souvenirs. Steward found out and his assistant took me to one side and she said, "We have been told that you guys have run out of spending money, so we are giving you £100. Give it to your teacher to take care of – we just want to make sure that the rest of your holiday is not ruined because you don't have any money." I wish I could track those two people down to say thank you.

As you can imagine, I was thrilled, so I did as I was told and sought out one of the teachers, whom I shall call 'Miss Arkwright', told her what had happened and gave her the money to look after for Victor and me. She told me that when I wanted any money I should come and ask her. This was a big mistake! I should have kept hold of it myself. When we got to London I saw a camera and thought it would be a lovely idea to buy it so that I could have some memories of the trip. I duly went up to Miss Arkwright, told her about the camera and asked her if I could have some money to go and buy it, to which she replied, "I am sorry Henry, there is no money. We used it all up the other day buying hot dogs for the kids because there was no money left in the general kitty."

"Huh?" I was devastated. This money had been given to us and now we couldn't go home with even a single souvenir of our holiday.

When we got home and returned to school, Miss Arkwright was conspicuous by her absence. It transpired that, quite apart from misappropriating our money, she'd allegedly been having sexual relations with some of the boys on the trip – these were 12-year-olds and she was in her early 20s.

The whole affair was exposed when one of the boys sent a letter to the school addressed to her during the school holidays. The headmaster, at the school in preparation for the term ahead, was surprised to find a letter written in a child's writing addressed to a teacher in the holidays. His curiosity peaked, he opened it to discover the salacious details of the boy's infatuation and sexual relations with the teacher. I didn't find any of this out until many years later and I don't mind telling you that even then I was blown away that this had happened. She was a sporty individual who used to take charge of hockey lessons and I would never in my wildest dreams have considered that this woman was capable of what she did. The thing is that she was a teacher for whom I had an affinity because after Miss Sher left the school she took me under her wing. I used to sit on her lap too, although nothing sordid happened to me.

CHAPTER FIVE: SPORTING AWAKENINGS

We were stopped by a white policeman at a roadblock; he treated us like something that was stuck to the bottom of his shoe.

My first introduction to the game which would go on to shape my life came when I was about eight or nine years old, and a New Zealander called Bob Blair came to our school to do some coaching.

Bob was a fast bowler who had had the misfortune to be at the peak of his powers at a time when New Zealand probably had their worst Test side. Poor old Bob, who was born in 1932, played in 19 Tests and never tasted victory, losing 13 times. Despite that, he took a highly respectable 43 wickets and once scored 64 not out against England in Wellington. Bob was in his 50s when he arrived at my school but he still had a tremendous passion for the game.

He brought with him a load of Bob Blair-endorsed plastic cricket bats and plastic balls. It was important that it was all made of plastic because you know what kids are like – we had no appreciation of how expensive proper cricket kit is. So if a downpour arrived we would just run indoors and leave the bats and balls lying outside. I remember Bob showing us how strong these bats were by hitting the trunk of a nearby tree quite hard to prove it wouldn't break. And it didn't, but the challenge had been laid down and within weeks there was a plastic bat in pieces in the kit bag.

Before Bob arrived I had very little knowledge of cricket. He showed us how to hold the bat properly, telling us how important a correct grip was, and I enjoyed smashing the ball. However, because I was fast at running I loved bowling too and I quickly realised that I was pretty good at it too.

Bob showed us how to spin the ball, how to seam it and I was one of the few children who were able to hit the stumps with a leg-spinner. He congratulated me and, you know what, I should have stuck with spin. It would have been much easier just taking four or five steps before spinning the ball down the wicket than the fast-bowling route that I followed which involved running 40 yards at full pelt and punishing my body for years on end. Anyway, thanks to Bob I had discovered that this cricket thing was good fun.

Nevertheless, there was no indication at this stage that I would become a professional cricketer. If anything, of all the team sports we played at school, rugby was the game that looked to hold the brightest future for me.

Another great influence on my sport was a guy called Colin Osborne, who came out from the UK to give us some rugby coaching. We could tell immediately that he was something special but at the time we didn't realise just how good he was. He went on to become director of coaching and development with the Zimbabwe Rugby Union and spent three years as coach of the national side. At the time of writing he is a coach at Harlequins.

Osborne came to our school just a handful of times but his visits had a profound effect on me and I loved rugby from then on as I learnt how to side-step and dummy and discovered how to make it all click into place during a match.

I made it into the first XV team aged 12 and we had a pretty good side. Whenever we played a home match the rest of the school would come to watch, resplendent in their purple blazers, and cheer us on with the traditional school war cries. We beat most of the other schools at home most of the time as we had speed in our back line. I played at centre for most matches but sometimes I would play on the wing because of my speed.

Whitestone, a private school, had good coaches, as did Hillside, but we had been running for our breakfast for months so they were usually no match for us. We considered them the softies from the big city. We had this bizarre ritual where we would scoop sand out of a bucket as we ran on to the field and throw it into the air. To this day I haven't a clue what it was all about or when it started but I always hated being at the back of the line as invariably someone would scoop sand straight into your face. What a great way to start, spitting grains of sand out of your mouth.

At the age of 12 I was selected to represent Zimbabwe Schools at rugby and, ironically, we played Kenya, the land of my father's birth, and I scored the winning try. I also played for the Zimbabwe Schools cricket team when I was 12. It's funny but at that age you don't fully appreciate the significance of pulling on an international jersey or wearing your country's colours. Sure, you know that you are good at whatever sport it is, but you just want to go out there and score a try, hit some runs, take some wickets. I'd come through the provincial set-up, and you just take it for granted.

That attitude all changed one day when, while travelling back home after having been just selected for the Zimbabwe under-12s cricket team, my brother said, "Henry is an asset to the family." I didn't really know what the word 'asset' meant but I think it is the greatest compliment he has ever given to me. And it was probably the last, too, because from that day on my brother became my biggest critic.

In those early years, even though I was being selected to represent my country at both rugby and cricket, I was still just playing for fun. I can remember scoring plenty of tries and taking lots of wickets but, as much as I enjoyed playing those sports, it had never once entered my mind that I was going to be good enough to represent my country at senior level. At no stage did I go to bed at night dreaming of becoming a professional cricketer or rugby player. Athletics was my passion.

I also recall that we never seemed to have enough cricket kit, which meant that players had to share bats; as if that weren't bad enough, there weren't sufficient protective boxes to go around either, so we had to share those too. It was something that we all just got used to, and that didn't change until much later.

I actually can't remember the details of many of the rugby and cricket matches I was playing at this time, but I clearly remember Halley's Comet which came into view of the Earth in 1986. We had a fabulous view of it in the bush because there was no ambient lighting, so we could sit and watch it clearly in the night sky. It sent shivers down my spine and, thinking about it all these years later, it still does.

Throughout all of this, my relationship with my parents was pretty distant because of the isolation boarding school brings. But thankfully my stepmum used to bring the kids, Lionel and Yolande, to visit us on the weekends and also to sports events. What was nice was that they always brought some delicious food to eat that trounced the boarding school meals. They were always our biggest supporters, faithfully attending any matches that Victor or I were playing in.

While I was at junior school I was solid academically, always aiming to be in the top five in my class and I had some other clever rivals who spurred me on. I also discovered that I had a love and particular talent for art. Mr Mudavanhu was my teacher in grade 5 and, under his guidance, my painting and drawing flourished. He was easy to work with, the sort of teacher who never over-complicated things, he just kept it simple and explained things in a way that we could all understand.

I still paint today, and the way I tackle it even now is down to him. "Just take the paintbrush and paint," he used to say. "Paint what you see. Draw what you see. Start with the stuff in the background. If you are going to paint a landscape, you don't start with that tree in the front, do you? You start with the sky and the land, and then you gradually fill in the detail, putting the layers on top."

Art would also be my main subject at high school. It helped me to develop my creative leanings, which would come out in my love for photography. I also enjoyed science, and learning about the things around me, although later on in life the challenge would become reconciling the claims of science with the claims of my faith. At the age of 11 or 12 I can remember thinking, "Which is the right way? Who is telling the truth? Who best explains the meaning of life?" Many years later I heard the claims that someone knew the way, the truth and the life and it would change my life.

When I was in junior school I was also challenged about cruelty, through listening to church sermons and to certain things that teachers said, and that's when I came to realise that shooting lizards and birds for fun, setting broken glass traps for dogs or dissecting frogs and watching them squirm as you did so is fundamentally wrong.

In the mid-1980s I also developed a love for rap music, in particular Grandmaster Flash and the Furious Five. I used to love listening to their music. I had a friend who was also into it, and we used to rap against each other. There was nothing original going on, we would just copy the words of the songs we were listening to and try to outdo one another. Then there was Michael Jackson, whose music was basically the soundtrack to my life as a kid. My father loved Jackson, too, and on one occasion we drove all the way to Botswana and back listening to Jackson's *Thriller* and *Off the Wall* albums.

Epic car journeys became a feature of my life. On one occasion we all piled into Dad's car and drove all the way to Zambia to buy our first colour television set. We got a big Sony Trinitron. Even then, there were problems finding good-quality foreign goods in Zimbabwe. We were travelling in a small van and the clutch gave up in the hills of Zambia. Somehow my dad and his mechanic friend, who luckily was with us, managed to get it going again and we came home with a brand new colour TV. It was worth us all going on the trip because when you crossed the border back into Zimbabwe you got an import allowance for each family member in the car. Amazingly, 20-odd years later, that TV set is still working today in my dad's house in Zimbabwe.

When we told Mum about the TV, she decided that she wanted one too, although we went to South Africa to buy hers. That was a memorable trip – there was Mum, my Uncle Joseph, Veronica, Victor and I – but mostly for the wrong reasons. I vividly remember being struck by the reality of apartheid. At the age of 11 I saw these signs that said things like "Whites only" and "Blacks not allowed". At one point we were stopped by a white policeman at a roadblock; he treated us like something that was stuck to the bottom of his shoe. I was old enough to know that this was a dodgy country, that South Africa was not a place I wanted to be. We couldn't even book into the hotel of our choice, or stay in the rooms of our choice: everything was segregated. This wasn't the heart of South Africa either: we stopped just across the border at a place called Petersburg.

Just prior to going on that journey I had seen the film *Cry Freedom*, in which Denzel Washington stars as Steve Biko. I had wept when I watched it, but that wasn't unusual. I cried at lots of films. I saw one at school called *Old Yeller*, which was about a dog, and that also reduced me to tears, as did several others including, I am almost ashamed to say, *Annie*. But the truth of *Cry Freedom*'s story hit me hard now that I was actually in South Africa. It wasn't a great time for me because this movie had given the impression that all white people hated all black people, and then I had gone to South Africa, for nothing more serious or more sinister than to buy a television set with my mother, and I had witnessed apartheid with my own eyes. I was so happy to get back home and watch TV in colour but because we lived in a hilly area, after all that effort it was still a fuzzy picture.

My overwhelming sense of what we had seen in South Africa was that it was what Zimbabwe used to be like in the 'bad old days' before liberation. I had a horrible feeling that refused to go away because what we had experienced made me feel like a second-class citizen for no reason other than the colour of my skin. Even at that tender age I knew it was so wrong. How could people treat each other like that? What I didn't know was that at that time a lot of white people were leaving Zimbabwe because they felt that, in Mugabe, there was a madman running the country and that they were about to be subjected to the same discrimination experienced by the black population of South Africa for so many years. I wouldn't have agreed with them at the time but then, aged 11 or 12, I knew no better. To me Mugabe was, and remained, the hero I was being told that he was.

Throughout my schooldays I perceived him to be a genuine and honest man who wanted the best for his country and maybe that is how it started out. I continued to feel that way about him until well into the 1990s. Remember, too, that it was well known that Zimbabwe was supporting the ANC during the 1980s and, in my young mind, I figured that if we as a country were giving money and practical help to the people who were being oppressed in South Africa then that had to be a good thing – as, indeed, it was. Mugabe was denouncing apartheid and demanding reform, FW de Klerk and PW Botha were the hate figures.

Having said that, there were lots of things about South Africa that were cool to a 12-year-old boy. Just about all their fruit juices and crisps were better than the equivalent produce made in Zimbabwe, and you could get fizzy drinks in cans from South Africa whereas we had to make do with bottles.

South Africans also excelled at sport and we were aware of that, even though apartheid meant that an entire generation and more missed out on the chance of competing on the international stage. I loved a lot about the place, but hated it at the same time. How could there be so much beauty and also horror in one country?

Trying to find answers I turned to church. There was a chapel at school, where attendance was compulsory and we would sing traditional hymns. It was beautiful and had wonderful acoustics so when you had a group of children in there singing their hearts out it sounded amazing and was incredibly uplifting. I used to go there on my own, sometimes to quietly sing, sometimes to sit in silent contemplation. It was a place where I felt incredibly comfortable, a place of solace.

I have always loved churches and even way back then, as a young boy, I felt that these were places where I could meet with God. I loved the serenity and the peace I could find there, even in a church in a large busy city. I have always been a deep thinker. I would describe my personality at this time as perhaps phlegmatic–melancholic. I was moody on one hand, but creative and buzzing on the other, full of ideas: introverted and then extroverted. I have changed now, partly through the process of growing up, partly through the help I received from the teachers I have mentioned and partly due to my faith.

Churches and chapels were always open, of course, which meant that you could go any time you wanted. I didn't really click with the Anglican Church way of doing things. It was very traditional and you had really old songs and hard pews! Though the lyrics were often meaningful it was a very dated sound. In spite of this I took a lot from the messages. I enjoyed the sermons because they were often relevant to youngsters, giving advice on how you could live a more holy life.

I was fortunate that REPS was a school at which the headmaster embraced spirituality and good behaviour. In particular he espoused honesty as the best policy, hard work and respecting other people's property. We had assembly every Monday at which we would sing a hymn, say the Lord's Prayer, hear announcements and then off we would go and begin the school day.

The Gideon Society regularly visited the school and handed out tiny Bibles, and over time I managed to get my hands on three of them. Every time they came to the school I got one. I mistakenly thought that simply owning it was like a badge of spirituality. But I did learn to sit down and read from it sometimes. I used to get confused when Benedicto would tell me that if you ever dropped the Bible it was an unpardonable sin and it meant you wouldn't be going to Heaven.

So I went through junior school going through the motions, not really committed to any particular faith. I thought the Bible was a fascinating collection of stories, but I wasn't sure if they were true, or if they were especially relevant. The bulk of my heart believed in God, though. I just felt it had to be true, but how was I to reconcile it with my academic mind?

I was treated unfairly on a number of occasions at junior school, which pricked my heart on the notion of justice and indeed injustice. On one occasion I was just sitting in a dormitory, not breaking any rules when Mr Mudavanhu walked by. I don't know what conclusion he came to, or what he thought we were doing but he launched into the most extraordinary outburst against us. He said we were all full of pretence, and then he turned to me and said that I pretended to be a good child but really I was full of wickedness and evil. I have no idea where it came from but resulted in him giving all of us there five of the best. He was a Rastafarian and perhaps that night he had smoked something a little stronger than cigarettes.

It was totally unjustified but what could we do? We were just school kids. I also struggled to cope with blanket punishments, which were meted out to an entire class or dormitory just because one or two boys were not pulling their weight. I guess it taught us the value of teamwork and encouraged us to do all that we could to ensure that anybody who was underperforming was brought up to scratch. The thing is that sometimes the people who underperform do so because that is the best they can do.

We had inspections of our dormitories all the time, and if things weren't good enough we got punished. The punishments were varied but the toughest of them all was facing the wall. This meant you had to just stare at a blank wall for minutes on end. Sometimes teachers would inspect the dormitory when none of us were there and everybody could be punished for the mistakes of just one person. It focused the mind on cleanliness.

There was a boy Dzavakwa who always got us into trouble. He didn't often do his fair share and we used to suffer blanket punishments because of him. Because of this we were all pretty cruel to Dzavakwa, calling him names and endlessly taunting him because he always got us into trouble. However, I don't want anybody reading this to run away with the idea that I was an angel, because I was not.

I was rightly punished several times for doing naughty things such as using swear words or lying and I had no complaint about that. I was reported on one occasion for using a word I shouldn't have used to describe a woman's private parts. In truth I hadn't a clue what the word meant but I was aping some senior boys. The result was that I received six of the best for the first time. This was the most you could get, administered by Mr Connick, the headmaster. It was almost like a badge of honour. But it hurt and I never committed that misdemeanour again. If you were white your backside turned blue, then purple, then black – it meant that if white boys got the cane you could see the after effects for weeks, but with me it was hardly visible.

The school had cold wooden floors that would give you a splinter if you were careless and the communal showers had concrete floors, so it was all pretty basic. The toilets were outside and were a pretty unattractive proposition in the middle of winter when the wind was howling. On one occasion I remember the school was hit by an outbreak of food poisoning and, at the same time, we ran out of water.

During the outbreak everybody had a dose of the runs. The toilets were fairly simple and none of them had lids, so you can imagine what it was like after a day. The smell was appalling, and it attracted huge flies, the biggest you have ever seen. We used to call them green bombers. The youth militia that would run amok in the country years later went by the same name. It turned out that the school had been given a bad batch of mincemeat and everybody had eaten it, pupils and teachers alike. After that outbreak, my stomach became immune to food bugs. During numerous cricketing trips to India and Pakistan I never once fell sick with the dreaded Delhi belly.

My attitude towards girls at this time was pretty weird I guess, but understandable when you consider we were shut up in an all-boys boarding school for months on end. You find that you haven't a clue how to speak to a girl that you really like. Well I didn't, at any rate. I didn't know where to start, so for most of my young life and into my teens, girls were not on the agenda. The only exception was a neighbour's daughter whom I would play kiss chase with when I came back from school when I was about eight years old. We were great friends until they moved to another area. So on one hand there was a part of me that was quite confident, but there was another part of me that was terrified because I just didn't know where you would start to form a relationship with a girl. I also had hang-ups due to having very few stable relationships in my life to go on, so I had the unbalanced view that relationships hardly last.

On a par with my shyness of girls was my hatred of water as I was a very poor swimmer. When we first moved to Bulawayo we stayed in a hotel that had a swimming pool. I clearly remember that there were several white families also staying there and they wanted to talk to us: they went out of their way to speak to Dad and to involve us in conversation. There was a certain amount of integration in Zimbabwe at this time, and it was certainly never as bad as South Africa, but it was still pretty unusual for white people to go out of their way to engage black people in conversation. Anyway, having spoken with these people by the hotel swimming pool, I decided to jump in. Don't ask me why. Naturally, I sank like a stone, straight to the bottom, so one of those people had to jump in and pull me up when I didn't surface. I had never had proper swimming lessons.

On another occasion I went to a public swimming pool and sat on the side, not wanting to jump in after my traumatic experience but one of the lifeguards kept encouraging me to go in, telling me the water was great. I said "No", so he picked me up and threw me in. Again, I went straight to the bottom and he had to jump in and save me. He tried to make light of it, but I was bawling my eyes out. Benedicto then arrived on the scene and had a furious argument with the lifeguard.

Third term in school was the one where they used to get us up for 6 am swimming sessions, and I hated it with a passion. The worst thing you can do to a child who can't swim very well must be to wake him up so early and force him to get into freezing cold water, but that is what they used to do. I am sure that some of my friends loved it, but I certainly didn't.

The over-chlorinated water used to go up my nostrils and I could never understand why that didn't seem to bother anybody else. When it happened to me I felt like my nose was on fire, and it hurt like hell, quite apart from the fact that you couldn't breathe underwater. Of course I have since learnt to swim, but even now it is not something that I enjoy for fun or training. I was to have another very, very frightening experience in water later on in my life.

Life became harder when Victor left REPS for senior school. I was lucky enough to be appointed head boy, which helped. Being head boy in a Zimbabwe boarding school is a big deal. It meant I had the power to give fellow pupils detention. Believe it or not, until about 18 years ago a head boy in high school could actually cane pupils. I was careful never to let any of this go to my head: for me, it was never about being on a power trip. I just felt lucky to have been chosen.

And my final year at REPS was a wonderful year of sporting achievement as I once again got picked for the Zimbabwe schools rugby and cricket teams and set some athletics records that may well still stand to this day. That saw me receive my colours – a school honour which meant I got to wear a different kind of badge on my blazer – for cricket, rugby and athletics.

With regards to cricket in particular I had done well to be selected for the national team at the Rothman's trials week. I couldn't stop taking wickets for the Matabeleland junior team that week and made the Zimbabwe under-12s team despite holding a Kenyan passport at the time. I took 7 for 35 against Mashonaland and four wickets against Harare East and Harare Central – it seemed that every time I bowled a ball I took a wicket. In four matches I picked up 18 wickets. Trevor Madondo, the Murphy twin brothers, Gavin Rennie and a few others also made that team and we would be reunited again a few times all the way up to Test cricket.

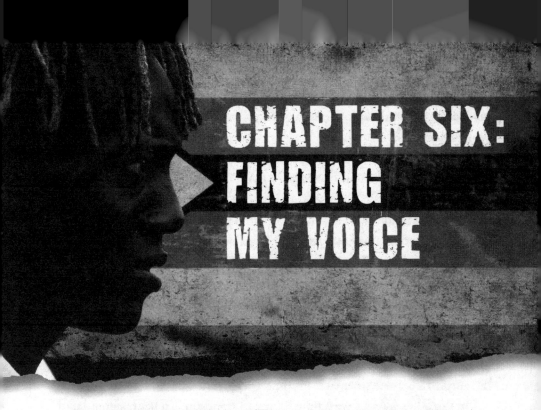

CHAPTER SIX:
FINDING
MY VOICE

At around this time I watched a West Indies side that included Jimmy Adams, Carl Hooper and Keith Arthurton, a team consisting entirely of black cricketers, smashing Zimbabwe to all parts. It was inspiring to me to see that cricket wasn't just a white man's sport.

At the age of 13 I started high school at Plumtree, and from day one I was quick to realise that it would be very different from REPS. For a start it had 450 boys so was three times as big. I wasn't going to be teacher's pet here but at least I would have Victor to appeal to if trouble beckoned.

On my first day at Plumtree an older boy, Smith, came up to me and my classmates and said, "You guys know you're not in junior school any more, don't you?"

"Yes," I replied.

"No, you say 'Si' when you answer me. Do you understand that?"

"Si."

It was a tradition that, to this day, I still don't understand but we had to use it as a term of respect. He was a horrible boy who took great delight in frightening us. Victor had also warned me that I was going to find it tough, so I arrived there not exactly looking forward to what lay ahead. The young boys in the school were called 'lighties'.

It was made clear to us that we had to show respect to all pupils who were older than us. There was a pecking order, and it changed for nobody. I have always believed that it is correct to show some respect to your elders, but surely they have to earn it in some way?

On the other hand, I was quite happy to stand up when a teacher came into class, and I knew that it was the right thing to address them as 'Sir' or 'Ma'am'.

Anyway, we were given our places in the dormitory and guess who was with us? Dzavakwa. I couldn't believe it. I thought that I had finally seen the back of him when I left REPS but no, here he was again, in a position to make my life and the lives of those around me thoroughly miserable. I came to the conclusion that we hadn't a hope. The dormitory was basic – we each had a bed, a foot locker in which we stored our shoes and towels, and a cage with various levels where we kept our clothes and uniform.

As at REPS, we had frequent dormitory inspections which were very solemn occasions. We weren't allowed to talk as the prefects walked down the aisle, stopping to inspect our beds and lockers, looking us up and down from head to toe. If they found anything against you they wouldn't say anything, but would just write something down, and you could feel everybody's eyes boring into you. It was incredibly nerve-racking. Faults could be anything from a bed that they decided had not been made properly to a pair of shoes that hadn't been polished to their requirements, even dust on a window sill. We were responsible for keeping the dorm clean and if they found anything wrong they had the power to punish the whole dormitory – and they frequently did.

But this was no longer junior school, so the punishments were a lot more severe than standing up and facing the wall. The prefects' favourite was 'holding the wall', where you were made to squat with your back to a wall and your knees bent and you had to hold your hands out in front of you and flick your fingers continuously. Do that for a couple of minutes and your legs start to hurt, do it for three minutes and they start to tremble, after four minutes they start shaking uncontrollably and after five minutes you can't stay up any longer. But if somebody collapsed, the prefects would give everyone another five minutes of it. It was barbaric and needless but it had been done to them when they were new to the school so now they were doing it to us. I am convinced that our house had the worst prefects, and that we were punished more than any other kids. Or maybe it was just because we had poor old Dzavakwa.

On one occasion they woke us up early in the morning and took us down to the athletics track. It was a cinder track and they made us run round and round it barefoot. It felt like running on razor blades. It was total agony. Then they made us take a shower and it was even worse. Our legs were numb, our feet felt frozen and red raw and when the heat from the shower hit the soles of our feet the pain was beyond description.

"Well, it's easy enough," chimed one of the prefects. "If you guys don't want this to happen again you will pull up your socks, follow the rules and keep your dormitory clean." We learnt pretty quickly and we took out our revenge on those who were letting the group down when the dorm prefect introduced us to 'running the gauntlet', which was pretty much exactly as it sounded. We would single out the boy or boys who had caused us to be punished by the prefects, form two lines down the dorm and the boys would have to run from one end to the other. We would be holding our pillows, inside which some boys would put cricket balls, shoes and suchlike, and as the poor victim ran past we would hit them as hard as we could.

Eventually the boys got the message and stopped letting us all down, but not before one occasion when we all laid into Dzavakwa and he broke down and sobbed uncontrollably. Like everybody else, I had bought into the fact that it was OK to pummel somebody we felt had let us down but seeing him in tears stirred something in me, and I felt genuine compassion for this poor boy. My attitude changed towards him from that moment. He still got us into trouble from time to time, but hey, so what?

Despite my continuing sporting endeavours, I had a love for the arts and was developing an interest in drama. I'd been bitten by the bug at REPS thanks to Alistair Lowe, who produced a show called *Bits of Broadway*, featuring songs from *Grease*, *The Sound of Music* and *The King and I*. It was taken around Zimbabwe but I hadn't been good enough to get any decent roles. This left me feeling very disappointed, so when I got to Plumtree I made up my mind that I was going to redress this. They were holding auditions during my first term and I went along, not even knowing what production they were going to put on. I just had to be in it.

Felix Westwood was the choir director and the moment you met this woman you knew that she was an influential person. Some people have an aura about them. She used to play piano during assembly and the organ during church services, and was very strict. During the fortnightly full-school hymn practice she would shriek at the top of her voice if we made an error. She taught English and everything about her and her classes was very proper.

We had another teacher Craig Hepburn, who was a hyperactive man and nobody used to take him too seriously. He was full of energy and bobbed up and down a lot. Nice guy, though, although he never gave me a chance with my O-level maths; I confounded his expectations by getting an A. He is the current headmaster of Plumtree. We would take the mickey out of him, but nobody took the mickey out of Felix Westwood or misbehaved in her classes. You spoke only when she spoke to you.

She was in charge of the auditions and I was asked to sing something on a sheet of paper and I believed that I had nailed it with my high falsetto voice. I walked off the stage feeling ten feet tall, convinced that I was going to be given the lead role, especially as lots of nice comments had been made about my singing. The next day I went to the notice board to find that I had been indeed landed a part in *Oklahoma*. As a girl! Well in an all-boys boarding school they had to find girls from somewhere and the boys in form 1 with high voices made prime candidates. That brought me back to earth in a hurry.

I wasn't good enough to take one of the lead roles again, but I knuckled down, learnt my lines and we put on the production on sports weekend, which is when all the houses compete against each other in track and field. We had already staged the show for the school, but this time was for the parents, and it was quite an undertaking. It involved a lighting crew, sound crew, musicians and the cast. There was an outstanding black drummer, Nyakudarika and a few other black boys in the cast, so it was pretty encouraging for me that I wasn't the only black boy in the show.

Getting made up was the weirdest feeling I can tell you. Looking at myself in the mirror was a revelation. The make-up was way over the top of course so I reckon I may well have been better placed in the cast of *Priscilla, Queen of the Desert*.

I should single out a fellow pupil, Mark Green, who is the person responsible for getting me into the world of solo music and singing the way I do today. He had the most wonderful tenor voice I had ever heard, with perfect pitch and vibrato. He was 18 years old and he was the god of singing to me at the time. I wanted to sing like he did. We all wanted to sing like he did.

After each performance there was always the opportunity for the cast to have a coffee and a bun and talk about our performance and perhaps let our hair down. As I was standing there in the vicinity consuming my iced doughnut, I heard a conversation that would change my music ambitions quickly. Felix Westwood, who'd clearly had something strong to steady her nerves said to another teacher as she laughed, "I hate to admit this but Henry is categorically one of the ugliest girls we've ever had in any production." She'd been at the school for more than 30 years so I made up my mind right there and then that I would never play a girl in any other production. Having said that, I also took her comment as a compliment because you don't want to be too pretty in a boys-only school!

During my first term, as well as my traumatic dramatic debut I performed well on the athletics track, breaking lots of age-group records, many of which had been set by Victor. By the time I was 16 I held 13 records, and I think it was 21 by the time I left. This, of course, was something that my Kenyan-born father was happy to encourage. Kenya has produced dozens of long-distance athletes over the years, although my preference was for the sprints.

Everything I achieved on the track was down to my athletics coach Atherton Squires, who was amazing. He had first turned up when I was at REPS, scouting for potential talent. He had been to university in South Africa and studied training techniques, and really knew what he was doing. He had heard about my early athletic prowess and came to REPS when I was in my final year and asked me what senior school I was going to be attending.

He knew that Plumtree was going to be sending an athletics team on tour a couple of years later and he told me that he thought I was good enough to be on that team and that he could maybe even get me a scholarship or a bursary. So it was that Squires took me under his wing at Plumtree and for the first time in my life I knew what it was to train properly. At REPS we just used to rock up and run or play rugby or whatever, but no longer. Now it was serious. If I was going to be an athlete, I was going to learn to do it the hard way.

The training was intense. Have you ever tried running while pulling a tyre behind you for a mile or two? It makes you strong but it hurts a lot. Then there would be jog–run–sprint repetitions known as 'fartlek' training or 'speed play' and over time it certainly worked in turning me into a lean, mean fighting machine.

Plumtree used to clean up at all the inter-schools athletics meetings and I gradually set my heart on becoming a professional athlete. I enjoyed winning and the euphoria of leading the pack although I also discovered the emptiness of it all. It was the same with rugby. There was nothing to beat running in the winning try or putting in a man-of-the-match performance where your teammates would look up to you, but the anticlimax afterwards would see me wallow in deep melancholic despair. It was hard to figure out.

The Plumtree under-13s rugby team captain was Sydney Sithole and I was his vice-captain – both of us had played for the Zimbabwe Schools team the previous year. Sydney was the life and soul of whichever team he was playing for. A big guy with a big heart, he loved telling jokes, especially those at other people's expense. All in all a good guy and a very good captain.

In 1989, at the start of the rugby season, I said to Sydney that it would be fun to see how long we could go unbeaten. Blow me down but for three years we didn't lose a single match. It's amazing how setting goals can work for you. Mind you, that run may also have had something to do with the fact that Atherton Squires was also the rugby coach.

At around this time I watched a West Indies side that included Jimmy Adams, Carl Hooper and Keith Arthurton, a team consisting entirely of black cricketers, smashing Zimbabwe to all parts. It was inspiring to me to see that cricket wasn't just a white man's sport. During the 1970s, black people had not been allowed to play cricket in white clubs in Zimbabwe. In those days, you had townships for black people and suburbs for white people. It was really just like apartheid South Africa, where the white population played cricket, bowls and golf, and the blacks played football. End of story. All the cricket clubs and cricket grounds were in the suburbs. Even if you were an educated black person like my dad, in those days you just didn't break into the suburbs. If you had tried to play tennis at any of the mines where Mum worked, you would get funny looks. There were certain clubs where even the black waiters would give you a sideways look if you turned up to play. It was built into their psyche.

Independence changed all that eventually, but it took time, and it needed a steady flow of black kids coming through and learning how to play cricket and rugby. Don't forget, too, that black kids did not have role models they could look up to because the entire Zimbabwe cricket team consisted of white players, so we had to look to the likes of the West Indies to find bats-men and bowlers to provide us with our inspiration.

Throughout this period we were building up to the tour that Squires had told me about at REPS. It turned out that it was going to be to England, Northern Ireland and the Republic of Ireland in 1990. We ran a 24-hour marathon to raise money for the trip. It was an awful, although worthwhile, experience and we were all knackered at the end of it. We all walked about like zombies from Michael Jackson's *Thriller* video for a few days after.

On the tour we visited Bryanston College, Worcester Grammar School and a few others whose names elude me. The weather was so odd compared to what I was used to and we wondered who had stolen the sun! There were these overcast, dreary, drizzly, drab days. I would have been 13 at the time and I was competing against 15- and 16-year-olds, but we managed to do pretty well in the athletics, although we were hammered in the tennis. But what a fabulous, cultural and educational experience for me once again.

It was a great trip, although I was almost kidnapped again. We were in London and some of the older boys, including Victor who was almost 16, said they wanted to go to a nightclub. I didn't want to be stuck in the hotel alone so I told them I would tag along but they said I couldn't because I was too young. I knew where they were going – it was a club called the Hippodrome. I waited a while and then I followed them there, but as I stood outside I quickly realised that there was no way they were going to let me in.

So I started walking back to the hotel and out of the corner of my eye I became aware that somebody was following me, a slimy-looking man wearing a black leather jacket. I stopped, and so did he, I carried on walking, and so did he. I came to a shop and stopped and looked in the window, he also stopped and looked in the window.

By now I was scared, so I decided to go inside a shop and made up my mind that I would stay in there for as long as it took. This man followed me in but after a while he got fed up and left. It was not a good experience. Here I was, aged 13, in a city I didn't know being trailed by a shady character whose possible intentions scared me witless. All I can say is that I was glad to get back to the hotel. What is it with these Europeans wanting to kidnap me all the time!

Apart from that experience, it was a good tour, during which I won my fair share of races. But the most memorable part of it for me was when we went to Northern Ireland. It was a big deal, not only for us but also for the locals. We were staying in Belfast and we went into the city centre – you can imagine how odd this group of black African children looked. We stood out like a sore thumb, but people made a fuss of us; they wanted to know where we had come from and what we were doing in their country.

My hosts for the short trip were the Hanvey family. Their daughter was called Joy and their son was Ryan. I didn't know anything about the religious issues in Northern Ireland as we just didn't have access to the information. It was 1990, at the height of the Troubles, but I knew nothing about Roman Catholics versus Protestants, bombs, terrorists or anything like that. Jack Hanvey, the father, asked me how much I knew about what was happening in his country and I had to be honest and admit that I hadn't a clue. So he asked me what religion I was and I told him that I was a Catholic, just like everybody else. The Hanveys were devout Protestants!

The day before I left Claire asked if she could have my cap, so I gave it to her. She was delighted and we have remained friends to this very day. We exchanged addresses and became pen pals from that point on. It is peculiar how as you go through life you meet certain people with whom you just click.

At one point I got Claire's number and we began to chat on the phone which didn't help my dad's bills. I loved her Irish accent and learnt to loosely imitate her inflections. The conversations with her, apart from being always enthralling, made me mentally study how to project the voice to sound different. I then started to study other people's quirks and attempt to mimic their accents. Claire is married now, with kids, and whenever I am in Northern Ireland I go and visit her. But what were the odds of two people, from such very different backgrounds, striking up a friendship and keeping it going for all these years?

This time there was no teacher to misappropriate my funds so at the end of the trip I brought back something to show for my time away – it was a boombox, or ghetto blaster, which had a CD player and two cassette decks. It was my pride and joy for many years until it finally packed up. But Blackbox, Rebel MC and Soul II Soul sounded awesome through this guy, and even better I could dub tapes in high-speed mode and make my own recordings with the built-in mic.

Not many children from Zimbabwe got to go on trips to Europe, but Victor and I did, twice, and I felt really privileged. It also got me interested in travel and in seeing other parts of the world, another passion that has stayed with me to this date. At the last count I had visited 35 countries.

Dad was always very generous with me. Victor, Benedicto and Stephen, my stepmother's brother, were always getting up to mischief. Victor mostly just wanted to have fun – he was into nightclubs by the time he was 15. In contrast I was quiet and generally well behaved, and my school reports were often good.

But I loved the rewards of studying hard. My first ever school prize was an illustrated book called *How Things Work in the City*. I got it for being in the top three in the class. Once I got one prize I wanted to achieve more and the desire to do so became a strong driving force for me.

1990 was also the year when the football World Cup was played in Italy. It began with a concert performed by Placido Domingo, José Carreras and the legendary Luciano Pavarotti, a musical experience that had a profound effect on me. Oh, and I also loved the football. The memory of Paul Gascoigne crying remains with me, but not as vividly as hearing Pavarotti singing *Nessum Dorma*. It was spine-tingling. There was so much passion, so much joy. I watched it and thought, "I want to do that." And thus began my mission to get hold of as much music by these guys as I could. This led me on a road of discovery. Don't laugh, but I also came across Aled Jones when he was still a chorister with the voice of an angel. How Aled Jones? Well, I found that Carreras sang a lot of Andrew Lloyd Webber songs and from there I wondered who else was singing these songs, and I discovered that Jones was. I was something of a one-off among my peer group. I can assure you that none of my friends were listening to Aled Jones singing *Walking in the Air*! I was still listening to music by Sting, Madonna and the like, but it wasn't the same.

This was also the year when I fell in love with painting. I was in my early teens, was doing art as a subject and asked my dad if he would buy me some oil paints which he duly did. I painted a few pieces for him as a result. The teacher who had inspired me to pursue this line was a man called Mr Piltcher, who was also my housemaster. He was a stern man and had a wife who was quite a strict woman who tended the gardens of Gaul House and hated anyone walking on the lawn. She sadly died of a terminal illness recently.

That same year I was also cast as Marco in a school version of *The Gondoliers*, a Gilbert and Sullivan production. It was pretty leftfield for a black guy to get the lead in any big show, but the reason I landed the part was that I was the only one who appeared capable of hitting the top note in a song called *Take a Pair of Sparkling Eyes*. Nobody else could come close to hitting it.

It was a scary experience because for the first time in my life I was singing solos. It's the story of two brothers who fall in love with a couple of girls and my girlfriend was played by a young boy called Johnson who made a pretty convincing female!

Plumtree was on the border with Botswana, 100 kilometres from Bulawayo, and every Christmas we would travel to the City Hall to sing in a carol concert. The format at the concert was that one of the schools would sing a piece, then everybody would sing together, another school would do its piece and so on. It would all end with up to 500 children singing *We Wish You a Merry Christmas*. It was always a fantastic way to end the year.

Our choir mistress, Shirley Smith, used to screech at the top of her voice like Felix whenever we got anything wrong. She would relish the chance to conduct us and she had very high standards along with amazing energy. I ended up working with her a number of times and she was just the most wonderful person, along with her husband Basil.

As a result of singing in the carol concert, I was asked to perform a solo in a concert entitled *Music of Many Moods* at the Robbie Sibson Hall in Bulawayo. I'd had back problems and went to see Mr Armstrong, a homeopath, who told me that he thought I was going to go a long way in life. I wondered what he was on about. He attended the concert at the Robbie Sibson Hall as a patron of the arts and he heard me sing that night. It was 1991 and I was 15 years old. I sang *Memory* from *Cats*, and I never looked back from that point. I was asked to sing at weddings, at parties and the like, and Shirley Smith was instrumental in helping me, right up until I left school. The last time I worked with her was in 1997 when I sang the arias from *Handel's Messiah*.

I kept pushing the musical boundaries, taking on the emotive Irish folk song *Londonderry Air* when I was still at school, and I continued performing in plays, in musicals and solo performances. I always had a fear of forgetting my words but once you get over that there is a tremendous buzz to be had from being up on stage and from hearing an audience burst into applause as a direct result of something you have sung. The sense of achievement was enormous.

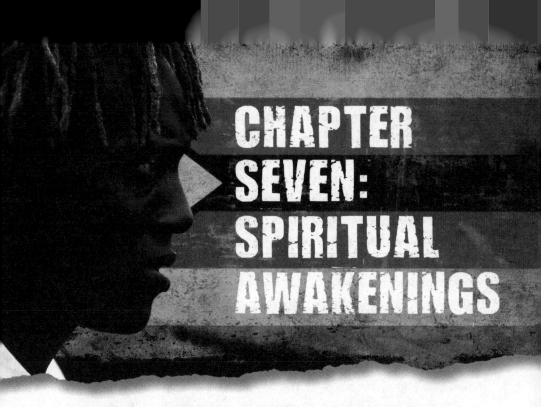

CHAPTER SEVEN: SPIRITUAL AWAKENINGS

If I'm honest I envied something they had. These were solid guys who weren't weird in any way and they had a quiet peace that I didn't have. But I wanted it.

My headmaster at Plumtree was Mike Whiley, also known as Spike. He had a passion for sport, especially cricket and rugby. He was headmaster when I arrived at Plumtree and he left when I was studying for my A-levels, as did Atherton Squire.

In 1991 Whiley led the Plumtree rugby team on a tour to Namibia. We visited Swokopmund and walked on the fabulous beaches there, with the Atlantic Ocean lapping at our feet. It was a beautiful misty evening, the sun was setting and there were huge sand dunes behind us. Just standing there, watching the sun going down, it was almost like having an epiphany.

Namibia was also where I came across the biggest elephant I have ever seen in my life. We were driving down a road one day and came round a corner and there he was, standing defiantly. It was almost as if he was challenging us to keep coming. I wondered what would happen if he decided to charge but, fortunately, he had better things to do and walked off, swishing his tail behind him.

From a sporting perspective the tour was a disaster. The Namibians played hard, physical rugby and we lost just about every game. Our transport amounted to not much more than a truck with do-it-yourself beds in the back. We went through Victoria Falls via the Caprivi Strip and had to cook out in the open as well as do all the other essentials for life in the bush without running water.

We also visited Windhoek, the capital city. While we were there I was walking through the streets with a teammate when a white guy threw an egg at us for no reason. Namibia was still very racist at the time. It struck me that there were some pretty dreadful things going on in the world if you could be singled out just because of the colour of your skin.

Our team was a mix of black and white players and, for us, skin colour really wasn't an issue. But it soon became apparent that none of the Namibian players – who were all white – would speak to any of our black players. One of my teammates on that tour was a white guy called Wayne Weedon and he eventually asked one of them why. I had tried to strike up a conversation with the Namibian player, but he just blanked me. Anyway, he told Weedon that he had ignored us because it was what his father had taught him. I thought it was just about the saddest statement that I had ever heard. He wouldn't mix with us because his father had told him not to. I didn't blame him. His father had obviously had the view drummed into him as he grew up and it was only natural that he would pass on the sentiment to his son. They didn't actually regard us as human beings.

I went to a school that wasn't segregated. Here we were playing sport in teams that contained black, white and coloured boys. If you were good enough, you were picked to play. I had also been to Europe, where we had been treated as equals, so I knew that it wasn't the whole world that regarded black people with such disdain, but it troubled me deeply. It was sad that the Namibian rugby player was brainwashed and it never occurred to him that his father could be wrong.

This was my first taste of playing first-team rugby for the school and I was only 15. Rugby was a sport I thoroughly enjoyed throughout my schooling. I had always been inspired by a match I watched in the late 1980s when a French rugby team called Côte Basque came to play at Hartsfield, the main international rugby ground in Bulawayo. They were absolutely awesome. Their handling skills and pace were so impressive and they took the Zimbabwe national team apart. I dreamt of being that good one day.

Rugby had a great tradition at Plumtree. The entire school would attend the matches, all dressed in their green blazers, and we would launch into a series of 'war cries' that had been carefully rehearsed. There was a war cry for every incident, whether it be a crunching tackle, a try, a conversion or whatever. It must have been pretty intimidating for the opposition to hear 400 boys screaming in unison, but we lapped it up.

The rugby field, called Kabot, was like concrete, so you knew that coming off after a match you were guaranteed lots of grass burns and bruises that would only reveal themselves in the shower. They would seldom water the pitch and if you landed head first after a tackle, boy did you know about it. It wasn't a game for softies.

In the open age group, I used to love playing for Matabeland in the inter-provincial matches that took place at Hartsfield, where the pitch was rather more forgiving. Plumtree would also play our provincial selection matches there, often against the Christian Brothers College, Milton or Falcon. It was during one of these games that I experienced my first major sports injury. At the age of 15 I was running with the ball when suddenly it felt like someone had shot my left hamstring muscle. I was rushed off the field and treated by a young physiotherapist called Sue Bailey whose brother had been a Plumtree head boy. I was sad to hear that that was the end of my match and after a slow recuperation I was back playing the game. Sue was to later become a great family friend.

In 1991 I also played my first winter league cricket. During the rugby season, which runs through May, June and July in the Southern Hemisphere winter, there are some people who continue to play cricket, and special leagues are set up to accommodate them. It is a way of keeping your hand in all year round. During one of those matches I broke my middle finger while trying to take a catch from a guy called Brown. He hit a low drive and I dived for it. I didn't even manage to catch it, but I did break my middle finger. Yes, my hamstring had troubled me but I could live with that. This really hurt. Stupidly, I then went on to play rugby while still suffering from the injury. The result is that now I have a slightly deformed finger.

I had a bad cricket experience later that year. I played in a Zimbabwe schools selection week and I wasn't chosen, even though I had bowled well. The selectors thought, not for the first time in my life, that I was too erratic. The team would go on to tour Namibia and do well, and I made up my mind that it would be the last time I would be left behind. I had no intention of settling for second best. Being left out of a team is not a pleasant experience so I resolved to play harder cricket.

So the Zimbabwe schools team went to Namibia without me. It was the school holidays and I refused to feel sorry for myself and immersed myself into my art. By this time my mother had moved to another mine, Mazoe, where she was the head nursing sister. The Mazoe area was famous for its citrus produce and to this day produces some of the best orange cordial in the world, and it was a great place to spend the holidays.

Victor and I used to spend some days fishing, using a homemade line. Why spend £50 on a rod when you could make your own for next to nothing and have exactly the same result, namely catching nothing? You didn't need a license either. Our rods used to consist of clear twine, a hook and a piece of wood, which we would cut and trim and twist to make sure it was both strong enough and sufficiently flexible.

As far as bait was concerned, we used to dig up worms from the back garden. So off we would go, filled with hope and optimism. Sometimes we actually did catch a fish or two and cook them for our dinner, although I have to admit that on occasion we would come across fishermen on our way home and buy what they had caught. Either way, mother was always impressed.

Victor and I also built a little golf course, using cans as holes and bits of wood as flagsticks. We made our own fun because we had to, but they were great times and I wouldn't swap them for anything.

In the early 1990s my mother adopted the daughter of Esneya, one of my cousins, who got pregnant by a flashy guy with lots of money who drove a Mercedes. When Esneya told him she was expecting a baby, he didn't want to be responsible so Mum ended up taking the child in. Grace's natural mother could have been more careful with her choices and died in the 1990s. Grace was a wonderful child whom I came to regard as a sister.

Mum was amazing. Life was difficult for her after she split from Dad. She had hoped that they were going to be together for the rest of their lives, but it wasn't to be. I found it amazing the way she adapted to situations. She didn't need to take Grace in but she did so because she believed it was the right thing to do and she always tried to do her best for us kids. I looked up to her while I was growing up and always regarded her as one of my heroes. I still do.

I had a couple of good friends, Dina Nyandora and David Machazire, who had both gone to REPS with me and were both committed Christians. I always admired their resolve, faith and upstanding morality. There was also Khakha – a guy with one of the most unfortunate names in Zimbabwe because his surname means 'poo' in the vernacular, which meant he was subjected to some pretty wicked mickey-taking.

The three of them constantly wanted to discuss Christianity with me and challenge me about my beliefs, but at that stage in my life I found it irritating. We did Easter and Christmas at home but I wasn't ready to go beyond that, although by now I had figured that Christmas wasn't about a big fat guy climbing down a chimney with a sack. How does he end up staying white after going down billions of chimneys anyway? But I was starting to look for answers to life's big questions. I'd always had a nagging sense that there was far more to life than I was experiencing. It wasn't that I wanted more material things or more friends or anything like that, but I suppose I was not entirely satisfied spiritually.

I never believed in the theory of evolution. I never believed that everything we see around us came out of nothing, for no reason or cause. I did not want to be a dissenting student so I passed science without causing a stink. But Sunday church services told me there was a God who loved us. Monday science class said there wasn't. So who was telling the truth? The tension made me very uncomfortable. All I knew was that if God did exist, I wasn't in accordance with how He wanted me to live.

Yet everywhere around me I saw the presence of evil and I thought, if there was radical evil, why couldn't there be radical good?

I was 15 and I bought a book called *Teach Yourself Yoga*. I thought yoga would provide the answer, but it didn't. Perhaps I did it all wrong but I was encouraged to sit in the lotus position and open my mind, but nothing was happening for me. It didn't help that I couldn't do all of the stretches after my growth spurt but I never got the visualisation exercises either. They went something like this: *Imagine an apple. Then imagine that you are sitting in an apple.* Eh? So I imagined I was sitting in an apple. Next I had to imagine that I had become an apple. Pardon? And that was that. I threw the book in the bin.

I'd started off at Plumtree on a scholarship but by now I had been given a bursary, which meant some of my fees were paid and that they recognised something special in me. You would have thought that would help to stimulate me, to make me more satisfied, but no. I just had this uncanny feeling that I never made the grade in God's eyes and I couldn't shake it off. Unlike sport, there was nothing I could do about it.

Perhaps my friends could sense that I was searching so one of them invited me to attend a Christian holiday camp. These guys were well known in the school for their involvement with the Christian group. It was unlike the church services. They sang modern songs and shared really good stories of how God was involved in their lives. If I'm honest I envied something they had. These were solid guys who weren't weird in any way and they had a quiet peace that I didn't have. But I wanted it.

So finally I decided to go to the youth camp one holiday and it was an amazing experience. We had lots of fun and games, but we had great talks and conversations, covering many different topics. After hearing the message of salvation called the Gospel, I was converted. Up to this point I'd heard all about Christ dying for the sins of the world. I knew all about the Christian festivals but I'd never before reached the point where I felt it was something I would appropriate in my own life.

I felt in my heart that I had heard the truth I was seeking.

So, at the age of 16 on 12th December 1992, I decided to become a

Christian. I felt free and at peace with God. No more did I have to wrestle with the scenario of what if I lived like a heathen and died only to find out that God did exist?

I went to the youth camps for two years or so and I look back on them as the key beginnings of my journey towards relating to God. However, some sad things did happen at these camps.

At one of the camps I attended, possibly my second, somebody died. He wasn't a strong swimmer and had jumped into the pool. Nobody missed him until the following day, when his body was discovered at the bottom of the pool. We were all horrified. How could something like this have happened?

After I had left school I heard that a scandal had broken out surrounding the behaviour of the guy who ran them, the camp director. It emerged that some of the day-school kids who attended the camp had complained about some of the things he had been doing. Beatings, skinny dipping and communal showering, that kind of thing.

To a boarding school pupil these things did not seem odd. We regarded corporal punishment as normal and living so close to other boys seven days a week, I never gave it a second thought when the camp director used to come into the showers with us.

But some of the day scholars went home and told their parents what had happened and they were absolutely livid. The parents got together and decided to sue him, so they hired a lawyer called David Coltart. He was a human rights lawyer at the time and he got in touch with me to see if I would be willing to tell my side of the story as a former camp leader.

On meeting him I was given a dossier that had been compiled in England and focused on the camp director and his past life there and some legal issues he had had, again involving alleged inappropriate behaviour with children. By this stage I would have been about 20 years old and I was asked to appear as a witness in the parents' action. As it turned out, it never went to court but I had been introduced to David, who would go on to play a hugely important part in my life.

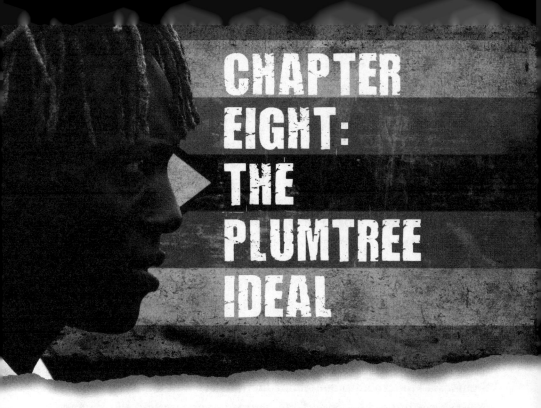

CHAPTER EIGHT: THE PLUMTREE IDEAL

God, grant me the serenity to accept the things I cannot change; courage to change the things that I can; and wisdom to know the difference.
Reinhold Niebuhr

During 1992, aged 16, I ran the 100 metres in 10.6 seconds, threw the javelin 60 metres and cleared seven metres in the long jump. These achievements were all down to Atherton Squires. OK, maybe I had something to do with it too but without his cajoling, without his training regimes, I wouldn't have got close to any of those achievements. For a time I thought that it might really be possible that I could represent Zimbabwe at athletics and get to an Olympic Games.

But at the beginning of 1993 I was gutted when I returned to school after the Christmas holidays and discovered that Squires had been head-hunted by a private school called St John's and left Plumtree. If ever there was a man I looked up to, a man I wanted to do well for, it was Atherton Squires, and now he was gone. My sporting dreams were shattered.

However, a few weeks after he had gone I received a call from him, saying that he wanted me to join him at St John's. He told me that he still believed I had huge potential as an athlete and that I could go all the way. He also said he could arrange a scholarship for me. I had a massive decision to make. I was happy at Plumtree, but this man had been my mentor in sport, which played a huge part of my life.

I asked my dad what he thought and he advised me against going as he felt Plumtree was the best place for me. I also talked to my teachers and they said that Squires wasn't the only one who could coach us and insisted that I would be able to run just as fast as I had done before, faster even. Some of them felt that Squires wanted to take all of the credit for the success achieved by the school on the athletics track. I believed that Squires had just about single-handedly transformed Plumtree's athletics programme and so he was perfectly entitled to claim the credit as far as I was concerned.

With all this pressure on my shoulders, and with Dad saying that he had spoken to the head and agreed with him, I decided to stay where I was.

So I gave up on the opportunity to go to a better school where I would have been able to concentrate on my athletics and my cricket. Later in my school career I developed a problem with my bowling technique which I am convinced would have been ironed out at St John's. But there is an uneasy tension involved with this part of my life because had I gone to Harare I would have become a 'shifty'. Most Matabeleland schoolboys considered that to be a fate worse than death!

The other thing is that I loved Plumtree. It had a great tradition and because none of the boys were from really rich families they tended to be down to earth. I had also made a ton of friends there and when I told them of my dilemma they all played a part in persuading me not to go. Overall I lean towards believing that I made the right call to stay at Plumtree.

Squires took over the athletics programme at St John's and, guess what, they started winning everything. Plumtree, meanwhile, never attained the same heights again. There was a group of kids, myself among them, who had been trained by him and who managed to continue competing at a decent level, but we no longer had the strength in depth and nobody came through to challenge us and then follow in our footsteps when we left the school.

More changes were to come to the school. Mike 'Spike' Whiley, the headmaster, left and was sorely missed by us all but was ably replaced by the deputy head Mr John 'Jub' Shaw for a term. Gone was the man with his three Dalmatians and bicycle roaming the school and calling students 'peanuts'. Mr Shaw was renowned for always saying the Prayer of Serenity after school assembly. And the words have never left me.

Mr Whiley was replaced by Ian Glover. Glover was a highly experienced teacher and had an entirely different approach to Spike, who used get on convivially with his pupils and would happily umpire cricket matches. Glover came to us from Harare and his arrival coincided with me being appointed head boy.

Mr Glover had a wife whose name was Denise. She was a cuddly lady, and the two of us became the unlikeliest of friends. I nicknamed her Ma G and it has stuck to this day. I bumped into her one day and told her I was hungry – I often was as I didn't really like the school food. Without hesitation she told me to come inside her home and she would make me a sandwich. She made me a cheese and bacon toastie, and it was delicious, much better than the overcooked school porridge.

Before I knew where I was, this had become a regular habit, and then I found out that she had a fantastic collection of classical music, so we listened to that together too. Food *and* music – I was in heaven! One of my most cruel pranks but one that gave me the greatest kicks was to sneak up behind Ma G in her house and giving her a fright by making a loud noise. I am sure that I almost gave her a heart attack on more than one occasion. She had two dogs, but they were old and deaf, so they never heard me coming.

I did have a few run-ins with her husband, however, because he kept insisting that I attend my lessons, which was a pretty reasonable request from your headmaster. But in my final years I spent more time away practising or playing cricket. We were often at loggerheads over it.

It didn't help that a lot of the teachers didn't get along with the head as when he first came to the school he was a 'no man'. By that I mean often before you had even finished asking a question, he would say "No." Spike

Wiley wasn't like that so it was difficult for many to adjust to the new regime. Admittedly Mr Glover had to place his stamp of authority early on but he eventually mellowed down. Ironically he is now a good friend.

Some boys go through the teenage rebellion stage when they are 13 or 14, but with me it occurred when I was 17. Maybe I was just reacting because he was never receptive to any of the ideas that came his way and I decided that if he wasn't going to give anybody else the time of day, then why should I give it to him?

Luckily I passed my exams anyway, and we did find some common ground in cricket. He loved the game and I was good at it, taking lots of wickets for the school, so in the end we established a grudging respect for one another.

An incident I remember sums up his outlook. Glover enjoyed rugby and on one occasion we were playing another school, Peterhouse, at a rugby festival and we got a penalty behind the halfway line. I decided to kick for goal and could hear the collective murmurs in the crowd. I knew I could get it because the team had been staying at Lilfordia School and I had practised that exact distance successfully.

Yes, it was a long kick, but I had a chance. I gave it everything I had, caught it perfectly and watched as it fell between the posts, just clearing the bar. It was a big moment for me, but we went on to lose the match. We were coming off the pitch and Glover came up to me and said, "I didn't think you would get that kick, well done." I wasn't surprised at his reaction because he was a natural pessimist.

Ma G could not have been more different from her husband. She was full of optimism and was hugely encouraging towards me. Here I was, an 18-year-old boy, striking up a relationship with a 50-something woman and discovering that we had a lot in common. I was black, she was white; I was young, she was old. It was an unlikely alliance but I can still relate to this hospitable woman. I sometimes related better to my elders, such as teachers and coaches, than I did with students my own age.

Just before my final year, in the last week of term 1993, a prefects' camp was held at a place called Willow Creek. It was the sort of place where companies would send their employees for team-building courses . It had a lake, obstacle courses and all that sort of stuff. The camp was a blast, but the overwhelming thing that came out of it for me was the challenge of creating a different kind of prefect.

The camp director, Mark Klukow, made the suggestion that we do things differently from how they had been done in the past. Traditionally, prefects were bullies who threw their weight around and ruled with a reign of terror. I had been appointed head boy, which gave me the perfect opportunity to try to leave a positive legacy and I thought it would be great to try to change that. Wouldn't it be better if the prefects worked at mentoring the younger pupils rather than bullying them? It simply wasn't right that prefects should be allowed to cane younger pupils, or inflict any form of physical punishment on their fellow students.

There were some who didn't want to change things but they were in the minority so we put it to the vote and agreed that the following term would see a new approach. It was the right thing to do.

Towards the end of the camp, Mark recited a poem – *Risk*, by a poet called Leo Bascaglia – that left a huge impression on me. On hearing it I realised that it encapsulated the essence of how I felt about life.

To laugh is to risk appearing the fool.
To weep is to risk appearing sentimental.
To reach out for another is to risk involvement.
To expose feelings is to risk exposing your true self.
To place your ideas, your dreams, before a crowd is to risk their loss.
To love is to risk not being loved in return.
To live is to risk dying.
To hope is to risk failure.

But risks must be taken.
Because the greatest hazard in life is to risk nothing.
If you risk nothing and do nothing, you dull your spirit.
You may avoid suffering and sorrow, but you cannot learn, feel, change, grow,
   love, and live.
Chained by your attitude, you are a slave.
You have forfeited your freedom.
Only if you risk are you free

The prefects' camp had a positive effect on us and before we went back to Plumtree we wanted to thank one of the men who ran it called Rowan. So myself, Busisa Moyo, the deputy headboy, and another friend, Garth Lester, went to seek him out before we left. As we approached him he said, "Welcome you three who have been drawn here by the Holy Spirit."

We looked at him, and then at each other, and wondered what on earth he was talking about, but he continued talking. He started making prophecies about things that were going to happen to us in the future. He said, "There will be many who will come to seek the comfort of the fire and you must not turn them away, you must give them peace and give them comfort."

We were all in a state of bewilderment but it was about to get a whole lot stranger because the next thing he said was, "I am going to blow on you the Holy Spirit." As he said this a whirlwind blew up outside. It was very, very odd, like being in a scary movie, but it had a profound effect on me and I resolved to be more spiritual from that day on.

I was determined that as head boy I would really make a difference to the school. A former pupil of the school called Mr Anderson had written a piece of prose called *The Plumtree Ideal*, which basically summed up the characteristics of the ideal Plumtree student. This was how it described the perfect Plumtree pupil:

A young man with manners, of honesty and integrity, respectful of his own and others' property, respectful of his elders, and in particular those who give of their time for his benefit, proud of himself and of Plumtree, always determined to acquit himself well even when the chips are down.

It moved me to such an extent that I suggested that the whole school should learn it. Now I am not going to suggest that, as a result, the whole school became well behaved overnight but I hope that there was something that was placed in their psyche that made them aspire to bigger and better things.

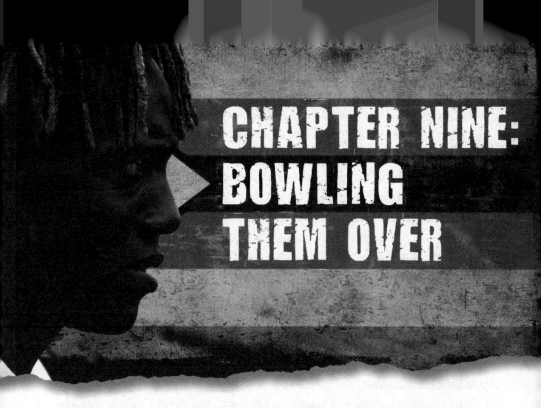

CHAPTER NINE: BOWLING THEM OVER

"We do not have a really fast bowler, Henry, and I believe you are good enough to become that player," he said. He also pointed out that I could be the first black cricketer to play for the country.

With Squires gone I kind of lost my way a little. Although I loved my athletics, without my mentor my passion for running began to fizzle out.

Meanwhile, I had played my way back into the Zimbabwe schools cricket team and during this period the country had been awarded Test status for the first time. In 1992 the country played its first official Test against India and this was followed by a series against Sri Lanka.

But there was one thing missing from that first Zimbabwe Test side – there was no black player in the team. Of course the vast majority of the population were black, so it seemed odd that no black player, either batsman or bowler, had been able to break through. Indeed, the Zimbabwe cricket team had never had a black player. On top of that, the team had no out and out fast bowlers. Yes, we had some fast medium pacers such as Heath Streak, who could occasionally deliver the odd quick ball, but we did not have a genuine quickie.

The cricket coach at Plumtree at this time was a guy called Roy Jones. One day Roy, who now teaches in Bristol, sat me down by the side of the basketball courts and told me that he thought I had the talent to play for Zimbabwe at Test level.

"We do not have a really fast bowler, Henry, and I believe you are good enough to become that player," he said. He also pointed out that I could be the first black cricketer to play for the country.

"If you put your mind to it, you could be playing for this team before you know it. Imagine travelling the world, playing a sport you love and getting paid for it. You will have to work hard, but there is no reason why it can't happen."

I was 17 when Jones delivered this verdict and I decided that I liked the sound of what he'd said. It made sense and I began working towards achieving my new dream.

For a start I decided to bring my rugby career to an end after I suffered an ankle injury whilst throwing the javelin. It flared up again on the rugby field and I realised that I had to stop playing rugby if I was going to be successful at cricket. So I wrote a letter to the rugby coach, Doug Lake, in which I told him I was no longer available, and had a younger pupil take it over to him. It is not one of the proudest moments of my life. I should have gone to see him, face to face and had an adult conversation.

Although I was pretty good at it, throwing the javelin was at the root of more than just physical problems for me when it came to my cricket. One or two people told me that sometimes when I bowled a cricket ball it appeared to them that I was bending my right arm during my delivery, exactly as I did when throwing the javelin. In cricket, they call this "throwing" or "chucking" and it is illegal because it allows bowlers to find a bit more speed. Nobody made much of an issue of it and, because of that, neither did I. Looking back I would have benefited from specialist bowling coaching but it wasn't available to me, and I was taking wickets, so why worry about it?

I began to develop as a cricketer, taking lots of wickets and even scoring a few runs. I struck up a friendship with Donald Campbell, who was the captain of the schools team, whose brother Alistair played for the national team, and I ended up spending quite a bit of time with the Campbells.

The Plumtree team would often stay at Lilfordia School just outside Harare – where Donald's dad, the late Poll Campbell, was the headmaster – on the way to and from sports festivals there. On other occasions Donald would arrange for us to stay with his family if the events were more than a day's drive from the school.

They were the nicest family I had ever come across. They had a genuine love for each other and were really nice, generous and open. They had tons of fun and joked together, and anyone was welcome with them. I cannot heap enough praise on this family. It was a cause of sadness to me as well in a way because I was observing how a normal family should behave with each other, while I had a degree of dysfunction in most areas of my life.

The Campbells were always generous when it came to accommodation and just a phone call to the school and an appeal for a lift and a place to stay would lead to Poll giving instructions to Kinross, the school's driver, to fetch us from wherever we were. So it was that we often stayed there for the cricket or rugby festivals in Harare when all the schools assembled together at the beginning of each season to play each other to get everyone into the mood for competition.

On occasions like this you were expected to have your own gear and it was also important to look the part if you wanted to impress the Zimbabwe schools selectors, so it was embarrassing to be scrambling around trying to borrow stuff. I didn't even have a bat until Alistair Campbell handed me one and told me that I could keep it. Imagine that – being given a cricket bat by one of the best players in the country. It was one of the best gifts I ever received. It was an SS Jumbo and it had the biggest sweet spot you could imagine.

While I was with them I picked up a cricket catalogue by a British company called 3-D and took it back to show to my father. I pointed to a pair of boots and told him that I would love to have a pair just like them along with some other cricket gear. I always believed that if you don't ask you won't receive. Up until that point I had only ever bowled with trainers and they are not ideal for fast bowling.

Dad had a UK bank account with Lloyds and when the order was placed I was over the moon to receive a real pair of cricket boots. My dad had never been demonstrative with physical affection but he was generous. It wasn't like that all the time, mind you. When we were young he was very frugal and with reason, but as we grew older he became more giving. When he bought that kit my love and appreciation for him as a father who provided deepened exceedingly.

In the Plumtree team we always shared bats, pads and such like and it was nice to be able to lend my kit to others instead of asking teammates if I could borrow their bat or their box!

That SS Jumbo that Alistair Campbell gave me was a beast, and suddenly I was starting to make lots of runs. For the first time in my life I was performing like a proper batsman. Roy Jones taught me to tighten up my technique. Then I got into the habit of getting out to leading edges, usually when I was on 49, but I had a word with Donald Campbell and he told me to watch the ball onto the bat and I started turning those scores into 50s.

I was bursting with confidence now and Roy Jones kept reminding me that I was good enough to become Zimbabwe's first black Test cricketer. I had discovered the secret of batting (or at least I thought I had), so I began to turn my focus to cricket more and more and, before long, I was starting to score centuries and was even harbouring ambitions of becoming a genuine all-rounder.

My first hundred came earlier in 1993 against Milton, a rival, government-run school. They would often play for a draw but we wanted to beat them. It was difficult to get a result in a game that started just after lunch, but we always looked for a way. You have to force a victory. They batted first and gave us a big target to chase, something in the order of 250 runs. In reality, it was impossible.

I was batting with a boy called James Harhoff. We were batting pretty well and reached 100 for the loss of a couple of wickets, when the coach got the message to us that he felt we had a chance of reaching the target. So I wandered down the wicket and said to James, "Right then, James, let's go for this. We can do it."

This match featured a guy called Mpumelelo Mbangwa, who was their kingpin. He was an ex-REPS boy as well and now he had attended Milton for a number of years. He had been given a scholarship by an English school called Dean Close, which had toured Zimbabwe, played against him and been impressed by his ability as a cricketer. When he came back, everybody called him 'Pommie' because he returned to Zimbabwe with an English accent. Pommie was their main man. He wasn't very quick, but he bowled naggingly accurate out-swingers. He ended up playing for Zimbabwe with me and has since done really well for himself working as an internationally recognised commentator; everyone still calls him Pommie.

Anyway, after I'd reached my 50, James and I launched into their attack, hitting sixes and fours almost at will. It was carnage, and in the end we reached our target easily. It was the first time I'd experienced high fives on a cricket field, and I loved every second of it. Nobody had expected us to get there, we had beaten our big rivals and I had batted brilliantly, scoring my maiden ton. I felt I had arrived as a batsman, and afterwards every single member of the opposition team wanted to look at my Jumbo bat.

That match against Milton was a turning point for me in my cricket career. From then on, if I didn't score lots of runs I would take a bunch of wickets, and my self-belief grew with every passing match. Doors started to open for me. It was a confirmation that I belonged in this sport.

Brighton College came out from England on tour in 1994 to play a few Zimbabwean schools. I was captaining the side and I hated declaration games, when the opposition would bat negatively right from the off, so at the toss I asked their skipper if we could play a limited-overs match. But he wanted to stick to the traditional format and I was livid. They won the toss and opted to bat, but an hour and a half later they were back in the hut, all out for not many, after I had taken eight wickets for 15 runs. When it was our turn to bat I made 103. There was so much time left in the day we allowed them to bat again. That is hands down the best day's cricket I have ever played at any level.

Brighton had a player called Claire Connor in their team and we thought it was hilarious that they had turned up to play us with a girl in their side. I am not being sexist at all: this just never happened in Zimbabwe. We had no idea that women even played cricket. What were we going to say if she overstepped the crease? We had that figured out – 'No balls'! Unfortunately she had broken a finger in an earlier match so was unavailable for selection. Later on in life she became the captain of the England women's team and led them to a victorious Ashes campaign. She also ended up playing for the Lashings World XI with me and, guess what, she was the leading wicket-taker that season!

By this time, Victor had left Plumtree. He'd had an argument with a teacher and it was made clear to him that he would not be welcomed back. Victor took it to heart because he felt he had been picked on unfairly and that Dad should have stuck up for him. It is amazing how something that can seem insignificant in your teens may go on to shape your entire life.

From that point, Victor's life went in a different direction and he started having brushes with the law. Dad tried to get him to go to college but he refused, although he did carry on playing rugby and went on to represent Zimbabwe. He scored a magnificent try in a match against Wales and then became captain of the country until having a conflict with the authorities in 2001 when he led a player boycott in a bid to get the team's training facilities improved. He was banned from playing for Zimbabwe so he moved to England and played rugby for the Penzance and Newlyn Rugby Football Club in Cornwall.

Right up until the mid-1990s very few black men played rugby or cricket. Victor was the first of a wave of black players who started to be picked on a regular basis for Zimbabwe. He was capped more than 30 times. He hated losing and he also hated being asked to play out of position, which the Zimbabwe selectors frequently got him to do.

He spent most of career as a fullback but I know that he longed to play fly half. Later on in life he also made it abundantly clear that he did not agree with the stance I took against Mugabe and stated so publicly, which was very disappointing for me. Having said that, I have always tried to give him the benefit of the doubt. Perhaps he reacted the way that he did as a defence mechanism. He wanted to return to Zimbabwe after all.

Victor is a livewire, and has been all his life. He is a free spirit who lives his life the way he wants to. Perhaps it would be helpful if he were more circum-spect. I really got on well with him when we were younger but beyond a certain stage in our teens we didn't get along. I really miss those days. I suspect that beneath the tough exterior he has a good soul inside him. Sadly we hardly talk now due to our different points of view but I am sure that one day we will be reconciled. He is now settled in Bulawayo, although there is not much available for a retired rugby player in a small country like Zimbabwe.

Music continued to play a major part in my life. Often I would tell Denise Glover that I wanted to sing a particular song but I wasn't sure if I could hit the high notes, but she would always tell me that I could, and that I should go for it. I had two musical friends, Sifiso Makalisa and Michael Brownlee-Walker, who both went on to become music professionals. They would often accompany the choir and on the odd occasion my solo pieces. I sang at numerous weddings, including that of Doug Lake, my rugby coach, and Jane Westwood, the daughter of Felix. I was also singing at the occasional concert, and that continued as my cricket career progressed.

Felix was another teacher with whom I struck up a rapport. It developed after I gave her a painting I had done. We were never really close, but from time to time I used to open up to her about some personal stuff. She was a lovely lady with a very warm heart, although she was pretty strict too.

We were talking one day, not long before I was about to leave school for good, and she suggested that I go for an audition. The London Academy of Music and Dramatic Arts had sent a talent scout to Zimbabwe and she believed that I should go and sing for him. The audition was being held at Girls' College in Bulawayo, so off I went and sang *The Holy City*. The scout was impressed with me and told me that he would love to see if he could give me a scholarship. He felt that there were not a lot of young black singers available for the West End in London and that he thought I had what it took. In a nutshell he was offering me a scholarship if I were willing to pursue it.

But soon after leaving school cricket came to dominate my life to the point that I was unable to take advantage of the offer. Of course, there would have been no guarantees of success, especially in England, where there are so many other very fine singers, but it would have been something else to have had the opportunity to further my music.

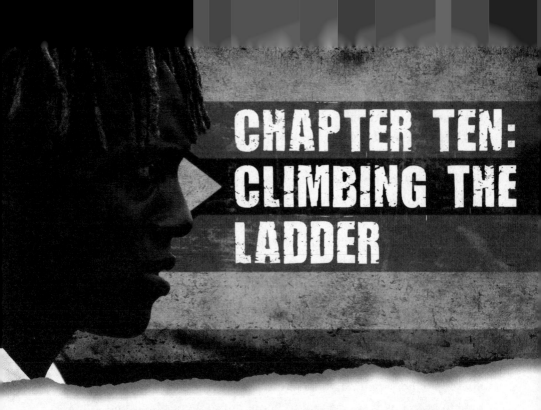

CHAPTER TEN: CLIMBING THE LADDER

I'd been told that the national selectors had wanted me to make my test debut against Sri Lanka when I was still at school, but I felt I wasn't ready.

In my final year of high school I suffered an eye injury when, during a cricket training session, we returned to the damp wicket to continue a net session after a slight downpour. One of my teammates decided to bowl a bouncer that reared up off the damp surface and caught me flush on my right eye. I was rushed off to hospital and had to have eye drops that made my pupil dilate for a few days. Thankfully I never did have the detached retina that they suspected and in a few days I returned to school with an eye patch. That was a scary time and realised how easy it is to lose one's sight. To this day the right eye has never been right and requires a stronger prescription with my glasses.

When I could get away from school I was playing for the provincial team, Matebeleland. This was the full men's team and included players like Heath

Streak whom I had played both alongside and against in provincial and schools rugby and cricket.

Heath's dad Dennis ran the winter league club called Good Hope Country Club. It was a club that was based at their farm, where they also reared wildlife. I played for them a few times in matches against touring teams and also played winter league games. I remember the Christians in Sport team coming out from England and playing us there once and I met Andrew Wingfield Digby, the chaplain to the English cricket team. In those days I was still a wayward tearaway bowler, really quick but not terribly accurate. Despite this, I clearly impressed the Streaks.

The Streaks also wanted me to play for Old Miltonians, the Matabeleland league club so I ended up bowling alongside them and one or two others who would go on to became fine cricketers. I was about 17 years old at this stage but I was still at school, which meant they had to pick me up and then drop me off back at Plumtree every Sunday.

I am indebted to the Streaks who, along with the Campbells, helped and encouraged me to get stuck in and develop and improve my bowling. Without their support, who knows whether I would have improved as I did?

I then established myself in the Matebeleland team, under the captaincy of Plumtree old boy and wicketkeeper–batsman, Wayne James, who would transport me to and from games. Wayne had a wonderful girlfriend called Jenny, who would later become his wife. He was very frustrated with life at that stage because he worked for his father and eventually he had to make a choice between family, business and cricket. He wanted to be a full-time cricketer, but he would often be chosen to go on tour with Zimbabwe and then find that he spent the whole time sitting on the sidelines watching the action, cursing Andy Flower, the first choice keeper, under his breath.

I have mentioned that people like Heath and Dennis Streak, Wayne and another humorous teammate called Roscoe would drive me to and from cricket matches, but I probably need to put this in perspective. Often this would mean that they were faced with journeys of around 100 kilometres to and from Plumtree and sometimes more if we were playing in and around Harare, so the sacrifices they were making on my behalf were considerable.

During my last year at school I spent very little time in the classroom – my year was dominated by cricket, playing for my club, Old Miltonians, and the province. I found myself playing against senior professional cricketers, the likes of Dave Houghton, Grant and Andy Flower and David Brains to name a few. Despite my inconsistency, I did enough to impress these guys and I kept being picked and kept taking wickets here and there. By this time, any thoughts I might have entertained about being an all-rounder had been laid to rest. When you start to face accurate fast bowlers who propel the ball towards you at speeds in excess of 85 mph you quickly find out whether or not you really can bat. And I couldn't.

And as I began to make a name for myself in the game, people were also beginning to sit up and take notice of the minnows of Zimbabwe on the international stage and we had some serious players like Eddo Brandes, who took lots of wickets against England. But there were still no black players.

In the mid 1990s, however, cricket was becoming for everybody, and I was in the thick of it. Old Miltonians had a formidable pace attack. There was myself, Heath Streak, John Rennie and Ethan Dube, who was the other joker of the team. Ethan had been shortlisted as the black player most likely to play Test cricket for Zimbabwe along with another talented black bowler called George Thandi. But things never quite materialised for those two.

We also had a couple of decent all-rounders, including Guy Whittal, and some superb batsmen, the pick of whom was probably Mark Dekker. I had watched Mark play against New Zealand at Bulawayo Athletics Club (BAC), which was the city's international ground until Queens was renovated. He was flaying their bowling all over the park. The facilities at most of the grounds we played at were pretty basic. There was a pitch, a pavilion and a boundary, and that was about it. BAC, however, had tennis courts and when the West Indies played there Carl Hooper hit a huge six that disappeared onto the courts, never to be seen again.

Dekker was a phenomenal left-handed batsman. I discovered he had been a believer at one point but he decided he did not believe in God any more. As far as critics of my faith came he was the most vociferous and he would often question my beliefs publicly. In Mark's case I was to hear that personal tragedy had led him to that place. I had heard that somebody close to him had died and Mark had failed to reconcile what had happened with his religious belief. I have heard that Charles Darwin also followed a similar path after the death of his daughter Annie.

I got on well with most of the Old Miltonians team. By the time I started playing for them they had already faced lots of black cricketers and as I mentioned we had a funny guy called Ethan Dube playing as well, so they embraced me. All that they were interested in was whether or not I could bowl.

Between matches, I sat my A-levels and prayed that I would manage to get some passes. I ended up with an A for art, C for geography and E for English, and I also managed to scrape an O-level pass in biology. I have no idea why I stuck with four subjects. Had I just done three my results would surely have been better.

There was a system of recognising consistent achievement at Plumtree. If you played in the school first team at any sport you would receive something called "99s". You were presented with a little badge. I am sure that there is a logical reason for the term 99s, but nobody I came across ever knew what it was. Almost there perhaps? If you were chosen to represent the province you received something called "colours", which allowed you to wear a blazer with red stripes, but the ultimate recognition was 'honours', which took the form of a cream blazer – you received this for achieving something extra special, such as representing your country.

I'd already received my colours when I was 16 but I really wanted honours. I had represented my country at cricket and rugby and I had set all these records and, to be honest, by the end of my final term at the school I was a little put out that I hadn't had them already. You were never told that you were going to receive colours or honours: it was announced just before you broke up at the end of term. I was beginning to despair of ever receiving honours, but, sitting at the back of the chapel just before I left the school for ever, my name was finally called out. It was the proudest moment of my school life. After my final examinations I left Plumtree School and I had already decided that I wanted to continue with my cricket and try to forge a career in the game.

I attended a Zimbabwe schools cricket selection week, held at St John's

School, where Atherton Squires had gone to work. It was a week-long tournament in which all the provinces played against each other, and it was attended by the national schools selectors. I was playing well, taking wickets and scoring runs, but I sprained my ankle just before the last game and Andy Pycroft, one of the national schools selectors, approached me and asked if I intended to bowl the following day. I told him that I was really hurt and that I didn't think I would play. "Well, if you don't bite the bullet and play, we might not pick you, Henry." he said. "We need to see you take wickets."

So I strapped up my ankle and bowled through the pain, taking a few wickets in a rain-affected match but nonetheless impressing the selectors in the process. It was a lesson to me that sometimes you just have to play through discomfort. I'd had back problems since I was 16 because of all the cricket I was playing and from that point I was playing with a back support and I was popping Ibuprofen tablets like sweets. In England and other parts of the world, they wouldn't allow that sort of thing from a young fast bowler, but I soon realised this was my lot as a pace man.

During that week, Bill Flower (the father of Andy and Grant) took me to one side and told me he thought that I was a good player, but that I was too erratic. He was the convenor of selectors for the schools side, so he was an influential figure and when he spoke, you listened. I knew that he was correct. He told me that he was impressed with my pace though.

Things were moving very fast in my cricket career, and some people were starting to whisper that I might become Zimbabwe's first black cricketer. One potential stumbling block to this was the fact that I had a Kenyan passport and was still officially a Kenyan national, so I knew that at some point I might have to make an important decision about where my allegiance lay. It wouldn't be difficult because I had spent most of my life in Zimbabwe.

The next thing that happened was that a journalist from England called Geoffrey Dean sought me out for an interview. He wrote a fabulous article for *The Daily Telegraph* all about my life – the kid whose father wanted him to run for Kenya but who could be about to make history as a cricketer. By now I'd been told that the national selectors had wanted me to make my Test debut against Sri Lanka when I was still at school but felt I wasn't ready.

Following on from the selection week, I attended the Coca-Cola schools cricket festival in Pretoria with the Zimbabwe schools team. The trip to South

Africa was not the best. We travelled down in a coach and early on during the trip the on-board toilet stopped working, and the air-conditioning also packed up. Try to imagine how awful it was, especially after the last person to use the loo before it died had left a particularly stinky one. The pong soon permeated the entire bus, so we had times when the coach would be travelling along the road with all these teenage boys standing up on their seats and sticking their head out the windows and the sunroof to get some fresh air. Heaven alone knows what we must have looked like, and that's without stopping to consider how dangerous it was. We reckon it was Trevor Madondo or 'Mad Dog' as he was affectionately called who was the culprit. We all just wanted to get out of there, but we couldn't. I have never felt so claustrophobic in my entire life.

And things didn't really get much better for us when we arrived and started playing cricket. The standard in South Africa was so much higher, even at schools level, than anything we had been used to. We would play against provinces and they would eat us for breakfast. I remember we faced these huge pace bowlers and being frightened for our lives because we weren't wearing helmets. There was one huge fast bowler we had to face as the sun was going down and the ball was fizzing around our ears. Fun it was not. The game was eventually called off for fear that somebody would end up being seriously hurt by this big brute.

While we were in South Africa we went to see a day-night match at Centurion Park. It was the first time I had ever seen a day-night match live. They love their cricket in South Africa and every match is a huge social occasion as they cook barbecues (braais) with music thundering out in the background. I wanted to be involved in this. During the game one of the batsmen skied a shot high into the air and as it disappeared into the floodlit night sky the entire crowd let out a massive "Oooh". The saying "money on the ball" comes to mind and it seemed that everybody in the ground held their breath as they waited to see whether any of the fielding side would catch this ball as it made its way back to earth. The fielder didn't get anywhere near it. The atmosphere was fabulous.

We returned home a few days later after the tournament ended and when we got back on the bus to return home to Zimbabwe, we realised all too quickly that the toilet had not been repaired.

Within a few weeks of returning from South Africa I found myself back there again, this time having been selected for the full Zimbabwe B side. The B side was the team just under the national side and most young talented cricketers were blooded in this team. It was to be a two-week tour and we would play a few provinces and the South African A side.

We were staying in a luxurious hotel in Johannesburg in a posh part of the city. Now back in those days we used to have to share our rooms with a teammate although later on that would change and we would have total privacy. I was sharing with a senior player, with whom I would go on to play several tests, and one night he brought a girl he had picked up back to the hotel room. I wasn't sure what she was doing in the room but then it became obvious when the two of them climbed into his bed and made love. I was in the bed next to him with a blanket over my head pretending it wasn't happening. I wanted to die.

As if that hadn't been bad enough, on the second night he phoned an escort agency and told them he wanted a brunette. Soon afterwards there was a knock on the door and a girl came into the room, looked at me and the first thing she said was, "I don't do black guys". We were in South Africa, remember. I actually wasn't offended by her remarks, but I was mortified that he'd had the audacity to bring a prostitute into our room. He didn't ask me if it was OK and it was too late for me to go anywhere else. I couldn't just sit outside the room.

So again I just had to lie there; eventually he paid her and she left. There was a total lack of respect and I thought it was beyond the pale. But I was only 18, a junior on the tour, and I didn't want to rock the boat. After the woman left the room, I lay in bed, not saying a word, when he turned to me and started attacking my Christian values. The truth, I guess, is that he felt some guilt over what he'd done. We had a discussion about faith in which we debated a few issues. I didn't report it to anybody, but it never happened again.

It was an incident that reinforced my views on sex. When I was 15 I had been involved in a brief relationship with a city girl who had been in the dating game way longer than I had. She was the same age as me, had seen me play a rugby match and had taken a liking to me. So she wanted to become pen pals and we wrote a couple of letters to each other. I remember how beautiful her writing was; the feeling of falling in love was incredible.

But I couldn't get over how fast everything was moving and my conscience bugged me. This was mainly to do with the fact that Mum had sent me to a sex education class and all they spoke about was the dangers of HIV and AIDS. They also showed us some dreadful photographs of people in the advanced stages of the disease and I already knew a few people who had died from the "slow puncture", as AIDS is called in Zimbabwe.

I also remembered a young schoolmate who kept complaining that every time he went to urinate it was like agony, like his privates were on fire. So they sent him for some tests to discover that he was suffering from gonorrhoea. At 12 years of age! And there were boys younger than him who were sexually active. In my eyes it was a frightening prospect to consider crossing that line so young. I had been brought up to believe that premarital sex was wrong so I resolved to wait until I met the right person and within a few weeks the relationship was over.

As part of an AIDS awareness campaign in Zimbabwe they had used the slogan "True love waits". In other words, abstaining from illicit sexual affairs is the best way for a young person to conduct himself. It teaches self-control which is needed for marital fidelity and most of all it prevents the spread of disease. That was one of the hardest sermons I heard but I responded by deciding that I wanted to develop that kind of character and that I would avoid casual sex. It seemed out of swing with the rest of the world but in Africa this can save your life.

Falling in love was never going to be easy for me. But when I was 17 and still at school I met a young woman whom I shared a great deal of my formative years with. We went to my last prom dance together before I left school, we fell madly in love and would go on to become engaged. Because she has asked me not to talk about our relationship in this book I will respect her wishes, but she was a Christian girl with high ethics, was very respectable and a genuinely wonderful human being. Though we were young we did genuinely care deeply for each other. We both loved music and she had a very musical voice. It was a turbulent, on/off relationship and we both broke it off a number of times, but for a time we were very much in love.

On that trip to South Africa with Zimbabwe B we faced Shaun Pollock,

Dale Benkenstein, Neil Johnson and Jacques Kallis. This was before they had made their full Test debuts but, even then, it wasn't difficult to work out that these were going to be wonderful Test cricketers. We returned to Zimbabwe with nothing to show for the trip as we were resoundingly thrashed in every match.

On my journey to the top I had learnt over time to develop aggression, it wasn't something that came naturally to me. When I did harness it, though, there were some disastrous results. I clearly remember a game we played against Milton when I was at Plumtree, I think it was for the under-15s. They had a player called Mhlaumbe Ncube and they always used to pick him in the wrong year, so he went right through school playing against boys who were younger than he was, which gave both him and his team a slight advantage. I used to hate it when they picked him to face us.

Anyway, this guy was a bowler so he came into bat as a tail-ender and perhaps all I had to do was bowl a straight yorker to dismiss him. But I was really fired up about Mhlaumbe being in the team and bowled him a bouncer that caught him flush in the jaw. He immediately grabbed his jaw and went off the field. There was some bad swelling and he was taken off to hospital. We later found out that I'd broken his jaw and I was absolutely gutted.

These kids could not afford to buy helmets, so he'd had no protection. But at the end of the day I had only bowled him that bouncer because I had felt a sense of injustice that he was being allowed to play against us when he should have been playing against older boys. But was that justification enough? That incident had a profound effect on me. If I hadn't broken his jaw, I think that I may have turned out to be a more ruthless fast bowler. You always get the sense that the likes of Geoff Thomson enjoyed breaking bones; for him, making opposing batsmen dance about in their crease was what Test cricket was all about, and that may be true.

But I never played any form of cricket to break anybody's bones, so from the moment I shattered Mhlaumbe's jaw I erred on the side of sportsmanship. Fancy that – a fast bowler with a conscience. I knew that I could bowl fast and that I could hurt people, but he was defenceless and injuring him remains one of my biggest regrets.

The sad thing was that I had actually gone to REPS with him so I had known him for ages. He used to win the cross country and one day he almost died when a pole accidently fell on his head. After the match Roy Jones suggested that it might be a good idea for me to write to him and I wrote a sincere letter of apology.

I am not suggesting that I was never again able to find a ruthless streak – clearly, I would not have been able to make the progress I did if I had bowled within myself, and I knew that if I didn't bowl flat out against top batsmen then they would punish me, but I retained my humanity. I bowled hard, but I bowled fair, and I got no enjoyment out of trying to hit a tail-ender unless they started getting smart. A cricket ball is hard and, in the wrong hands, it can be a lethal weapon, so my philosophy was to bowl fairly. I guess for similar reasons I was never into sledging either because I thought the ball should do my talking for me. And I also reckon you have to be a good bowler to sledge. No point sledging a batsmen and then he hits you for consecutive boundaries.

Having said all that, I did break a few more bones in my professional career, but the key difference was that it never came from a sense of anger or resentment. Unfortunately, one or two teammates suffered at my hands. I managed to break a bone in Brian Murphy's hand during a net session on the final day of a Test against Bangladesh and he never played for Zimbabwe again. It wasn't totally my fault, mind you, because the nets were just a rolled part of the outfield that had the odd divot here and there. The ball reared up from one of them and broke his left hand. D'oh!

The most unfortunate broken-bone story of my career concerned a guy called Greg Loveridge, a right-handed leg-spinner who was playing for New Zealand in 1996, making his Test debut in the Hamilton Test. I bowled a bouncer at him that caught him on the hand and he retired hurt with a broken finger. Sadly he never bowled a ball in that match and was never considered for international selection again. Greg, if you get to read this, I'm really sorry mate!

On another occasion we played a club match and I bowled another bouncer which caught the batsman on the elbow. He was taken to hospital, where it was discovered that he'd suffered a broken forearm, so they patched him up and put him in a sling and, lo and behold, he returned to the ground and came out to bat with one arm in a sling when they were nine men down. That was guts, although they still lost the match!

None of these injuries were intentional but they happened because I possessed the pace to cause that kind of mishap. But true power is not having the ability to do something and doing it: it's having the ability but knowing when to do it and for good motives. Perhaps this is the true tragedy of someone like Mugabe because he has the power to ruin people's lives and he uses it, when he could alternatively have used that power as a force for good.

We are given skills and abilities to use at the right time but with wisdom. But shattering people's bodies with a God-given ability to bowl quickly, just because you can, is not one of the things that you are supposed to do in my humble opinion. It is crossing the line and perhaps, in the thick of battle when the adrenaline is pumping, our natural desire to win takes over. But at the heart of this lies a 'win at all costs' attitude, be it ball-tampering, match-fixing or excessive appealing. Perhaps what I was starting to realise is that the game of cricket has a unique vantage point in all of world sport. In similar fashion to golf or tennis, it has a soft, somewhat unwritten moral compass. It is called the 'spirit of cricket'. It elevates our desire to be true sportsmen and tempers our natural tendency to have an unfair advantage.

The International Cricket Council has adopted the MCC's recommendations on the spirit of cricket into the laws of the game. The spirit of cricket was instrumental in some major decisions I was to make in later life. Did I make mistakes? Of course I did. Did I cross the line once or twice, like not walk when I should have? You bet. But I didn't do it often, always felt awful about it and subsequently always aspired to the highest levels of sportsmanship.

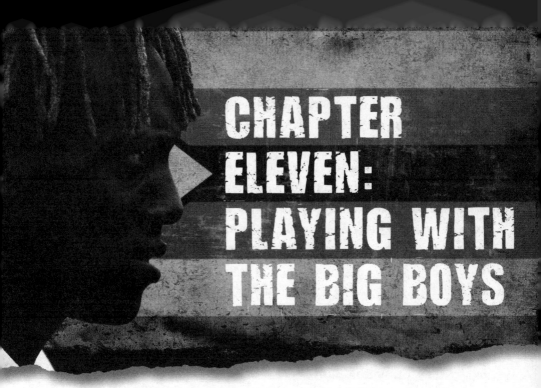

CHAPTER ELEVEN: PLAYING WITH THE BIG BOYS

All of a sudden, from being called a hero I was in disgrace because I had brought the name of Zimbabwe cricket into disrepute. In my first Test!

Months after leaving school I was still living at home with my dad, stepmum, younger brother and stepsister but without a real job. The world of cricket had embraced me and though I wasn't a professional, the fees I was receiving on the various club, provincial and national side tours were enough to live off and improving all the time. It appeared that cricket might turn out to be a viable profession for me.

During the 1994/95 season Pakistan arrived in Zimbabwe to play a Test series, and I was picked for the President's XI to face them in a warm-up match. It was mid-January and I had been bowling very well, but this would be proper cricket, against world-class opponents. Pakistan possessed batsmen who destroyed poor bowling and had fast bowlers who were among the very best on the planet, and I was about to face them at the age of 18.

This was the team I had watched winning the 1992 World Cup – Salim Malik, Wasim Akram, Saeed Anwar. Legends. The only one missing was Waqar Younis as he was suffering from a stress fracture of the lower back. It is an understatement to say that these guys were icons to me. We played them at Harare Country Club, which is just outside the city, a nice, picturesque ground next to a golf course. India had toured Zimbabwe, as had Sri Lanka, but this was huge and the media were out in force, including the BBC.

When the game started I thought I was bowling well enough, but the Pakistan team put pressure on the umpire to call me for throwing. It started as a faint complaint, then a loud whisper, then a clear accusation. Aamer Sohail had started the murmurings, saying, "He's throwing the ball." When I dismissed him I said, "Do you think I threw that one as well?" He stopped halfway to the pavilion and shouted back, "You are dead."

I felt a little bit of fear then. "Perhaps if I have to bat Wasim will knock my head off," I thought. I was playing with the big boys now. But I too was bowling fast, probably as fast as anybody else in the game at the time. Then I got called for throwing once or twice. The umpire was a man called Kantilal Kanjee and he was posted at square leg at the time. My bowling action had been questioned once or twice in the past, but to be called for throwing in a match of this significance was pretty traumatic. In effect, I was being accused of unintentional cheating.

Naturally, the fact that I had played made the news. I ended up being interviewed by Barney Spender for the BBC and he questioned me about how I would feel if I was picked to play for Zimbabwe and asked what would happen about my Kenyan citizenship. Naturally, he also quizzed me about my action. I was 18 and had never been schooled in media relations, so I answered his questions as honestly as I could. It was all new to me.

I returned home for a few days and despite the throwing furore, I got the call from the team manager: "Get up to Harare, Henry: you have been picked to play for your country in the first Test against Pakistan." I was to be the youngest player to represent Zimbabwe, at 18 years and 212 days, and I was the first black cricketer ever to be chosen. What a moment that was for me.

Our coach was John Hampshire, the former England, Yorkshire and Derbyshire player. He was terribly English and I always had problems understanding his northern accent. For the first time, I was in a professional environment, and Hampshire was a proper, dedicated professional. When he took catching practice with us he used to smash the ball miles into the air, and I had never experienced anything like that before. My hands stung for days after I caught the ball. Net sessions were a revelation, too, as I was given a new ball. A new ball? Surely you were only handed a new ball when you went out to open the bowling in a match? Apparently not.

Here I was bowling in the nets to Andy and Grant Flower, to Dave Houghton, to Guy Whittal, to Streaky and they were now my teammates, my international teammates. I was as high as a kite.

Before the match I was presented with my cap and what a moment that was. I still had a Kenyan passport but I was given special dispensation to play for Zimbabwe. It would take another two years to become a Zimbabwean citizen. Mugabe came to the ground, although I did not meet him. In all probability he came to see me make history. If only he had any idea of how different things would be years later.

The atmosphere in the ground was fantastic. We had our own version of the Barmy Army who congregated in a part of the ground called Castle Corner. Castle is a bottled beer in Zimbabwe; they were one of our sponsors and owned a thatched bar in a corner of the ground. The fans enjoyed their product to the full, getting drunk and singing songs all day long. Most of the spectators were white, but a few black people came along to see me take my bow.

So it was that on 31st January 1995 I made my Test debut for Zimbabwe at Harare Sports Club. Andy Flower was our captain, having just taken over from Dave Houghton. Andy was the consummate professional and a tough taskmaster. He didn't suffer fools gladly: he had no time for players who didn't train properly and we had a couple of those in the Test side, guys who simply were not fit enough to play international cricket. One of them was a guy nicknamed Rumpum. Andy had played overseas for a number of years so he knew what it took to perform at the highest level.

Andy was not to be messed with. As a captain, what he said went, and he was not the sort of guy who would put his arm round your shoulder and encourage you. So if you are playing for him, don't give your wicket away and bowl the ball in the right place or else you will know all about it. He knew what he wanted, told the team what he wanted and off we went to face Pakistan. We won the toss, batted first and it was totally surreal. Grant Flower scored 201, Andy Flower 156 and Guy Whittal 113 as we declared at 544 for 4. We were on cloud nine. After batting for the best part of two days, we genuinely believed, expected even, that we could bowl them out twice, and what a result that would be.

Every person in the ground knew the significance of Henry Olonga being given the ball. It was a moment of reckoning for me. As I walked out there was a standing ovation from the crowd, and the hairs on the back of my neck stood on end. I was a bundle of nerves.

I should explain that I didn't come from a family where we watched Test cricket on TV. I knew it was a longer version of the game even than the one we played at high school. But even in inter-provincial cricket we only played for three days and tried to get a result in that time. We usually had to contrive a result. But five days? Wow, this will take a while! I knew what it was like to be in the field for a day, and walk off knackered, but in Test cricket you could be out there for two days – or more. This was a brave new world for me. I didn't even know who WG Grace was. The tactics and intricacies of the game were a whole new ball game for me.

Heath Streak bowled an amazing opening over and suddenly I found that I had the ball in my hand so I marked out my run-up, thinking, "Right, how am I going to bowl this?" At the other end was Saeed Anwar, one of the finest left-handed batsman in world cricket. You would hope that your first delivery would be unplayable, would catch an outside edge and be caught by the keeper. Well that's how I imagined it, but my maiden delivery turned out to be a wide that went for four byes. Andy Flower was one of the finest wicketkeepers in the business but he didn't get anywhere near it. Put it this way, I know how Steve Harmison felt when he bowled that awful ball to begin England's defence of the Ashes in Australia in 2006.

Talk about a sense of anticlimax. A hushed silence went around the ground with the odd snigger here and there. I was mortified.

Anwar must have been licking his lips. My second ball was a bouncer. It was a good ball, quick and accurate, and it forced the batsman to take evasive action. The crowd were back on my side. Next came an outswinger that started on leg stump and moved away. Anwar made an involuntary flick at the ball and got the slightest of contacts as it flew past and into the hands of Andy Flower, who leapt up to appeal. I wasn't sure, but I appealed sheepishly and Merv Kitchen, the umpire, wagged his little index finger and the crowd erupted. So I got a wicket with my third ball in Test cricket. The crowd went wild and perhaps they were thinking that maybe this Olonga kid was a decent bowler after all, even if it hadn't been the greatest ball.

Salim Malik was next in, and by this time I was really fired up and was bowling with a bit of heat. After I'd bowled a few balls to him and I was returning to start my run-up, I saw that Malik was conferring with the umpires. I wasn't sure what was going on, but I got the feeling that it wasn't good. It turned out he'd been telling them I was throwing the ball. I bowled a few more overs and then I was called for throwing by our local umpire, Ian Robinson, and to make matters worse I pulled a side muscle and had to go off the field for treatment.

I bowled ten overs in total but they did not want to risk me again because if I got called a second time I would not be able to take any further part in the game anyway. All of a sudden, from being called a hero I was in disgrace because I had brought the name of Zimbabwe cricket into disrepute. In my first Test! Zero to hero to zero. It was devastating and during the lunch break I sat there stunned by what had just happened.

Mark Dekker tried to reassure me by saying that the Pakistani batsmen had just been trying to find a way to get rid of me because I had a lot of pace. The manager was saying that all fast bowlers chuck their quicker bouncer. The rest of the team were equally supportive. I knew they were trying to be helpful but it didn't really change how I felt. I had just embarrassed the country. And worse still I had made it appear like black Zimbabweans couldn't play the game properly. That was the most bitter pill to swallow. But we had a Test match to win so there was no moping around.

Heath Streak was on fire, claiming six wickets as we bowled out Pakistan for 322 and enforced the follow-on. Second time around we dismissed them for 158, with Streak taking another three wickets as we completed a historic innings and 64-run victory. It all kind of passed me by, not helped by the fact that I didn't bowl at all in the second innings and dropped Inzamanul-Haq, incurring the fury of Andy Flower. It was Zimbabwe's first Test win, but it was overshadowed by my demise.

It was a very embarrassing moment for me in my life, and a point when I had to make some serious decisions. What was going to happen to me next? If I had an illegal bowling action, would I be allowed to carry on playing? It was almost as if my career had been short-circuited before it had begun. I had worked hard in schools cricket, I had represented Zimbabwe as a schoolboy, played for my province with the odd question being asked about my technique, but I never thought it would come to this. If my action was so bad surely this should have been addressed and sorted out long before now? Just imagine how I felt, playing my first full international and being called for chucking. It was a slap in the face, a devastating blow.

I had been hoping that somebody might come along, put their arm round me and give me some words of comfort, but instead I got this nugget. I was sitting in the pavilion when the father of a former Plumtree deputy head boy wandered over to me to speak with me. He informed me that the last person who had been called for throwing while playing for his country 32 years earlier had never represented them again. It was exactly what I wanted to hear! Thanks Mr Bourdillon, your sense of timing was just impeccable.

In one sense I am thankful. The game had not been shown on television in Zimbabwe although if it had been at least it would have given me an opportunity to see my action in anger and work out for myself what I was doing wrong. It was also the age before widespread Internet access, so it didn't spread all over the world.

As I sat down to try to analyse it, I realised the issue with my action was probably connected to my javelin throwing. You throw a javelin side-on, and there is every chance I was doing the same thing with the cricket ball. I do know that I started having the problem the year before I left school, which was also when I started bowling my quickest, and that was what put me on the international selectors' radar. I remember tinkering with my action at high school, and my coach telling me he believed that there was a problem with it.

But unless you can get an expert in biomechanics who can come in and fix it for you, or at least point you in the right direction, you are just going to keep doing what comes naturally to you, whether that be right or wrong. And you are certainly not going to repair the problem overnight.

I am not making excuses, and I certainly didn't bowl incorrectly all the time, but I now recognise that when I tried to bowl a little bit quicker that is perhaps when my action became suspect, and in international cricket you have to bowl as fast as you can for as long as you can if you want to avoid being slaughtered by the world's best batsmen. No bowler wants to go for three or four boundaries per over.

Naturally, because of the question marks surrounding my action, I played no useful role in the rest of the Tests or One Day Internationals. A photographer had taken pictures of my bowling action and yes, even I could see that it wasn't right. He gave me some copies so that I could go away and study them.

That Test series was a major triumph for Zimbabwe but a few months after it ended I was sent to an Indian academy, the MRF Pace Foundation, in what used to be Madras but is now known as Chennai. The reason they sent me there, of all places, was because Dennis Lillee had been involved in the setting up of an academy specifically aimed at producing Indian quick bowlers. They always had great spinners, but no world-class quickies. Cricket is like a religion in India, so if they identified a problem, they were going to spend whatever it took putting it right. The authorities in Zimbabwe felt it was the place where I would be put back on the right road.

Joel Garner, or "Big Bird", the legendary West Indies bowler, was one of the coaches at the academy, and he and Lillee were to come over for a week so we would be taught by the very best in the business.

Cricket was the last thing on my mind, however, when I first arrived in Madras. I was struck by the poverty, which was at a level that was beyond my comprehension. I saw things that horrified me and still live with me today. Families scavenging for food on rubbish dumps, fighting for scraps with dogs and rats, and everywhere you went were beggars. It is in your face at all times. I remember one tiny child, with snot running down his face, grabbing hold of my leg and crying, and then he went to touch one of the Zimbabwean guys I was with and this bloke kicked out and told the child not to touch him, to go away. When you meet people in such desperate circumstances you realise what an unjust world it is that we live in. I didn't know what to do as it seemed so hopeless. You could give a few rupees but how far would they go?

And yet we were invited to a dinner with the sponsors where we ate amazing food and sipped champagne. And that is the way it is in India. There is abject poverty and there is extravagant wealth, and little in between. And despite it all, the Indians are the most amazingly friendly and warm people, most of whom would happily give you their last rupee. The smallest act of kindness means so much to them.

It saddened me deeply and it put the problems of my bowling action into some kind of perspective. During my time at the foundation we stayed in a guest house. I was with fellow Zimbabweans Brian Strang and Darlington Matambanadzo, the latter of whom never quite developed into the player he could have been. We would go jogging and training every day and video our actions. We could then watch it again, from various angles and at different speeds, identify what we were doing wrong and then try to put it right. It was so much easier to be able to actually visualise it

Dennis Lillee arrived, and I remember standing next to him and Garner and feeling like a midget. These guys were giants, in every sense. The coaching was great, and Lillee looked at my footage and was very kind to me. I got the feeling right from the start that he was on my side that he knew it was not a nice thing to be called for throwing, so he was very compassionate towards me. "I don't think you're throwing," he would say. "Oh, yes, well maybe there is a slight flaw, but don't worry about it because we can sort it out. You can be quick, bloody quick." To hear this from one of the greatest fast bowlers who ever lived did wonders for my self-confidence and made me think that maybe, just maybe, I could resolve my problems and get back on the field.

I returned home a week later. Now, I hadn't been to church for a long time because so much else had been going on in my life, but a while after I came back from the academy some friends told me about a church they had discovered and insisted that I go with them to experience it. I was quite sceptical but as soon as I walked in I knew I was meant to be there. They were singing praise and worship songs, the music was being played by proper musicians – not just somebody on an organ – and the guy who was preaching was just a normal man. It didn't seem contrived in any way: there was no sense of us having to do certain things, like kneeling down, standing up, sitting down – you know what I mean.

All churches have their issues but the second I walked into this one I felt that I had entered a place where the Holy Spirit was. I had continued to experience back problems and, on one occasion after I had been two or three times, the pastor said if anybody had any health issues then they should tell him and he and the rest of the congregation would pray for them. So I told him about my back and asked if he would pray for me. It may sound melodramatic, but nobody else had managed to find a cure, and the one thing you didn't want as a fast bowler was a dodgy back.

So he did pray for me, but nothing happened. And he prayed for me a couple times more, but still nothing happened, until one day he sat me down and said, "I have a prophecy for you, son." I thought, "Oh, here we go again." He then went on to tell me that he sensed that God was going to use sportsmen to tell people about the Lord in the last days. He added that if this truly was the word of God it would be confirmed to me by another witness.

Unbeknown to him at this stage I was considering whether or not I wanted to continue playing cricket for a living because of all the problems I'd had with my bowling action. Yes, Dennis Lillee's clinic had given me hope but months after returning I began to suffer from depression and had decided I was going to walk away from cricket. The only thing that was stopping me was how I wanted to be remembered. I didn't want Mr Bourdillon's words to be the last word in my career. I didn't want to be the player who played one Test match, got called for throwing and left the game in disgrace. My personal life had had its challenges and I had recently broken up with my girlfriend. I was so confused and eventually decided that I was going to throw in the towel. Then something out of the ordinary happened to me.

I went to church one day, although on this occasion I really hadn't felt like going, but there was something in the back of my mind telling me to go. A couple called Joyce and Charles David used to take me to church every Sunday, but they were late and I was just about to head home when they came screeching round the corner and off we went, arriving in the nick of time for the start of the service.

In the church were a couple I didn't recognise, Colin and Jeannie Janjetich, who were visiting the area from South Africa and had been staying in a flat nearby. Jeannie revealed that she had heard this beautiful music coming from our church, so she had asked if she and her husband could come in and join us. Part of the service was where people pray for you. I stood before the pastor who prayed for me and the next thing I knew I was sitting up on the floor and wondered what on earth was going on.

Then Jeannie, this strange hippie-looking woman, walked up to me. She was wearing bright multicoloured clothes, a headband and bangles, and she tapped me on the shoulder. I was mesmerised by what had just happened to me, but she told me to stand up. I had never seen this woman before in my life but she looked me in the eye and gave me a prophecy.

She told me she saw me playing a sport and that I was also going to be a singer and speaker. The summary of the message was that God had seen where I had come from, He knew what I had been through but He was calling me because he had a purpose for my life. The whole utterance lasted about three minutes and then it was over. Woah! Although it was one of the strangest things to happen to me I found it irrefutably comforting. It suggested that God knew what I had been through.

She could not have known that I played sport. She could not have known I had a passion for singing. I was completely overwhelmed by it all. Right there and then, however, I knew that God was part and parcel of my life. She then anointed me with oil, prayed for me and the service continued.

I left that church with a renewed sense of understanding. The pastor had told me that if his prophecy had been the word of God it would be confirmed by a second person, and it had been. I determined that it was my destiny to remain in cricket, and decided that I would do whatever it took to get my bowling action sorted out.

The real test of any prophetic word however is not how good it sounds at the time, but whether it comes to pass or not and I have been flabbergasted at how exactly the things that were mentioned have in the last 14 years begun to take shape, just as the prophet said.

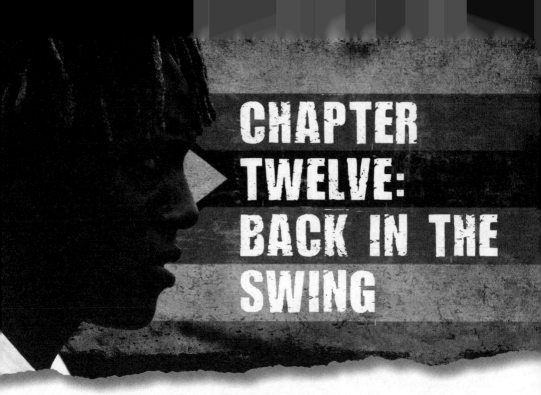

CHAPTER TWELVE: BACK IN THE SWING

These big waves kept knocking me under and the current was taking me further and further away from the beach. I knew that I was in serious trouble.

I spent months working hard on fixing my action – work that would continue for the rest of my career. I bought myself a camcorder and a tripod so I could film myself bowling and I worked closely with Heath Streak and John Rennie, my fellow teammates for Matableleland. Steadily my action improved and eventually there were no question marks surrounding it. All the hard work had finally paid off and I was chosen to go on the tour of New Zealand early in 1996. I didn't play a great deal of cricket while we were there, but it was enough for me just to be back in the fold, knowing I had put in the work and that I had convinced everybody I was back and as quick as ever.

I played in the Test in Hamilton and I bowled horrendously, but I did enjoy one moment of glory. I was fielding at mid-off when Stephen Fleming was on about 50. He hit the ball straight at me and inexplicably decided to go for a quick single. I looked up and realised he was out of his ground but the angle I was standing at meant I only had one stump to aim at. I let fly and the ball smashed into the stump, running him out. He was livid; I was delighted. As it turned out, I ran out quite a few New Zealand batsmen in Test matches during my career. They kept trying to run singles that weren't on, and I kept hitting the stumps. It is funny how things work out like that.

Next up was the World Cup, to be played on the Subcontinent in India, Pakistan and Sri Lanka and I made the Zimbabwe squad again. This was the World Cup when Australia did not want to travel to and play in Sri Lanka because there had been quite a few security scares. As it turned out this was also the tournament in which Sri Lanka truly announced themselves as the most entertaining one day side in international cricket. They proved that it was possible to attack from the very first ball and completely changed the way people approached 50-over cricket. The impact they made was similar to that which Twenty20 has had on the modern game. And, of course, they won the competition, beating Australia in the final.

As far as Zimbabwe was concerned, there is not much to say. We were thrashed by the West Indies, Sri Lanka, Australia and India, just managed to beat Kenya and then headed home after our ejection from the tournament. That Kenya game was bizarre. We were playing them at Patna and were 45 for 3 after 15 overs so it was a bit of a struggle. I have no way of saying which way the match would have gone but our run rate was not the best. Then there was a brief rain shower that meant the covers had to be brought on and the outfield became a little sodden. Then some bright spark suggested that perhaps they could use a helicopter to dry the outfield. The helicopter came and hovered for a few minutes before all of a sudden the wind from the rotor-blades blew the covers off, dumping all the water that had collected on them straight onto the pitch. Play was now impossible and the game had to be postponed until the next day. We returned to effect a comfortable victory but had it not rained the day before it might well have been a different result.

Then came the India match. I hadn't bowled a ball throughout the World Cup and I was informed that I was going to be picked for the final match against India. I told the selectors that in my humble opinion I wasn't up to playing as I simply wasn't match fit and feared I would let the side down as I had done in New Zealand. I was still making my shaky, unstable return to international cricket and I had been burned before.

Not long after we got back from that tour, I was sitting in Central Park in Bulawayo with a guy called Fred Sorrells, who became a sort of spiritual mentor to me. Fred was an American Southern Baptist who worked in sports mission, using baseball camps to preach. We ended up working together for a number of years; whenever I went on tour it was always good for me to know that I had his support. We often got together to catch up and this was such an occasion. As the two of us sat together in the park we were approached by a man who was clearly a down-and-out. He asked if we were praying and when we told him that we were, he asked us if we would pray for him.

Of course we did, and we asked him to sit down with us. His name was David, and he would become a central figure in my life for a brief while. He had nowhere to live and slept on the streets, so I kept tabs on him whenever I could, giving him money and checking that he was doing all right.

I had never befriended a street kid before but after spending a few hours with this young man I felt I had a responsibility to look out for him. I was devastated when I discovered the pain of his story. I could never understand why he was always falling sick and I assumed it was because he had a terrible diet. He was in and out of hospital with pneumonia. The first time it happened was about 12 months after I had first met him. I knew it was serious because I visited him in hospital but I had no idea he was that sick. I mean, you can treat pneumonia, can't you?

I used to take him to youth groups, because I thought he was a teenager, but he turned out to be some seven years older than me. In the end David was sent from one hospital to another and eventually he died while I was away on tour. It was sobering to have a friend of 32 die. He was so young, and it seemed to me to be such a waste of a life. Perhaps the worst thing of all from my point of view was that we only found out David had passed away by getting in touch with his relatives because he had disappeared off the face of the earth.

Some concerned friends and I tried to track him down and when we finally found his family they told us that they had already buried him. He was laid to rest next to his brother, who was only 40 when he died. I was mortified to discover much later that he had contracted AIDS by selling his body on the streets, but I had never put two and two together.

One of the great tragedies of HIV is that so many parents are now outliving their children in Africa. I took a photograph of the grave and, in keeping with custom, dropped a stone on it. David taught me a candid lesson. Everyone deserves a chance at redemption.

David's father was relatively well off in his area and I remember looking him in the eye and realising that my friend still lived in his father somehow, whose gestures were identical. His father told us that David's funeral had been announced on the radio and that he had been surprised and disappointed that nobody had come, but even if I had heard the broadcast I wouldn't have known it was my friend. It transpired that his name wasn't even David, it was Emmanuel.

During 1996 I was told that the cricket authorities in Zimbabwe wanted me to work with Dennis Lillee again, and this time I was sent to the Australian Institute of Sport's cricket academy in Adelaide. Rod Marsh, the great Aussie wicketkeeper, was the director of the academy and I spent three weeks there alongside some really talented up-and-coming cricketers including Brett Lee, who at the time was recovering from a back injury. This was the same academy that had been attended by the likes of Glenn McGrath, Shane Warne and Michael Slater, so if you couldn't get yourself sorted out there, you were probably in the wrong sport. The facilities were fabulous.

The elite training academies had all come about following a disappointing Olympic Games in the early 1980s – the Australians had been woeful and decided to address it by building the best facilities money could buy and staffing them with the best coaches on the planet. And guess what? It worked. They dominated Test cricket as a result of the academies turning out world-class players.

While there you get great healthy food, the kind of food I know is good for you but that I hate. I am not a huge fan of pasta and lettuce, so at any available opportunity I would find an excuse to leave the academy and eat a "real" meal. As well as teaching you – well, trying to teach you – about sports nutrition and how to look after your body, they also taught the best training techniques, supported by state-of-the-art technology. But the best thing of all was that we were being taught by men and women who were the best in their field, including psychologists and biomechanists.

Not so great was when we were told, "Right lads, in the pool, and I want to see you all do 50 lengths." Gulp! Thankfully they allowed me to go at my own pace. But the running and all the other fitness training meant that I was soon in the peak of condition. Lillee told me that I needed to model my action on Malcolm Marshall, the former West Indian quickie, who had a straight-on bowling delivery.

All our training took place at the Adelaide Oval and it is one of my big regrets that I never got to play an international match there. Adelaide is a beautiful city with wide-open streets. The academy was right on Henley Beach, overlooking the ocean. I was mesmerised. I love the ocean – I don't love swimming in it, but just standing there, taking it all in, that is something else. Zimbabwe, remember, is landlocked so this was a special experience.

While I was in Adelaide I gave a radio interview, during which I mentioned my beliefs. A pastor called Craig Bailey was listening and he invited me to come and hang out with him. I couldn't turn down the prospect of real food so off I went. I arrived and there were maybe ten or so people but they were all talking to each other so I sat down at a table on my own and a young lady came over and introduced herself to me. She said that her name was Tara. We chatted and soon discovered we had a great deal in common – we were both believers, we both had parents who had split up and most of all we both loved sport. She was a physical education teacher. We just clicked and it was so easy to talk to her. It really was like I had known her all my life. Eventually it was time to go and I said my goodbyes, going back to the academy completely oblivious to the fact that our paths would cross again.

Craig stayed in contact and one day he took me to meet a quadriplegic. He was a lovely, lovely man who had great spirit and a wonderful attitude to his infirmity. As you go through life you come across inspirational characters like this guy, people who have suffered the very worst that life can throw at them but who keep smiling, have a positive outlook and rise above it. Yes, people who make you realise how incredibly fortunate you are, people who leave you feeling humbled. He didn't last many years after my visit and quietly passed away in a hospice. Meeting this man put life into perspective for me.

The hard work continued at the academy and I was given a video of my bowling action and told what I needed to work on, and keep working on. It was a huge help to me and I felt immensely lucky and privileged to have had the opportunity to work with Rod Marsh, Dennis Lillee and the rest of the academy team.

Before I returned to Zimbabwe, Craig invited me to a service where I bumped into Tara again, and we arranged to meet up one more time before I left. So the night before I was due to go home I met up with Tara and we talked for hours. We both knew exactly where the other one was coming from. We just clicked in a way I never had with anybody else. So when I flew out of Adelaide I thought to myself that I had made a new friend, and that was the way it transpired, with the two of us staying in touch over the years that followed.

I used to phone her occasionally, but I would always miscalculate the time difference and end up calling her at 5 am! I had no concept of daylight saving because in Zimbabwe the clocks do not go forward or back, and once I phoned her and it turned out to be 4 am. We also wrote letters to each other but I didn't for one minute ever think that anything more would ever come of it – I lived in Zimbabwe; she lived in Australia.

After my time at the academy, I went home to Zimbabwe with a new confidence and belief in my action. It took a long time for my front-on action to feel completely comfortable – and I would actually end up having to attend another academy in 1997 to finally cement it – but overall I was bowling accurately, fast and legally. This really was a turning point for me and the beginning of my life being taken over by cricket. I lived, breathed, ate and dreamt about the game, especially how I was going to become a permanent feature in the Zimbabwe side.

In September 1996 we arrived in Sri Lanka for a two-Test series. The Sri Lankans were on cloud nine following their World Cup victory and we knew that we were going to be in for a tough ride. And so it proved.

While we were in Sri Lanka we stayed at a place called Ahungulla Bay, a few miles up the coast from Colombo. We had played a warm-up match the day before and we were enjoying a chill-out day on the beach, although even then we had to do some exercises on the sand, including press-ups and sit-ups and a bit of running. Malcolm Jarvis, a former player, was in charge of the tour and the player-coach was Dave Houghton.

After the exercises, Jarvis sent every member of the squad into the sea, telling us to stay there for a few minutes to cool off. You already know all about my previous experiences with water, but this was to prove the worst one yet. While I was swimming I was hit by a big wave and I went under, came back up, was hit by another wave and when I came up this time I realised that I was at least 30 yards away from everybody else. It dawned on me that I was in a rip current.

These big waves kept knocking me under and the current was taking me further and further away from the beach. I knew that I was in serious trouble. It was like being inside a washing machine. I waved my arms frantically and managed to alert the other players to my plight. They in turn alerted the beach rescue teams.

Remember that we had all been training on the beach for about an hour prior to this so we were all pretty tired. I was in the middle of a life-or-death fight and I didn't have the energy for it. I screamed out at the top of my voice, "God help me!" I kept being buffeted by the waves when I saw that Alistair Campbell was swimming towards me. Meanwhile, another team-mate had tried to get a volleyball to me, the idea being that I would grab hold of it and float, but that didn't work. His throw didn't reach me.

Alistair eventually reached me after what seemed like an eternity. "Right, H, we are going to do this," he screamed. "Now swim." With that, he swam behind me and pushed me, trying to help me. I was doing my best but I was shattered and we were going nowhere. Eventually, after a few exhausting minutes, the lifeguards reached us. One of them had swum out to us carrying a float, which he passed to me. I grabbed it and started working my way back towards the beach, before being picked up by a boat before I got there.

To my horror, I turned round and realised that Alistair and the lifeguard were now in serious peril themselves, struggling to make any headway against the waves. But the guys in the boat decided to take me back to dry land before going back to help them. It was almost as if they had forgotten about the other two. I lay on the beach with sand in my hair, in my eyes, in my mouth and in my ears – and that was on top of all the seawater I had swallowed. I was gasping for breath. Minutes later, Alistair and the lifeguard staggered out of the water and collapsed beside me, totally exhausted. By now a crowd of around 400 people had gathered. It is human nature, I guess: they wanted to see what the drama was all about.

I came round, walked over to Alistair and shook his hand. We didn't need to say anything to one another and I didn't have the energy. I have no hesitation in saying that Campbell saved my life that day. By the way, the lifeguard had expended so much energy getting out to me and returning to land that they had to take him to hospital. He was fine in the end though. We later found out that a Frenchman had died at the same spot earlier that year, similarly caught up in a powerful current, and nobody had thought to put up any warning signs, even after that. I think it was the last time that Malcolm Jarvis insisted that the players go in the sea for a swim. We stuck to swimming pools from then on.

The tour of Sri Lanka was pretty forgettable from a cricket perspective. The first Test in Colombo started well enough with Heath Streak getting Roshan Mahanama for 4 and me getting the great Sanath Jayasuriya for a first ball duck. I bowled well enough but the Sri Lankans made 349 and then bowled us out twice, for 145 and 127.

The second Test wasn't much better. They bowled us out for a paltry 141, scored 350 for 8 declared and then skittled us out again, this time for 235 (I scored 3 not out!) before knocking off the required 30 runs in double-quick time.

There wasn't much time to draw breath. On 17th October 1996, we were stepping out at Sheikhupura Stadium to face Pakistan in the first Test of a three-match series. There was no grass on the wicket, and there wasn't a lot more in the outfield. Grant Flower and Paul Strang both scored centuries and we were all out for 375, but the pitch was dead and I was not looking forward to bowling on it.

I only took one wicket, that of Ijaz Ahmed, LBW, and Pakistan piled on 553 runs. The thing is at one stage we had them 237 for 7 but then Wasim

Akram and Saqlain Mushtaq came together and it was carnage. Wasim was in imperious form and scored a quite spectacular career-best 257 not out. Saqlain contributed 79. Poor Paul Strang sent down 69 overs and went for 212 runs. We managed to hang on for a draw, but nobody who took part in that Test or witnessed it will ever forget Wasim's performance with the bat.

I suffered a groin injury which ruled me out of the second Test in Faisalabad. This time Wasim took ten wickets as Pakistan thrashed us by the same number. My injury meant that I had to leave early and while I sat in Faisalabad Airport I watched my teammates playing Pakistan in the first of the one day matches on the television in the departure lounge. I was gutted that I wasn't playing and feeling very gloomy.

Flying home from a cricket tour on your own when there are still matches to be played is a desperately lonely experience and it leaves you feeling very flat. You go to the physio, he assesses your injury, tells you that recovery is going to be long term so you may as well fly home. Then you tell the manager, who makes the necessary calls and sorts out your plane tickets, you say goodbye to the team and head to the airport in a taxi with nobody for company. As a sportsman, it is a very difficult place to be.

Apart from the cricket, one abiding memory of this tour is being racially abused by the Pakistan fans. Here were spectators with brown skin hurling abuse at cricketers with brown skin just like theirs. They were calling me and Matambanadzo "black monkeys". It was quite awkward but we could see the ironic side of it too. These people ended up throwing all sorts of stuff on to the field at us, including banana skins, coins and even small pieces of concrete.

It was also in Pakistan that I saw reverse-swing bowling for the first time, with Waqar Younis being the great exponent of the art, and I made up my mind that it was something I had to learn.

Groin injuries can be notoriously difficult to treat, and that was how this one turned out. It took me weeks to get over it, but when I got back to Zimbabwe I gradually rebuilt my fitness levels and got back into the province team.

CHAPTER THIRTEEN: BUMBLING ALONG

"We murdered them. We got on top and steamrollered them. We have flipping hammered them. One more ball and we'd have walked it. We murdered them and they know it. To work so hard and get so close: there is no praise too high. We have had some stick off your lads. We flipping hammered them."
David Lloyd, England cricket coach

England came out to Zimbabwe for their first official tour in December 1996 and as expected it was a huge deal for Zimbabwe cricket. I was working my way back to fitness after another injury and was drafted in to play in the warm-up game between

Matabeleland and the tourists. I was fielding at cover with Jack Russell and Robert Croft at the crease. They decided to take a quick single; the ball headed in my direction so I picked it up and dived as I threw it towards the stumps, extending my left arm to brace my fall. I landed awkwardly and immediately knew that I had injured my wrist, but I was not sure how badly so I went off the field, iced it and bandaged it up for support. I tried to drive home that night in my first ever sponsored vehicle, which was a van, but I struggled to change gears so I got some elastic and taped up my wrist as firmly as I could.

I didn't want to miss the Test series so I didn't tell anyone about it. This was going to be one of those times when I would just have to bite the bullet. I had always been told that you never really play at 100 per cent, and sometimes you just have to grit your teeth through the pain barrier.

The England coach during that series was a certain David Lloyd. Bumble has gone on to build a reputation for himself as one of the best commentators and analysts in the game, but as a coach he sometimes said things that I am sure he later had cause to regret.

The first Test was played at Queens in Bulawayo. We scored 376 in our first innings, with yours truly being bowled for a duck. Thankfully, Andy Flower and Alistair Campbell were in imperious form, Flower scoring 112 and Campbell 84. England then made 406 but I bowled reasonably well, claiming three wickets including that of Nick Knight. I was out for another duck in our second innings total of 234, with all dreams of being a proper batsman now consigned to the dustbin of history. I got the wicket of Michael Atherton in the second innings, clean bowled, and they ended up needing three runs off the final ball to win. I have to admit that I miscalculated (I thought they needed four runs to win), so when the ball came to me I was perhaps a bit more relaxed in fielding the ball than I might otherwise have been. I quite casually threw it in to our wicketkeeper as the England players attempted to score the winning run and we ran out Nick Knight for 96. It was fortunate that I had kept my wits about me.

In the post-match interview David Lloyd said, "We murdered them. We got on top and steamrollered them. We have flipping hammered them. One more ball and we'd have walked it. We murdered them and they know it. To work so hard and get so close: there is no praise too high. We have had some stick off your lads. We flipping hammered them."

Yes, England should have won the first Test, but they didn't. We felt we gave them a good battle, so the comments of Lloyd were rather inaccurate because after five days of cricket the teams could not be separated. The comments were not appreciated by Zimbabwe fans, either, with one banner in the crowd during the second Test reading "Wanted: David Lloyd. For Murder of Zim Cricket Team. Last seen with his finger up his nose talking complete bollocks. He knows it and we know it."

The second Test in Harare was another draw. We bowled England out for 156 to entertain thoughts of victory, with me once again taking the wicket of Nick Knight. They bowled us out for 215 and, guess what, for the third successive innings I failed to trouble the scorers and my wrist still hurt. In a rain-affected match, England then made 195 for 2, so we had drawn the series.

On the third day of the match, Robert Mugabe came out on to the field and shook hands with the cricket teams and in particular Michael Atherton, the England captain. It was a picture that was featured all around the world. As Zimbabwe players, we were proud to see our president at the match. It was the first time that I had been introduced to him, and I considered it an honour to shake his hand.

Like most of my teammates, at this point in my life I looked up to Mugabe. He had even been awarded an honorary knighthood by the Queen in 1994. We had no idea what the rest of the world was saying about him. Mugabe himself loves cricket and is on record as saying, "Cricket civilises people. I want everyone in Zimbabwe to play cricket. I want ours to be a nation of gentlemen." At this point I was still convinced that he was a good leader and that although we all have our flaws he wasn't too bad.

Then came a three-match one day series against England. I didn't play any part as Zimbabwe beat England 3-0 with Eddo Brandes, or 'Chicken George' as he was christened by the media on account of that fact that he owned a chicken farm, taking a hat-trick in the final match. It was heady stuff. This was England's first tour of Zimbabwe: they had surely expected to give us a cricketing lesson and yet it was Zimbabwe who had reason to celebrate at the end of it all.

At around this time I was also developing my love for all things electronic, and that was down to a friend called Scott Murray. I am fairly competent on a computer now whereas I didn't even know how to turn one on before. Scott introduced me to Windows 95 and fostered my interest in computers and everything that could be achieved with them. I didn't even know what a mouse was or why anybody would want to use a PC, but with Scott's help I set about buying and building my own computer. Before I knew where I was, I had started to make music on it and I then went out and bought a music keyboard I could use on my computer. That love for all things technical has never left me. Digital cameras, digital phones, digital music – I love it all. There is almost nothing you cannot do on a PC today. You can make your own album; you can make your own film if you want. Learning how to build, manage and troubleshoot computers has become a big part of my life now because I use them for a lot of my creative work. Most of what I learnt came from him but now I can actually help others. Subsequently I became the IT man of the team as many of my teammates would ask for assistance when their laptops were playing up.

Speaking of teaching others, in 1997 I was offered the opportunity to return to Plumtree and do some coaching. It was great to go back to my old school and catch up with some of my former teachers, and some of the pupils who had been juniors were now prefects. It was a reminder to me that time waits for no man, but it was extremely fulfilling to be able to spend time with young cricketers, teaching them how to improve their bowling and, yes, their batting too.

Early in 1997 I was sent to the Plascon Cricket Academy in Johannesburg to do some further remedial work on my action and also became a more holistic cricketer. I arrived a few days early and went to stay in a hotel and came down with tonsillitis. Whenever I stayed in a hotel that had air conditioning I always ended up coming down with a cold, and I am convinced that's what caused the tonsillitis. It got so bad that I couldn't even swallow my own spit so I arranged to see a doctor, who gave me a prescription for pills, but I was in such a bad way that I could barely even get the tablets down. After two days I went back to the doctor and told him the antibiotics weren't working and asked to have some more or something else.

"Where are the pills I gave you?" he asked.

"I've finished them."

"You've done *what*? Those were a week's worth of pills and you have taken the lot in just over a day. That's an African record."

He put me on to something stronger and, thankfully, they soon kicked in and I recovered. I have never suffered from tonsillitis since.

Fully restored to health, I turned up for my first day at the academy. One of the first things they do is to put you through a full medical, just to make sure that everything is in full working order. I was told that if there was anything that was troubling me I should tell them about it, so I mentioned that I was having problems with my left wrist, that it was still sore. I was instructed to keep an eye on it and to let them know if it got any worse.

This was another amazing academy. Clive Rice, the former South African cricketer, was the man behind it and it had been modelled on the one I had attended in Adelaide. There was one crucial difference. The previous academies I had attended had only lasted for three weeks, but I was in Johannesburg for six months. Most of the cricketers there were South Africans, but there was also a Ugandan and a Kenyan. I had some highlights while I was there, but I suppose chief among them would be the hat-trick I got in a practice game – these were proper games, taken seriously by everybody. For the first time in my life I was bowling away-swingers, which really helped in my development as an international cricketer.

There was an Afrikaner bowler among our number by the name of Pierre Joubert and he seemed to take great pleasure in sledging all his opponents. On one occasion he decided to have a go at me about my batting and shouted, "Olonga, how many Test runs have you scored?" Now I was the only player at the academy who had played Test cricket and though I had few runs to my name I was able to say, with absolute certainty, "More than you mate." He never bothered me again.

The first part of the course was all about getting our techniques sorted out and getting us in prime condition before we started playing matches, and by then we were really ready and raring to go. If you were a bowler you couldn't wait to run in at full pelt against an opening batsman, and if you were the opening batsman you were bursting to hit your first boundary.

During my time at the academy we went on a tour of the country, where I came across a batsman by the name of Herschelle Gibbs. Desmond Haynes, the former West Indies batsman turned coach in South Africa, had described him as the most talented cricketer he had ever seen. When you consider that Haynes had the chance to get up close with the likes of Viv Richards, Gordon Greenidge and Brian Lara, that is some testimony.

We faced Gibbs during our tour and he smashed 140 magnificent runs in 20 overs. It was an incredible display, leaving us clutching at shadows. It didn't matter where you bowled to him, he just stepped down the wicket and sent the ball to the boundary. It was a privilege to watch, even from the receiving end.

Word got round that he was also a pretty useful fielder and when it was our turn to bat one of our players smashed a shot through the air and Gibbs leapt towards it, caught it with one hand and then threw it in the air before he landed. Much debate followed about whether or not our batsman was out. My own view is that if you take a diving catch, the wisest thing to do is have the ball still in your hand when you land, just to erase any doubt. The umpire did not agree and our batsman was given out. Throughout his international career Gibbs has continued with this practice and, more often than not, he has managed to get away with it, but it came back to haunt him in one particularly famous 1999 World Cup match.

One of the matches we played on that tour took place in a small town called Potchefstroom on a pitch next to a mental asylum, and while we were playing there were patients screaming in the background, the kind of screaming that haunts you. Before we played we were warming up next to the asylum and were doing star jumps when a man who was obviously one of the patients came out and started to lead us. He started tapping his hands and feet in time to our exercises, and then he began to count: "One, two…" The poor chap didn't know what came next, so we all shouted out, "Three, four…" Don't get me wrong, we had compassion for him but it was also quite light-hearted.

Although Clive Rice was in charge of the academy, there were two other coaches who spent most of their time with us – Hylton Ackerman and a Kiwi called Mark O'Donnell whose nickname was Sack. Sack's favourite phrase was "You've got to try harder." He said it with such a strong New

Zealand accent that we would always end up making fun of him, but he knew his stuff. He used to get a tennis ball and racquet and hit the ball miles into the sky for us to catch. Johannesburg is at altitude and the ball flies through the air like a rocket, so there were a lot of finger injuries.

Because we were at the academy for six months, they focused on all sorts of things other than just playing the game. I have always felt sorry for sportsmen who suddenly find themselves thrust into the limelight without any training or preparation. We were taught how to handle ourselves in front of a room full of people so that when we would eventually face press conferences for real we would know what to expect and what to say. Once again, I also found myself being told what I should eat, and we spent time with sports psychologists. The whole thing was a fantastic experience that rejuvenated my interest in cricket.

Every possible area was looked at. We went running, we trained in a superb gymnasium in one of the best parts of the city. Boxing was on the agenda and the more of this I did, the more acute the pain in my left wrist became, so I asked to see the doctor again. I told her I was still feeling discomfort so she arranged an X-ray which revealed that I had broken a bone in my left wrist. The diagnosis came fully six months after I had first suffered the injury, so I was sent to see a hand specialist, a Dr Biddulph. I approached his surgery and there was a red Porsche parked in the doctor's bay so you can imagine how surprised I was when I met him and he turned out to be in his 60s.

He looked at the X-ray, grabbed my wrist and played around with it carelessly and I almost went through the ceiling because of the pain. So he muttered a few things to himself, made a few notes and then told me that I needed an operation. He said that if I didn't have it done it would end my career and cause me serious problems later in life. I was shattered. Here I was at the academy, I had just taken a hat-trick, I was swinging the ball, everything was great, and now suddenly I had to have an operation that would leave me in plaster for four months. This was the worst possible news I could have received. The academy had got me to the point where I couldn't wait to go home and start playing Test cricket for Zimbabwe again; instead, I faced surgery.

It was a month before Dr Biddulph could operate so in the meantime I continued to play, but now I was acutely aware that under no circumstances could I land on my left wrist. During this time I got a huge surprise when, in a match of no great consequence, it turned out that one of my team-mates was Hansie Cronje, who was a hero in South Africa at the time. He would, of course, destroy his reputation in the most spectacular fashion but here he was, the captain of his country, playing in one of our matches, and playing hard at that, risking injury to himself. It was weird. I guess he just loved to play cricket, which makes what happened to him all the more sad. I have since watched a film made by his brother Franz, simply called *Hansie*. It is about his life, his struggles, triumphs and, ultimately, his fall from grace and I must say he was an enigma. The movie tells the story of how he was baptised by Peter Pollock before his fatal plane crash so I believe that he did receive a form of redemption. In reality, the majority of the cricket-loving public still feel desperately betrayed.

Eventually I had the operation and when I came around I was in agony and my wrist was in plaster. The doctor gave me painkillers and they had the effect of making me as high as a kite. More accurately, one of the tablets he gave me made me feel as high as a kite; the other one was a suppository and that wasn't so pleasant.

There was a month left of the academy but my playing contribution was over. It was my fault – I should have had the wrist looked at when I was first hurt. Thankfully, the academy had insurance which paid for the operation, but before I left for Zimbabwe the doctor told me I would have to return in four months' time.

In the meantime, I continued to train with weights and bowl and I felt that I was in pretty good shape. Imagine my shock then when I returned to see Dr Biddulph and he cut off the cast – I looked at my wrist and I wanted to cry. After all those weeks in plaster it had withered away. I could not believe how skinny it had become and it looked even worse because the rest of my body was in such good shape.

He did a quick X-ray and told me that he wasn't happy, that it didn't look like my wrist had healed properly. When he had opened up my wrist he had removed a cyst, then he had shaved the two ends of the bone where they had broken, took another piece of bone, pinned it up, sewed everything up and put it all in a cast. Now it looked like the whole process hadn't worked and he said he wanted me to go for a special X-ray that would give a more accurate picture.

On my way to get the X-ray I prayed that everything was going to be all right. The consequences of failure were not something I wanted to consider. Forget my cricket career, there was a good chance that I would lose the use of my left wrist completely if arthritis set in. I waited for the X-ray. There was nobody with me as I sat there. Eventually I was given the slides and returned to Dr Biddulph's office with a sense of trepidation. He looked at the slides, breathed a sigh of relief and told me that everything was fine.

I was elated. And then he informed me that there was the small matter of the outstanding bill to be paid. I told him I thought the academy would be paying. He said, "I don't care who is paying, just make sure that somebody does." The bill was for thousands of dollars, way beyond my means. This turned out to be the bill for the operation, my time in the hospital, the anaesthetist and so on. Thankfully, the academy did agree to pay the bill but they immediately introduced a new rule stipulating that any foreign player who attended in the future must provide their own medical cover, so I spoilt it for everybody else. Sorry guys.

The doctor's parting shot was that I would have to return for yet another operation to have the pins in my wrist removed but in the end a doctor friend of my father sorted that out for me back home in Zimbabwe, and it turned out to be a minor procedure.

I was indebted to the South African Cricket Board so I wrote to them to thank them for everything they had done for me at the academy and for helping me through the operation. I then faced a long hard grind to get my wrist back to where it was before. There were months of physiotherapy and strengthening exercises to build up the muscle and regain my flexibility.

CHAPTER FOURTEEN: CHEATED OUT OF GLORY

I was twelfth man so I was sitting in the pavilion watching all this on TV. Your first instinct is usually the correct one and I was jumping up and shouting, "He's out!", only for the umpire to give the batsman not out. TV would then replay the incident, confirming beyond all doubt that the batsman had been out, plumb.

While I was still getting myself back to full fitness at the beginning of 1998, Zimbabwe went back to Sri Lanka for another two-Test series and I was in the squad, although I didn't end up playing much cricket. We lost the first match fair and square.

It was played in Kandy and they outplayed us from the very first ball. Marvin Atapattu scored a magnificent 223.

The second Test in Colombo was a different kettle of fish altogether. We scored 251 in our first innings and they replied with 225, giving us a slim lead of just 26 runs. Andy Flower then knocked off yet another wonderful century as we made 299 in the second innings. It meant that Sri Lanka had to score 326 to win.

Teams hardly ever score as many as 326 runs in the final innings of a Test match, but Sri Lanka did and it wasn't just because they outplayed us. There was something going on that just wasn't cricket. Decisions that should have gone our way simply didn't materialise. Rumours abounded that death threats had been made against the umpires should they had the temerity to give out Jayasuriya, Aravinda De Silva or Arjuna Ranatunga, the three heroes of Sri Lanka cricket. Jayasuriya made 68 and the umpires had no choice but to send him on his way when Andy caught him off the bowling of Heath Streak, but De Silva and Ranatunga remained unbeaten at the end on 143 and 87 respectively despite numerous appeals. Sri Lanka won by five wickets.

Some of the decisions that went Sri Lanka's way were extraordinary, to say the very least. De Silva and Ranatunga should have been out at least three times and it remains the most blatant swindling that I have ever witnessed in cricket, yet nobody ever talks about it. I was twelfth man so I was sitting in the pavilion watching all this on TV. Your first instinct is usually the correct one and I was jumping up and shouting, "He's out!", only for the umpire to give the batsman not out. TV would then replay the incident, confirming beyond all doubt that the batsman had been out, plumb.

Andrew Whittal was bowling to Ranatunga and the ball came off his glove and was caught by Andy Flower. Not out. Guy Whittal got De Silva leg before, halfway up the pad, hitting middle stump, not the slightest shadow of a doubt. Not out.

This was at a time when there was a local umpire and an overseas umpire. It has all changed now, of course, with neutral umpires standing for all Test matches.

Our pleas for the footage so that we could take it home and show it to the ICC fell on deaf ears. Although I wasn't in the team, I was with the players in the dressing room and you have never seen a sorrier, more devastated bunch of cricketers who have poured their hearts out to win a game. We just guessed that the governing authorities were guaranteed to back the umpires and not us. We were minnows and we had given our all but had zilch to show for it. At this point, our only Test victory had been against Pakistan. You play sport to win matches but what is so terribly wrong about losing from time to time? You just take it on the chin and admit that you were not good enough on that particular day. I am not saying that we definitely would have won but we did play better on the day and they couldn't accept that. It seemed as if losing to Zimbabwe that day was the worst possible thing that could happen to Sri Lankan cricket.

After the match, Dave Houghton called the squad together and said, "Guys, each one of you can hold your heads up high. Each and every one of us knows what happened today. We were cheated out of victory. Well done." We talked about boycotting the rest of the series but in the end decided to play on.

We had lost the Test and the series and later that night one of our players went to a bar, got very drunk and started bad-mouthing every Sri Lankan in the bar, calling them all cheats. Eventually the locals decided they'd had enough of him so they took him outside and gave him a hiding, breaking his jaw in the process. Thankfully, the Colombo Test was a one-off. The best way I can sum up that match is to say that to win a cricket match you have to take 20 wickets, but on that occasion we felt that we had to take closer to 25, and it still might not have been enough. Despite the bitter taste that this Test match left in my mouth, it did not change my opinion of the country it took place in. Sri Lanka is a beautiful, if troubled, part of the world, and I adore the people, so while I was there I spent some time visiting schools and doing a bit of coaching.

This slight bias against us when it came to decisions was one thing that really irritated me about playing for one of the relatively small cricketing nations. I don't think this bias was necessarily malicious or even conscious, more a case of an umpires giving the player with the better reputation the benefit of the doubt. But as a player for 'little' Zimbabwe it was highly irritating.

We had a couple of spinners, Paul Strang and Brian Murphy, and to my eye they consistently bowled balls similar to those that Shane Warne was getting leg before decisions for. But no, the umpire would often rule the batsmen not out. Reputations count for a great deal. It has pitched in line, hit him halfway up the pad and will go on to hit the stumps. How can it not be out? You're not Shane, that's why. Don't misunderstand me: Warney was a true legend of the modern game and deserved his wickets, but my point is that so did Brian and Paul.

There is one more murky area that I have pondered for a while. The laws governing bent arms have changed since I was called for throwing. It seems to me that there have been some throwers who have managed to get away with it over their careers with medical ratification. A doctor says that a player is double jointed or that they have a flexible wrist. As someone who had a problem with their action, I can tell you that I definitely gained an advantage by throwing the ball and if I could have found a doctor to say that I was double jointed and could carry on the way I was then I would have gladly continued. Enough said. But in truth I am pleased that the rehabilitation process is much more sensitive nowadays and the emphasis is to get players back on the field with as little embarrassment and disruption to their careers as possible. And of course I am grateful for the assistance I received from all the people who set me back on track.

I am often asked if I was ever approached to throw a match, if you'll pardon the pun. That question presumes that I had the kind of ability to affect a match in a big way in the first place. The answer is a resounding 'no' and in a sense it reinforces the idea that I probably wasn't good enough to make an impact in most matches.

Fortunately, we did not have long to dwell on events on the cricket field in Sri Lanka because we then headed straight to New Zealand for two Tests and five One Day Internationals.

The tour began with a couple of one dayers. I wasn't picked for either and we suffered two terrible hidings. The first Test in Wellington was no better – this time we lost by ten wickets – and then we lost the second Test in Auckland by an innings and 13 runs. We managed to win one of the three remaining one day matches but it was a pretty disappointing tour all round, and for me personally as I did not bowl a single ball in anger.

As you can imagine, spirits were pretty low when we returned to Zimbabwe but, again, we did not have time to feel sorry for ourselves because Pakistan arrived in March for a couple of Tests and One Day Internationals. I played no part. We drew one Test and lost the other, and we lost both one day matches.

After I became a Test cricketer and got my life on track I began to wonder what on earth had become of my former teacher, Derby Sher, so I phoned REPS. They were only able to tell me that she had got married but they didn't know what her married name was. Somebody told me that she had moved to Highland School in Harare so I contacted them and they confirmed that she had taught there, had got married and had kids, but she no longer worked as a teacher. The school gave me her father-in-law's number. By now, I was like a dog with a bone.

I called round at her father-in-law's house and introduced myself. Obviously, he knew who I was so he said that he would be happy to help. She was now Derby Derry. I explained to him that his daughter-in-law had made a huge impact on my life when I was at junior school and that I wanted to be able to tell her how much I appreciated the time and effort she'd put in with me, and to thank her for the part she had played in making me the person I had become.

Derby's dad phoned her and said, "Derby, you're not going to believe who has just walked into my house. It is an old student of yours and he wants to see you. You are never going to guess who it is." Sure enough, she listed a series of names, but not mine, so I quietly told him not to tell her who it was. He told her that he was giving this mystery pupil her address and he then told me how to get there. It was in the suburbs of Harare and not far away. I arrived, driving my sponsored car, a Ford Bantam pickup truck, with my name emblazoned on the side, "Henry Olonga, Zimbabwe Cricket Player, Sponsored by Ford." I was so excited and beaming with anticipation. I wondered how much she had changed.

I really wanted to surprise her so I hit the buzzer on the electrified security gates and when she answered I simply said, "I am here."

"Oh, I am looking forward to this," she replied, and let me in. She was genuinely surprised when she realised who it was. We said hello and had a chat, some 15 years since I had last seen her. She hadn't changed that much. But that first meeting was almost an anticlimax. It was very impersonal and obvious that she wasn't quite sure how to react to me. It was kind of, "Ah Henry, what are you doing with yourself?" Erm, I was a Test cricketer, surely she knew that? We spoke about the other teachers and she was talking about other students she had bumped into and I remember thinking, "I am not remotely interested in them; I have just come to thank you for the impact you had on my life." I don't know if I ever got round to that, if I did it didn't sink in with her. It was like, "Oh, great, you must come round more often." It's the sort of thing people say because they feel it is expected of them, and I didn't really believe that she meant it.

So I cleared off and forgot about it. But about six months later I met somebody at a gym who told me that Derby was back teaching at a school and he was working with her. He told me she had been delighted to meet me after all these years, and would love to see me again. I was very surprised, to say the least, because the impression she'd given me was that it had been a meeting that wasn't very important to her.

So I phoned her house and ended up speaking to her husband. He knew who I was and when I explained to him that I wanted to come round to see Derby again he suggested that I come to the house that Saturday, which was her birthday. I said I would love to come. I wanted to sing her a song called *Fill the World with Love*, from the film *Goodbye Mr Chips*. It had profound words.

I never pulled the song off but we got a chance to speak that evening, when she had let her hair down. All her friends were there, and she bragged, "Here's Henry, my old student, you know Henry from the cricket." It was as if a barrier had come down. Unfortunately, I wasn't able to stay for too long and on the way out Derby and I stopped by my car and I finally plucked up the courage to tell her what she had done for me all those years before. I said, "You know, one of the things I never got to say to you last time I was here is that you really had a profound impact on me. I really appreciate the fact that you spent a little time with me. So I just want to say thank you for what you did for me."

She said I was the first student to come back and thank her in that way. I was glad I did it because she helped to shape my life in a positive way and most good teachers don't often receive the appreciation that they deserve.

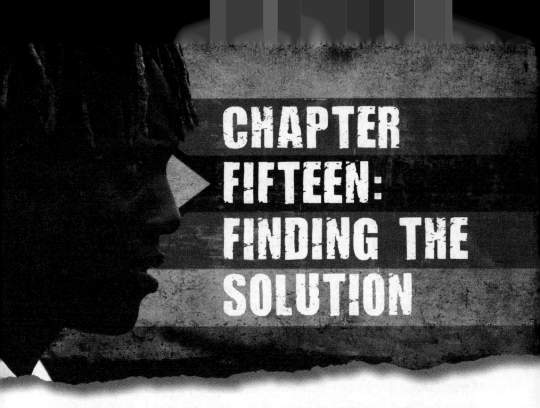

CHAPTER FIFTEEN: FINDING THE SOLUTION

Well, I figured that Allan Donald was my solution. If I could get anywhere close to delivering a cricket ball with the same pace and accuracy that he did then I couldn't go too far wrong.

When we returned to Zimbabwe in the winter of 1998 I was asked to do a lot of coaching in Bulawayo although I really wasn't thinking of taking my career in that direction. So I decided instead to get myself fitter than I had ever been by doing the "Cybergenics total bodybuilding programme". It was only a two-month programme but it was brutal – you train to the point of collapse, and it hurts like hell. You learn what it means to push your body to the limit, to put yourself on the line. It was the single most gruelling thing that I have ever done in my life, physically, and I reached a level of fitness I had never experienced before. I believe I had also matured just a little more as a person. If I wanted to get back in the team I needed to look like a proper athlete and be at my peak. After the programme I felt that I was ready for anything.

I also bought a home study course called *The Dynamics of Personal Goal Setting* by a man called Paul John Meyer, primarily because I wanted something that might help me to train my mind. It wasn't a cheap course, but it focused me and it helped me to set the goals I needed. I had to face all the negative vibes in my life and start a habit of positive affirmation. I began to believe that I had within me the ability to change my circumstances and I decided to take my destiny into my own hands.

I had continued to tinker with my bowling action even after my trips to the various academies, studying my action and bowling at the stumps to try to get it right. But I was struggling until I got it into my head that the action I really wanted to copy was that of Allan Donald, the great South African bowler. He had such an easy, stress-free streamlined action. After my course I kept hearing a voice in my head, over and over again, saying, "For every problem there is a solution, for every problem there is a solution." Well, I figured that Allan Donald was my solution. If I could get anywhere close to delivering a cricket ball with the same pace and accuracy that he did then I couldn't go too far wrong.

Incredibly, the results were almost immediate. I was bowling fast and I was bowling accurately. Something clicked and from a technical perspective it was spot on. Everything felt faster and easier. My comeback was taking shape very well and after the physical conditioning, now the technical side was coming good to a point where I couldn't wait to get out and play for real. As it turned out, it was to be the start of a purple patch for me that would last for three seasons.

In September 1998, India arrived in Zimbabwe for three one day matches and a one-off Test. Infuriatingly, before playing in a game for my province I had failed to warm up properly and suffered another groin strain. I felt I had done everything right but still I felt a tiny twinge that just grew worse. I was furious with myself because I really wanted to play against India. I played no part in the one day series, which ended 2-1 to India, and on the eve of the Test in Harare Andy Pycroft, one of the selectors, sat me down and told me that it was my last chance. He said that if I didn't go out and play the selectors would not look at me again and that they wanted me to pick up five wickets. I was in pain and discomfort but I figured, "What have I got to lose?" I had put on about four kilos of solid muscle and I figured that the rest of my body could support the pulled groin. Besides, if this was my last chance then I might as well go down with all guns blazing.

So I was selected to play, albeit with a very heavily strapped up thigh. Batting first, we only managed 221 runs but we bowled them out for 280. Opening from the pavilion end I was bowling fast and the Indian batsmen were soon dancing around on the bouncy Harare Sports Club wicket. To the Indian batsmen's dismay, the groundsman had left a little tinge of grass and they were not enjoying the ball seaming around. Everyone was amazed at the pace I was generating but my groin was always at the back of my mind. It felt like it could go any time. We managed it carefully and I had to ice it like crazy to keep the swelling down but, soldiering on, I managed my first five-wicket haul in Test cricket. I bowled 26 overs and took the wickets of Mongia and Sidhu, the openers, Mohammad Azharuddin, the captain, Sourav Ganguly and Robin Singh. Rahul Dravid scored a century; otherwise we would have skittled them out for next to nothing. I was on a high, wondering if we really could beat this wonderful Indian team. I had bowled flat out and I had bowled really well.

We managed to score 293 in our second innings, which left India a modest target of 235 to chase but the unthinkable happened and we bowled them out for 173, with the wickets shared among the bowlers. I only dismissed Mongia at the start but Neil Johnson claimed three including Tendulkar. We had won by 61 runs and I was named man of the match. It was a great victory against one of the very best teams in world cricket, and I felt that I had finally announced my arrival as a Test bowler, albeit three years too late.

I was bowling as fast as anyone else in the world in 1998, but the selectors did not know whether they could risk me in a one day tournament. However, on the basis of my performance against India I found myself selected for the one day tournament in Sharjah and by the time we got there I had shaken off the injury.

We landed in Dubai, the land of milk and honey, and I bought my first laptop while we were there. It was amazing to be in a place that was sandy, modern, clean and so fresh. They spare no expense when it comes to their sport and the Sharjah ground has to be seen to be believed.

It was a tri-nations tournament featuring ourselves, Sri Lanka and India. In recent matches we had been bowling far too many no-balls, and had even taken a number of wickets with no-balls, so the Zimbabwean selectors and team management had decided to fine any player who took a wicket with a no-ball $1,000. We thought it was pretty harsh but we accepted it. It would have been fairer if they also fined the batsmen for soft dismissals or careless run-outs.

Anyway, we reached the final, where we would face India. I hadn't played in any of the early games, however, but I was picked for a dead-rubber match against India before the final. Because the match didn't mean anything there was a very small crowd, but we were surprised when India fielded their first-string team and I went on to play a blinder. The surface of the wicket was perfectly flat, very shiny and quick. This meant that the ball did not get scuffed up, like it does on the Subcontinent, so I knew that if I was going to get wickets I would have to get them early. There would be no reverse swing here.

I got Ganguly with my first ball and was feeling pretty good. Replays suggested that the ball may have pitched outside leg stump. Then I got Dravid edging to slip playing a back-foot drive. Sachin Tendulkar, the little master, was next in and he made a streaky start to his innings. As good as he was and is, Tendulkar is a slow starter so if you are going to get him out you need to do it quickly. I bowled him a peach that moved away at the last second and he made contact with it. Just as Andy Flower was about to catch it I heard the shout, "No ball!" My teammates were furious. Hats were thrown to the ground and I heard somebody saying, "I can't believe you've just done that Henry." Meanwhile, I was thinking, "That's $1,000 down the drain."

I went back to my mark, looked at the ball in the palm of my hand and told myself that I was going to give Tendulkar the best ball I had ever bowled. I smashed the ball into the middle of the track, halfway down the pitch; Tendulkar made an involuntary flick at it; the ball looped up into the air and landed safely in the hands of Grant Flower, Andy's brother. I was ecstatic – I had just forced the best batsman on the planet into making two false strokes and I had got him out. I also got a run-out later in the innings plus the wicket of Ajay Jadeja, and finished with figures of 4 for 40. We won by 13 runs and I was named man of the match. Things were starting to turn for me.

More important from my point of view was that I was selected for the final. We made 196, which was never going to be enough and Tendulkar gained his revenge in some style, scoring 124 as India reached their target without loss. Ganguly chipped in with 63. I bowled lightning quick, firing in six overs and conceding 50 runs at 8.33 but although there were some close calls his innings was just about flawless. I was back to earth with a bump. I had made Tendulkar very angry by dismissing him in the previous match. Apparently after his dismissal he had vowed to his teammates that he would teach me a lesson. And he sure did.

We still picked up a decent prize fund and we had beaten Sri Lanka. The tournament prize money was split amongst the team based on the number of games played and level of involvement. For example, a twelfth man would get a smaller share than a player who took to the field in all matches, but it was still a very handsome reward. This was the start of my beginning to earn a pretty good wage from my cricket.

There was also a Champions Trophy Tournament in Bangladesh. In those days, these competitions were played on a knock-out basis, so if you lost your first game you were on your way home, and we lost our first game against New Zealand. The veteran Chris Harris managed to knock off 32 runs in the remaining two overs. We had felt we had it in the bag all the way to the end. On the plus side, I was one of the fastest bowlers in the tournament, my fastest ball being measured at 145 kph so I knew I was on top of my game.

On 17th November 1998, we arrived in Pakistan for a three-Test series and three One Day Internationals. Dave Houghton had said to us right at the start of the trip, "When you are in Pakistan you don't complain. You just get on with it. It is the same for every side that comes here, so it is going to be no different for us. I don't want to hear anybody moaning about the food or the conditions." Steve Waugh, the great Australian, had said something similar. Ironically, Houghton was ill for the first warm-up match at the Sahiwal Biscuit Factory and couldn't attend. We kicked off with the one dayers, played at Gujranwala, Sheikhupura and Rawalpindi, losing two and winning one, with me watching from the sidelines.

The first Test was at Peshawar, a ground on which Mark Taylor had recently scored a triple century for Australia on what was probably the flattest wicket in the history of Test cricket. We looked at the wicket and were told it was the same one on which Taylor had made his big score. The thought went through my mind that the match we were about to take part in was either going to be a boring draw or Pakistan were going to slaughter us.

As we were standing there somebody important from the Pakistan Cricket Board ambled out, took a look at the strip and said, "We are not going to play on that wicket again. We are going to play over here." And with that, he removed the stumps and put them in the wicket next to the one that had been prepared for the match. This new strip had been rolled, but there was a lot of grass on it our first thought was that none of our batsmen, or bowlers, much fancied facing Wasim Akram or Waqar Younis on this pitch; but then we realised that our side contained some pretty decent bowlers too, so it probably gave us our best chance of winning.

I looked at the Pakistan team sheet and it was filled with world-class players again – Saeed Anwar, Wasim Akram, Inzaman-ul-Haq, Waqar Younis, Aamer Sohail. I also remembered that the last time I had faced them I had been caused some unpleasantness by them on my debut so I was pretty fired up for this one.

Pakistan batted first and straight away the ball was seaming and jagging about all over the place. Their batsmen were hating it, but I was loving it. I got Moin Khan and Wasim Akram as we dismissed them for 296. Heath Streak had bowled really well for his four wickets and Pommie Mbangwa also chipped in with three. We managed to accumulate 238 runs in reply but had it not been for Neil Johnson, who made a wonderful 107, we would have been bowled out of the match. Waqar and Wasim accounted for nine of our wickets: they were simply too good for us.

At the start of their second innings Alistair Campbell wandered over and handed me the new cherry and told me that I wasn't going to get too many chances to bowl on a green wicket like this one at Test level, so I should go out there, make the most of it and have some fun. And boy, did

I have some fun. Unbelievably, we bowled them out for 103. I bowled 11 overs which cost 42 runs, but I also managed to pick up the wickets of Aamer Sohail, Azhar Mahmood, Inzaman and Saeed Anwar. I was bowling so fast that at the end of the day Andy Flower, who was keeping wicket, had to ice his hands. It was amazing to rip out the heart of their top order and all of a sudden we realised that victory was within reach if we could just knock off the relatively small total.

We duly went out and knocked off the required 162 runs, although it was pretty tense counting the score down run by run. Few of us had any nails left by the time Murray Goodwin hit the winning runs. We were just delighted. We had achieved something against all the odds; we had beaten Pakistan in Pakistan and few teams ever did that. I am sure that the poor groundsman got severely reprimanded for the underprepared wicket that was breaking up on the surface on day three, but he was just following orders.

Between Tests, Wasim Akram invited the entire Zimbabwe team to his home for a meal. He served us quail in some kind of curry sauce and it was the hottest, spiciest thing I have ever eaten. It nearly reduced some of the team to tears but it was so tasty that we kept eating it. It was great to be able to socialise with a rival away from the field; it was something that was quite rare in the Subcontinent, and it allowed us to see a different side to him. That is why I heard with profound sadness that his wife, Huma, had passed away in September of 2009. She had been a wonderful hostess. I had always thought of him as aloof but it was as if there was a new-found respect for us after we won that Test. Don't get me wrong: he still played very hard on the field afterwards.

I took another three wickets in the first innings of the second Test as the game ended in a draw because of fog – there was no play at all on the fifth day, but it had come down every morning on the four previous days and not lifted until midday. And when the third Test was abandoned without a ball being bowled, again because of fog, we had won our first ever series away from home. I do not believe any other Test series has been fogged off. People will say that we only won because of the weather, but we will never know what would have happened. And no matter what, the history books record forever that Zimbabwe went to Pakistan at the end of 1998 and won the series 1-0. And I was there. I was also named Zimbabwe's man of the series, on the basis of my bowling in one match. In fact it was on the basis of one bowling spell!

Ironically, the fog that had been our friend in helping us to win the series now became our enemy as we tried to get back to Zimbabwe. We almost didn't make it home in time for Christmas but, thankfully, there was a brief open window in the weather and we managed to get out. My Christmas present was knowing that I was now established as a Zimbabwe Test cricketer. I also had the comfort of knowing that most of the problems with my technique were firmly behind me.

CHAPTER SIXTEEN: BUILDING FOR THE FUTURE

I was informed that my sister had been on the phone to say that my dad had been involved in a car accident. I got in my car and immediately went to the United Bulawayo Hospital, fearing the worst.

Dad called Victor and I into his study at the beginning of 1999, sat us down and told us that he wanted to build a house for each of us. He knew how difficult it was for young people to get onto the property ladder. He insisted that we would have to pull our weight, however. He wanted us to get the plans drawn up and sort out the necessary planning permission, but he was going to buy the land and pay for the building for us. It was a wonderful gesture and very few children had fathers who could do something as amazing as this.

I was really keen, so off I went and found an architect. I had done technical drawing at school and I knew how to sketch out a plan so I put one together, gave it to the architect and he got it approved, and the building began.

Victor showed no interest until my house was nearly finished, when he said, "Listen Henry, the old man is not just building this house for you." I reminded him that what Dad had said was that he was going to build houses for each of us, and it was hardly my fault that Victor had sat back and done nothing. I knew that I couldn't really live with Victor as we were so different and incompatible and I was also caught between not knowing whether I should be living in Bulawayo, where the house was being built, or in Harare where the national squad was based.

A few days into the season I was playing a provincial match at Bulawayo Athletic Club when I got the call to come off the pitch and I was replaced by the twelfth man. I was informed that my sister had been on the phone to say that my dad had been involved in a car accident. I got in my car and immediately went to the United Bulawayo Hospital, fearing the worst, where I was met by Barbara, Dad's secretary.

It turned out that he had been delivering some building materials to the incomplete house and while *en route* he pulled out at a T-junction. My dad's polio meant that he used a stick on the accelerator to help him drive and as he was pulling out the stick had slipped off the throttle and an oncoming car had ploughed straight into him on the driver's side. He had broken several ribs, both legs and an arm, chipped a tooth and generally got a real working over. He had also lost a great deal of blood and when I arrived he was in a huge amount of pain. It was difficult for me to see this, as it was for the nursing staff because this was one of their doctors and here he was, facing possible death.

Later the same day he was transferred to a private hospital called the Mater Dei and taken to intensive care. I went in to see him and held his hand and he was clearly struggling to say something to me, so I moved closer, "The sheets that we wanted for the roof weren't available," he said. Here was my father lying in hospital perhaps on the brink and all he could think about was to tell me that he hadn't been able to get the roofing sheets he wanted for my house.

There was not much else I could do that day so I was expected to return to the cricket match I had been playing in and I somehow managed to get back on the field, focus and take three wickets to help the team to win. I felt quite numb through it all. I have been in hospital a number of times myself with operations of a sporting nature. But to be there for the sake of a loved one is totally paralysing in the face of being totally powerless to do anything to help. All one can do at a time like that is pray, I suppose. Pray that God will be merciful and spare their life and that He will guide the hands and minds of the attending doctors.

It was a very scary time for me and I found it very difficult to share my emotions with anybody. I wept a few times as I relived what my dad had been through in recent times. He was on his own again because his relationship with my stepmother had broken down and I was struck by how terribly lonely he had become. My dad had his fair share of responsibility in it all but I still felt for him. Judith happened to be in Zimbabwe at the time of the accident due to the death of her own father. It seemed like a double whammy but it was fortunate that she was there. It is amazing how much you appreciate people when losing them becomes a real possibility. Minor disagreements lose their importance. That week was a torrid time for me, during which I even received an award from Zimbabwe TV. To be honest I couldn't even tell you what it was for, but I guess it might have had something to do with the part I had played in helping Zimbabwe to beat Pakistan. I didn't turn up to receive it because I had too many other things on my mind, mainly my dad's precarious health.

A few days later I got another call which was more worrying, telling me that Dad had been moved back into intensive care because he was having problems breathing. The call came at 1am so you can imagine how I felt when the phone rang. I was convinced they were going to tell me he hadn't made it. He felt he was on the final stretch so he told Judith to gather the children around the bed. When I saw him again I felt helpless as he told me that he felt he was going to struggle to pull through. It would be bad enough hearing this from anyone you were close to, but to hear it from somebody who is a doctor was terribly upsetting.

I had to pull him together so I told him not to entertain such thoughts and think positively, he had to believe that he would make it. I went to church with a lump in my throat and prayed for him. My dad and I have never really spoken about matters of the heart the way sons and their fathers are supposed to. My guess is that this is because of the distance boarding school caused between us. But now I knew that there was so much more I needed to say to him. If he went now the song *The Living Years* by Mike and the Mechanics, which is all about a father dying and how then it's too late to say the things you want to say, would haunt me for the rest of my life. I gave him an incentive, or bribe if you like, by telling him that he needed to stay alive to see me get married and meet his grandkids.

I returned to the hospital the following day and Dad was complaining about pressure on his lungs, so he told the doctors that they needed to drain them. But for some reason they were reluctant until my stepmother, who had arrived to visit, informed them that if he died she would be holding them personally responsible. "He is telling you what's wrong; now just do as he says," she said. One of the doctors on call at the time was a family friend and perhaps he was in a state of shock but he kept procrastinating. But after Judith launched into him it was suddenly all hands to the pump and a chest drain was sent for. They cut through a muscle to get the tube into his chest cavity and immediately all this fluid poured out and he soon found he could breathe easily again. That was the point where we felt he was going to survive and that's what he told us too.

Dad later told me about a strange dream he'd had whilst lying in his hospital bed. He said that in the dream he had been standing at the edge of a cliff with a vast chasm ahead of him and a being was standing beside him telling him that it was time to go. He told me that he did not want to go and so the dream ended. I thought it was quite a profound spiritual experience he had just conveyed but I kept it to myself. They didn't know whether he would ever walk easily again, and his arm required a metal plate, but after many months of recuperation at home he more or less returned to normality. My good friend David from Plumtree had stood by me through it all but no one from the cricket fraternity knew. I thought they wouldn't understand or care.

All through this terrible time my dad's main concern was ensuring that we got the house finished. He told me that it was very important for him to see it built and I remember he even wrote out and signed a cheque with his broken right hand from his bed in intensive care. It looked nothing like his normal signature and I had problems persuading the bank to cash it but they eventually did when he spoke to them on the phone, even though he could hardly breathe at the time. With this money I was able to buy the rest of the materials needed to complete the house.

It is true that my dad has made his mistakes in life and he might have made wiser choices, but in that short space of time he became my greatest hero, role model, inspiration and mentor. You can have your movie stars, models, politicians, socialite celebrities and all the rest of them if you want but in my eyes the real icons are the unsung heroes of society. Yes, the doctors, nurses, firemen, teachers and so on but mainly the dads and mums of the world that do their best to give their children a better life. The way he conducted himself in that crisis was amazing to me and the love and concern he had for us all was heart-warming.

As Dad got better life soon returned to normality. However, I became acutely aware of a foot problem that had been nagging away for a while since the Pakistan tour. It seemed that the cricket boots I was using weren't that well suited to my feet and after bowling on so many hard pitches I started to experience some pain in my right foot. Eventually I sought medical advice and was told that I had developed an internal callous and it was arranged for it to be cut out by a well known surgeon called Mr Ncube in Bulawayo. The first thought that entered my mind again was "Why me again, why now?" The injuries that I was constantly suffering were the bane of my professional life as a cricketer.

My old friend Ma G was on hand to get a groggy Mr Olonga back home after the operation. I hadn't told anyone from the Zimbabwe coaching set-up about the injury or the operation because I didn't want to jeopardise my chances of going to the 1999 World Cup in England. Fortunately there was ample time for me to recover but by the time the tournament came round I had lost a little bit of weight and a touch of pace and in my head I knew that I wasn't 100 per cent.

With months of turmoil behind me because of my dad's accident and my injury I was up against it. Before we flew to England I wrote the following entry in my journal: "Let it be recorded on this day that I, Henry Olonga, declare my inadequate preparation and resulting unfit mental, physical and emotional state for the World Cup cricket 1999 held in England. If I were to have any positive effect on this World Cup let it be recorded that it will be by the grace of God."

So I was back in England many years after my previous trip, more mature now and relishing playing for my country again, despite my concerns over my fitness. We were in the same group as India, South Africa, England, Sri Lanka and Kenya, with not a single fixture that could be regarded as easy. Our first match was against the Kenyans at Taunton and we knew that if we couldn't beat them we were in serious trouble. They managed to get to 229 for 7 from their 50 overs, with Neil Johnson taking four wickets, and we cruised to our target with nine overs remaining. Johnson completed a memorable match by hitting 59 runs.

Then came our first big test, against India at Grace Road, Leicester. Sachin Tendulkar's father had died so he had flown home to pay his respects, but they were still an incredibly strong side and we were not fancied at all. However, confidence was high in our camp after our win over Kenya and Andy Flower made 68 as we reached a respectable 252 for nine from our 50 overs. My opening spell with the ball wasn't great and after bowling six wides and conceding about 20 runs in three overs the Indian fans started mocking me. "Bring back Olonga and the game will go on no longer," they were chanting. It was one of the moments in life that you just wish that a hole in the ground would open up and swallow you. To be fair to me the white reader balls were swinging all over the place and a lot of bowlers were struggling to control them throughout the tournament.

With India needing less than ten runs to win with three wickets in hand Alistair Campbell gave me the ball and, as he did so, there was a distinctive rumble in the crowd who were no doubt convinced I was going to be smashed out the ground and that this would be over quick. But I knew something they didn't: I had been working non-stop in the nets for such a time as this. I had been trying to get my yorkers bang on and attempting to master the reverse swing I had seen in Pakistan many years earlier. So I preferred the old, scuffed-up ball and by now the ball was more rough on the one side than the other, perfect for reversing. So I got to the top of my mark, took a deep breath and charged down toward the wicket.

The first guy to go was Robin Singh, caught at short cover by the skip-

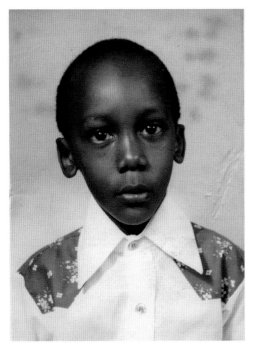

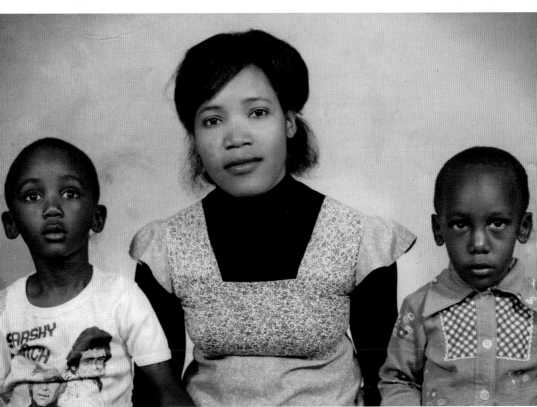

Top left. Me as a five-year-old in Nairobi

Top right. Dad relaxing in the garden in Bulawayo

Above. With mother and Victor in a studio shoot

Left. Pictured with Victor in our house in Nairobi

Above. Visiting Victor at REPS in the white Mazda with Benedicto, Mr Makoni and my dad

Above. The view of REPS from the school's rugby ground

Left. The REPS swimming pool – not my favourite place!

ZIMBABWE PRIMARY SCHOOLS NATIONAL CRICKET FESTIVAL

The Rothmans Week~

PRESENTED TO: *H. Olonga*

FOR *Representing Mat' Select*

DATE *16th Dec. 1988*

O. M. R. W.
13 2 31 4 vs. Har. Central
13 4 31 4 vs. Har. East
19 5 33 7 vs. Easterns
18 2 37 3 vs. Midlands

PRESIDENT, Z.C.U.

ROTHMANS OF PALL MALL,
Marketing Director.

Top. The cricket nets

Above left. Receiving the 'Sportsman of the Year' trophy at a prize giving at REPS

Above. A certificate presented to me after the cricket festival in 1988 in Harare where I impressed the Zimbabwe schools selectors

Left. The flag flying outside the Beit Hall at Plumtree

Top. The Plumtree first XI rugby team of 1992. That's me in the front row, second from the right

Above. Winning the hundred metres for my house at a Plumtree sports weekend

Left. Shields marking some of my sporting achievements, which as far as I know are still on display at Plumtree

Below. Playing Frederick, left, in *The Pirates of Penzance*

Left. The Matabeleland schools cricket team of 1993. I'm in the back row, third from the left.

Below. The Zimbabwe schools side of 1993. That's me second left. Also pictured are several players who became my Test teammates

Left. A picture taken for a Zimbabwean magazine in 1995

Above. Owzat! Taking the wicket of Nick Knight in a Test against England in 1996

Top. Appealing for a wicket vs Sri Lanka in 1996

Left. Bowling India's Srinath at Grace Road during the 1999 World Cup

Above. With the match ball after winning the match against India. I found that after the elation of victory I was often left feeling flat

Top. Happier times! Celebrations after I caught Daryl Cullinan as we headed for an historic victory against South Africa at Chelmsford in the 1999 World Cup

Above. A happy changing room after the South Africa win

Taking the wicket of England captain Nasser Hussein in Cape Town in 2000

Courtney Walsh breaks Kapil Dev's record for the most Test wickets. I am his 435th victim

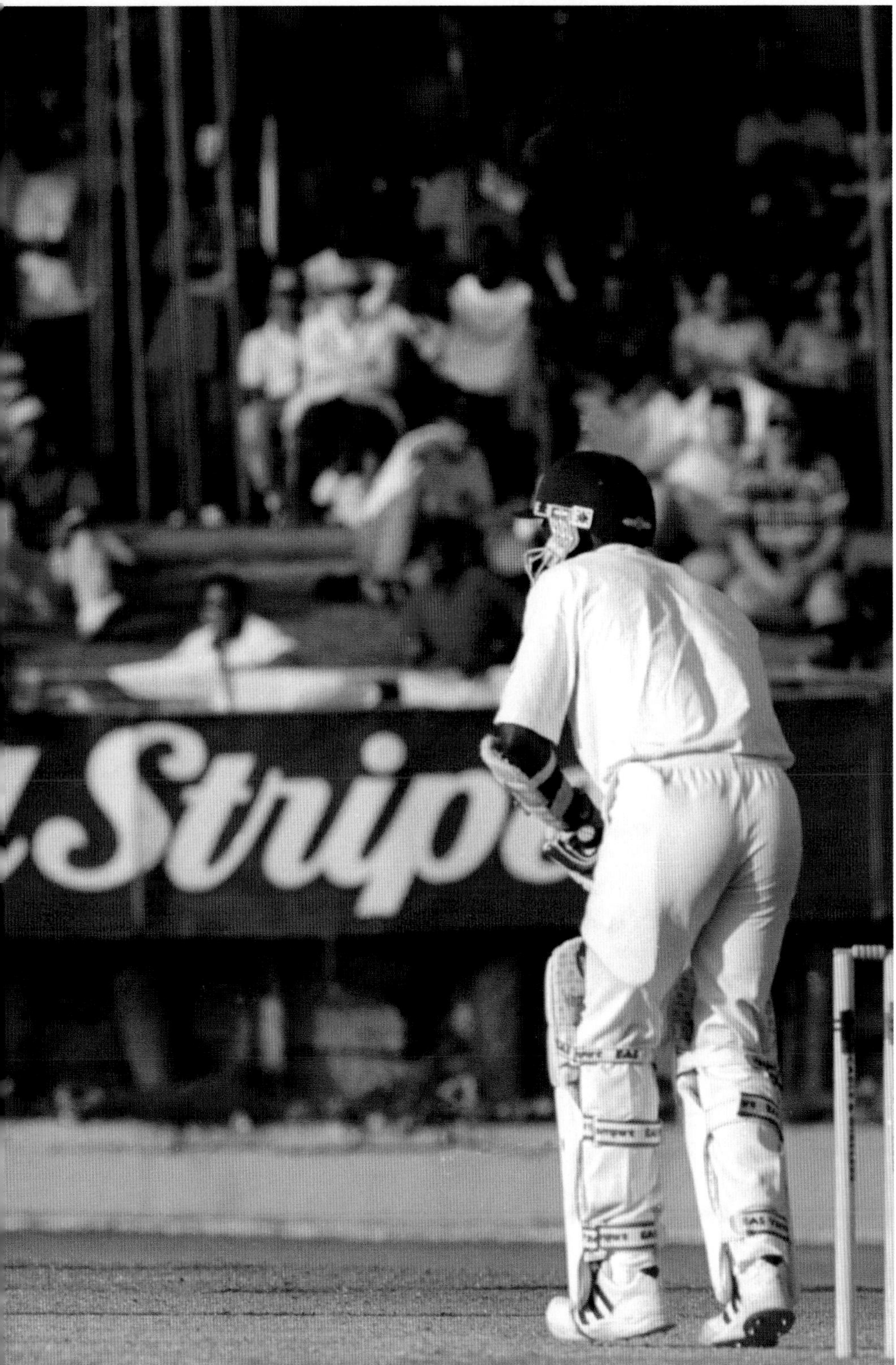

GETTY IMAGES

Guarding the wicket as Stephen Fleming is run out with a direct hit in 2000

We had some fun and laughs during nets after the protest, but I was starting to become very fearful about what would happen to me when the World Cup was over

My last ever wicket in international cricket – against Kenya in Bloemfontein

Others held up messages of support

Above. It wasn't long before some of the spectators at the ground began to join in with what we were doing

Left. Some wore hastily constructed black armbands like ours

Left. 'Cheesy' pizza ad
with Heath Streak

Below. Singing with
Prudence Katomeni
at the Miss
Zimbabwe event

Above. Picture taken during the *Our Zimbabwe* CD
cover shoot

Right. Commentating in India for the World Sports
Group when I was not picked for the tour

Top. Bowling in the first match of the 2003 World Cup against Namibia. Look carefully and you can just about make out the black armband on my left arm.

Top right. Andy Flower knocking up with his armband in full view

Above. Me on the balcony during the protest match

Above. David Folb, the chairman of Lashings and the man who offered me the chance of a new life in England

Left. Playing for Lashings and bowling spin in a six-a-side game. Alvin Kallicharan looks on in bewilderment!

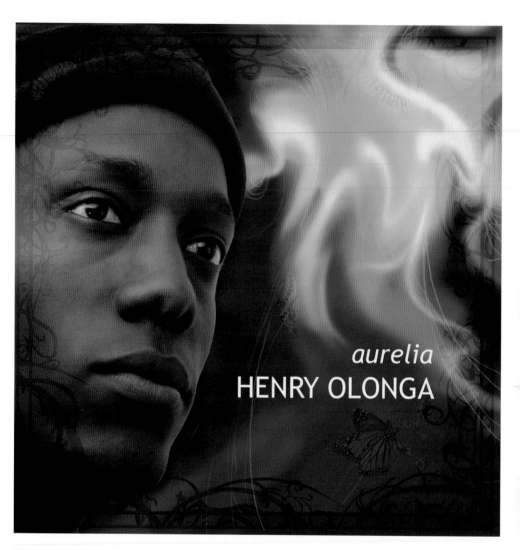

The cover of my first album, *Aurelia*

Tara meets the Kenyan side of the family in Nairobi

Tara and I on our wedding day in Adelaide

per with no runs added. Two wickets to go now and the crowd, mainly Indian supporters, were getting nervous although I am sure they still thought victory was assured. As I walked back to my mark I thought, "Henry, you can do this. Come on." Stuart Carlisle, one of my teammates, told me to seize the moment and make history.

I bowled a couple of balls to Anil Kumble and they managed to scramble a single. Srinath was now on strike, and he was a cricketer I have never clicked with. I don't know why, but ever since the Harare Test he gave the impression that he loathed me, so I was determined to get him. He had smacked a few easy boundaries in the previous overs from Paul Strang so he felt he was in. But I had only one thing on my mind. Bowl at his toes. As I ran in I fixed my eyes on them and sent down a perfect yorker which got through his defences all ends up. The crowd was now hushed and you could hear a pin drop. One wicket to go with just four runs to win and balls to spare. Surely India couldn't lose.

Prasad was in next and as he ambled up to the wicket I remembered that although we'd been together at the MRF Pace Foundation in Madras I had never seen him bat. I figured that he was probably a bit of a rabbit in the headlights like me who just needed a straight ball. I tried to repeat the previous delivery but it was on a length and it caught him on the pad. I didn't really think it was LBW but I thought to myself, "Hey Henry, that was actually a pretty close shout"; because I wanted to stop him running a single at all costs I headed off to retrieve the ball, but then stopped and felt it was worth a shout so I turned and appealed the biggest appeal of my life. To my delight and slight surprise Peter Willey wagged his left index finger to give Prasad out. I was swamped by my teammates and I can honestly say it was the greatest feeling I ever had on a cricket field because of the poetic justice of it all. We'd wrestled victory from the jaws of defeat and suffice to say I never heard any heckles from the Indian crowd after that. Not a word. But I did hear that the Indian bus was stoned by their own angry supporters as the team departed.

We then lost to Sri Lanka at New Road, Worcester, one of the prettiest grounds in all of county cricket and also lost to England at Trent Bridge, being outplayed in both games.

Next up were South Africa at Chelmsford and if we won this match we would more or less be through to the Super Six stage. South Africa were odds-on favourites and by this stage had qualified for the Super Sixes, being at the top of the table. Lance Klusener had been in immaculate form throughout the tournament, smashing everyone to all parts so we knew his dismissal would be key. But this South African team had great depth. They had Kirsten, Rhodes, Cronje, Cullinan, Pollock, Elworthy, Boucher and Gibbs in their batting line-up. It was almost certainly the longest in world cricket at the time with them having so many all-rounders in the side. However, fairly or unfairly, they had gained a reputation for themselves as chokers.

This was discussed in our pre-match team meeting and we felt if we could just place enough pressure on them we were in with a shout although we knew we would have to take all our chances. We arrived at the ground and there were a lot of Zimbabwe supporters there, either wearing the Zimbabwean replica shirts or flying the flag. Neil Johnson was in great form with the bat against his former countrymen and he scored 76 as we reached 233 for 6. Not a great score, really, and we knew it was unlikely to be enough. I knew that we needed nothing short of divine intervention to progress through to the Super Six stage. Then, during the break between innings, believe it or not it rained for almost the entire length of the interval – it was uncanny.

Just in time for our defence the rain stopped, we went out in the field and everything went our way. Now, of course, because of the rain there was just a hint of moisture in the wicket and Johnson got Gary Kirsten with the first ball of the innings, a snorter of a delivery that brushed his glove. Then Herschelle Gibbs was run out after a mix-up with Mark Boucher, the pinch hitter. Boucher himself didn't last long before getting out LBW to Heath Streak. When Jacques Kallis was out caught behind for nought off the bowling of Johnson and Hansie Cronje only made four, bowled by a stunning yorker, they were under real pressure. It seemed like every catch was going to hand and I took a stinging low, flat one at mid-on to dismiss Shaun Pollock. After the fall of Cullinan and the all-rounders we could then work on one side of the tail as Klusener went on his usual rampage at the other end. I took the last wicket by getting Allan Donald caught at mid-off by Heath Streak and so completed the biggest upset of the tournament. It was just one of those rare days when we were able to package a very good all-round team effort and in addition everything went our way. We finally dismissed them way short of the target for 185 and, unsurprisingly, Johnson was named man of the match for his 76 runs and three wickets.

The Zimbabwe team had qualified for the Super Sixes. I was bursting with pride as I stood on the balcony with my teammates looking down on hundreds of Zimbabwe supporters, all chanting, "Super Six! Super Six!" For a little cricketing nation like ours to get so far was unprecedented.

Sadly, that was as far as we got. Our first match in the Super Sixes was against New Zealand at Headingley, but the weather had the final say. We scored 175 between the showers and had them teetering at 70 for 3 when play was called off because of bad light. There was a reserve day but it rained all day and the game was abandoned as a 'no result'.

We faced Australia next, at Lord's, and they were simply awesome. My seven overs cost 62 runs, although I did clean bowl Ricky Ponting. Mark Waugh scored a ton and his brother Steve made 62 as they reached a formidable 303. Neil Johnson continued his amazing World Cup with a fantastic 132 not out but we could only manage 259 runs from our 50 overs.

Our final act came against Pakistan at the Oval. By now we were running on empty. Saeed Anwar, leading from the front, hit a century as Pakistan rattled up 271 for nine, with yours truly getting a couple of wickets. They then tore us apart, dismissing us for 123, 54 of which came from the bat of Neil Johnson.

There is a little-told tale that may have cost Zimbabwe a place in the semi-finals. Had we scored another 30 or so runs we would have progressed to the semi-finals as we would have had a net run rate superior to that of New Zealand, with whom we ended up being level on points. But our management team either hadn't realised that this was a possibility or didn't focus on it. In fact they made a couple of bewildering decisions.

I was out in the middle batting with Heath Streak and we were both struggling somewhat to score freely. Shoaib Aktar, Waqar Younis, Wasim Akram and Saqlain Mushtaq are difficult to get away at the best of times. First a message came out at a drinks break that we needed to up the run rate to try to win the match. We felt it was silly as it was way beyond us but perhaps we could have a dart at the end. Then another message came from the changing room that we would be excluded from selection in the next match if we did not hit out because the scoreboard was hardly moving.

With the threat of exclusion I was left with no choice. And the rest is history. Saqlain Mushtaq took a hat-trick and I was the first of his victims. Next was Adam Huckle and then finally Pommie Mbangwa. We were all out in the space of three balls. Streaky was livid when he returned and threw his bat down in disgust. Then the true reality of what we had thrown away dawned on us as the commentators blared through the speakers in the mostly silent changing room. Basically, the jist was "Zimbabwe have lost today to Pakistan and are out of the World Cup and it is such a shame that they failed to score just a few more runs as they would have been in the semi-finals."

Our hearts sank. We should have had someone who knew their maths. We needed a leader who reasoned that we needn't worry about the Pakistan result but improve or net run rate. Instead we had players threatened with being dropped. The players who were playing that day never forgot that incident, when a crazy management decision possibly cost us a place in the semis of a World Cup. I do not propose that we had what it took to upset Pakistan in the semis had we progressed. But it would have been huge for Zimbabwe cricket to get to a World Cup semi-final. So close but yet so far.

The feeling of purposelessness that accompanies being ejected prematurely from a cup tournament is quite depressing. You are left thinking, "What next?" Some of us visited friends, went sightseeing and finally made our way home. Australia played Pakistan in the final and bowled them out for 132 thanks to Shane Warne, who took five wickets, before knocking off the required runs in barely 20 overs. The tournament deserved a better final.

Despite our disappointment abroad we returned to a heroes' welcome, with a parade put on for us in an affluent area of Harare called Borrowdale. It was at this time that we began to become better known in the country as we started to appear in adverts and in the media. The World Cup had been shown on TV, the whole country had gone cricket mad and we had captured their imagination with our giant-killing performances.

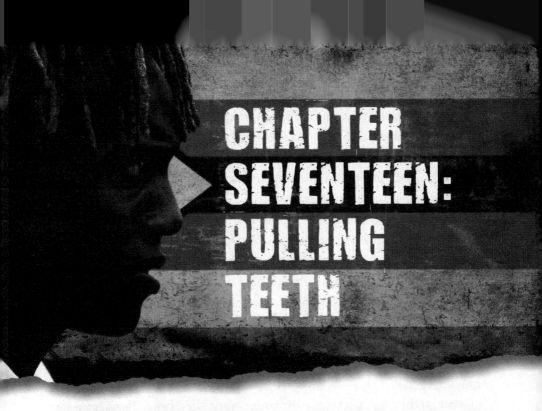

CHAPTER SEVENTEEN: PULLING TEETH

I didn't know what to do so I rang the CEO of the Zimbabwe Cricket Union and let's just say that he wasn't especially sympathetic. "Forget it. You are not going to miss a Test match because of a tooth. Tell him to do it afterwards."

had now made up my mind that, despite building the house in Bulawayo which was now finished, I was going to move to Harare, the capital city. The house was fully furnished and I had moved in, but more and more of the squad training sessions were taking place in Harare. I reasoned that I really needed to be there as I was now almost a permanent fixture in the side and spent more time there than in Bulawayo.

While I was looking for somewhere to stay I met a young man called

Bruce Izzett at a baseball clinic with Fred Sorells. We struck up a conversation and discovered that we had much in common including music and working with youngsters to try to mentor them. He was the youth pastor of a large church in the capital and he said he had space in the flat he was living in. So, in September 1999 I told my dad and my friends in Bulawayo that I was going to Harare and I took the plunge.

Things were beginning to go really well for me and one of the really cool things was that I had been awarded a Grade A national contract. In most countries, national contracts are graded and the better you are, the better your contract becomes. Previously I had been a Grade C player, so this represented a real boost for me, a promotion. I also had a new place to live, I was in a relationship and life seemed great. I would not have changed anything in the world at that point in my life. I was travelling the world, had a good wage, and I was even appearing in TV adverts in Zimbabwe.

I appeared in one television advert for a mobile phone company as a Biblical patriarchal figure and Tatenda Taibu, Zimbabwe's five-foot-five wicketkeeper, acted as my son. I got a lot of stick for that advert. It wasn't long before a clothing company also had some of us cricketers endorsing their products and I was asked to be part of a billboard campaign for a brand called 'Faithwear'. One more magazine advert campaign involved Heath Streak and I doing a shoot for a pizza company. The adverts were instrumental in increasing our profiles in the country.

No sooner had I moved to Harare than we flew to Singapore to play in a one day tournament. I wasn't picked to play against India but they did name me for the game against the West Indies. I was bowling some really good reverse swing at the time, having finally mastered the art, and when Brian Lara came in I got him to play and miss three or four times. Then he got fed up with it and hit me for six, straight over my head. We lost all our matches.

Singapore was a wonderful place and when we went there it was a warm humid climate. It is very clean and this is mainly because they dish out fines of $500 if you are caught littering. They also have a zero-tolerance approach to the importation of drugs, which is punishable by death. I was also impressed by the emphasis on family values to the extent that they even have billboards with posters that say things like "Spend time with your children!"

From Singapore we went to Kenya for the LG Cup. This was a special trip for me because of my family connections in Kenya – I hadn't been there since 1985. While we were there we were taken to a game park for the official photo and looking out over the African plains was so breathtaking, until you realised that there were creatures within a mile of your location that given the chance wouldn't mind having you for lunch.

During this trip I was taken around the tea estates by an uncle whom I had never met before and I began to get a picture of the true size of my dad's family as interesting trivia about them came up in the conversation. I also went for a meal with my Uncle Francis, my dad's eldest brother and leader of the clan along with my Auntie Florence, but at no stage did the revelation of my dad's earlier life come up in the conversation.

I didn't play against Kenya, whom we beat, or South Africa, who beat us, but I bowled pretty well in our third and final match against India and took a couple of wickets. Despite my contribution, India beat us by 107 runs and thus ended our interest in the competition so we returned home and prepared for the most inviting of prospects.

In early October we played against the world champions Australia in a one-off Test at Harare and it was probably the most unrewarding match of my life. Australia were the best team on the planet at the time and they bowled us out for 194, with Glenn McGrath and Shane Warne picking up five wickets each, and then it was Australia's turn to bat. It began promisingly enough, with Michael Slater and Greg Blewett being dismissed cheaply. I even managed to run out Justin Langer after he'd made 44, but that was as good as it got. Mark Waugh made 90 and his brother Steve hit an unbeaten 151 as Australian raced to 422. I bowled 17 overs and went for 83 runs.

Oh, and there was another significant blemish on my card when I dropped Steve Waugh off Heath Streak when he was in the 90s. Grant Flower also dropped him, as did Streaky himself and although it never makes you feel better it is clear that we were having a tough time holding our catches. The cricket saying 'Dropped catches lose matches' was certainly true on that day. We then made 232 but Murray Goodwin was caught on 91, just short of what would have been a well-earned century against the country he grew up in. McGrath and Warne did most of the damage again and they beat us comfortably by ten wickets.

A one day series followed, but I was told that I wasn't required. It was almost as if I was being punished for that dropped catch and, from that point, things started going against me in my cricket career. As quickly as I had ascended the ranks I was then dropped.

I was demoted to the B side and told to work on my bowling even though I'd only had one really bad match. I worked my butt off in the B team and started bowling well again, thanks to a lot of help from Trevor Penney, the coach. He was born in Zimbabwe but spent most of his career playing county cricket for Warwickshire and he got me back on the right track by just getting me to relax and enjoy the game again.

Sometimes you need somebody you can bounce ideas off and after all the problems I'd had with my action early on in my career I had never stopped fine-tuning and tinkering with it. I have always had mental belief in my ability to bowl quickly, but there were times when my action went walkabouts and very often there was just a small technical adjustment required. But knowing when to stop analysing and just expressing myself was always a tough balancing act.

The problem for bowlers in Zimbabwe was that most of our coaches had a batting background. One of them just used to say to me, "Go out and bowl fast." If a batsman had a technical issue then he was happy to spend hours working with them. They would often be advised on how to move their feet, keep their head still and so on but when it came to the bowlers the coaches did not have a lot to offer. So for most of my career we poor bowlers were left to fend for each other without any real bowling coach available. It wasn't enough.

In late October there was a Test against South Africa in Bloemfontein and I was quite surprised to be picked for the short tour. We had been caned by Australia and I think most of us expected a tough performance against Hansie Cronje's team. They bowled us out for 192, with Shaun Pollock being almost unplayable as he took five wickets in 21 overs that cost him just 39 runs. They made 417 and then I bowled 33.1 overs that cost 93 runs, although I did take four wickets. When they dismissed us for 212 they had won by an innings and 13 runs.

We had a return Test in November, played at Harare Sports Club. As soon as we were bowled out for 102 in the first innings we were out of it. The only reward for me was getting three wickets including the wicket of Hansie Cronje for 58. Within two and half years of this dismissal, he was to die.

It was around this time that I began to have problems with my eyes. I had been doing a lot of work on my computer and my eyes suddenly began to have double vision during the Test match. I went off to see an optometrist who informed me that I had a slight astigmatism in one eye and would need contact lenses or glasses to deal with it. It was the eye that I had injured at high school. I began using contacts for a while and then years later settled with glasses after one too many cases of mixing the cleaning fluid and the saline fluid. Anyone who has ever done this knows that it is not funny at all.

Next up was a three-Test series at home against Sri Lanka, but before I could concentrate on that I had to have some dental work done. I have always loved sweets and despite my best efforts to look after my teeth I had problems with a couple of them, so I went to see a dentist called Gerhard Lung, a German, who had been recommended to me as being the best in the business. He took an X-ray and when he came back in he was counting, all the way up to 13. He told me that he needed to treat 13 of my teeth. I thought he was kidding but he was deadly serious. There were six or seven amalgam fillings that needed to be removed and I also had a couple of cracked teeth and various other issues that had to be resolved.

He duly shaved down the teeth with amalgam fillings and replaced them with ceramic teeth. I wasn't terribly reassured when he informed me that he would be sticking these ceramics in place with the same type of glue that was used to hold the tiles in place on the space shuttle – didn't one of the shuttles crash because a tile fell off?

While he was treating me over the course of several weeks I kept bumping into people in his waiting room and discovered that they had travelled from all over the world to be treated by Mr Lung. He even had patients from England, who found that even after they had paid their air fare and hotel bills it was still cheaper for him to work on their teeth than it was to have treatment back at home.

Mr Lung took another X-ray of my bottom wisdom teeth and told me he wasn't happy with the way things looked. He thought there was an infection and that he needed to deal with it as quickly as possible but I wanted to wait, at least until after the series against Sri Lanka. I told him I intended to play in the first Test and he advised me against it, insisting that I complete my treatment first. I didn't know what to do so I rang the CEO of the Zimbabwe Cricket Union and let's just say that he wasn't especially sympathetic. "Forget it. You are not going to miss a Test match because of a tooth. Tell him to do it afterwards."

The first Test against Sri Lanka was to be played in Bulawayo. After we made 286, Sri Lanka passed 400 thanks to another double century from Marvin Atapattu. I took another four-wicket haul and we then batted out for the draw.

The second Test was played in Harare and yet again we failed to make sufficient runs in the first innings. Andy Flower scored 74 and Alistair Campbell 36 but we were all out for 174. This time it was Mahela Jayawardene and Tillakaratne Dilshan, with 91 and 163 respectively, who put us to the sword. They racked up 432 and I managed to get a couple of wickets. In our second innings, Andy Flower scored a superb 129 but he did not have a huge amount of support and they chipped us out for 292 before knocking off the 38 runs they needed for victory.

We reassembled in Harare at the beginning of December for the third Test but this time we were bowled out for 218. However, myself and Eddo Brandes took three wickets apiece to skittle Sri Lanka for 231. Unfortunately the match was hit by rain and we ended up losing a full day and several sessions so there was never going to be a result. We declared in our second innings at 197 for 7 and Sri Lanka had no time to get the runs they needed.

During the first match in Bulawayo I was invited to dinner with David Coltart. He was the human rights lawyer whom I had met after he represented the parents of the boys unhappy at the behaviour of the camp leader back in 1993. He was a passionate cricket fan and it used to inspire me to see him sitting in the pavilion.

Over dinner we got talking about Robert Mugabe. He explained that when Mugabe first came to power he had greatly admired the conciliatory stance he had taken, urging black and white people to work together to build a great new nation. He showed me a personally handwritten letter from Mugabe sent to him while he was studying at university in South

Africa, urging him to come home and play his part in building Zimbabwe's future. The note was on an official issue letterhead from the prime minister's office. Mugabe had been on television and made a memorable speech that had persuaded many white people to stay in the country.

However, Coltart's view had changed, and he was also the first person I ever heard describe Mugabe as a dictator. I had heard of Suharto, Idi Amin and Saddam Husain but I certainly wouldn't have put Mugabe into the same category. It just didn't bear out with what I had been taught all my life. He was a hero and that was unquestionable. But that view was about to change.

David handed me a concise dossier put together by the Catholic Commission for Justice in Zimbabwe called *Breaking the Silence – Building True Peace*. It was all about the Matabeleland massacres and had thousands of stories of the atrocities committed by the Fifth Brigade. Having grown up in the area where so many of the acts committed against humanity occurred, it was devastating to read some of the most awful testimonies of brutality and pain foisted upon human beings.

There are many incidents documented in the dossier and other sources about that time that continue to haunt me even today. This was the country I grew up in, this was the country I played cricket for and Mugabe was the leader who gave instructions for his citizens to be treated in this way.

There was one story involving two young girls who were gang-raped for days by members of the Zimbabwe National Amy and when they were done, the soldiers left by helicopter. Some months later they returned by which stage both girls were heavily pregnant. The soldiers split both of these girls' wombs wide open with their bayonets, removed the still moving foetuses and dumped them, leaving the girls to bleed to death. Fifty-six other people were tortured and beaten. There were many such stories in the dossier, each more harrowing than the one before.

Soldiers would cordon off entire villages and either shoot and torture all the inhabitants or they would starve the occupants to death by destroying food and preventing any more from reaching the area. It was like some sort of sick game. Mass graves have been found all over the countryside in Matabeleland, the province of my formative years. For fun, the militia would throw individuals down wells.

There was one more story that changed my perception of the president.

This was not in the dossier but I heard it from someone who had actually seen it happen. It involved a man who watched his mother being killed in front of him. The militia tied her legs, they hung her from a tree upside down, gouged her eyes out and they lit a fire underneath her and slowly cooked her to death. The man who told me this story has never been able to get over her awful screams as he watched her die.

The dossier explained that the Zimbabwean government had given the militia huge powers under a law passed by the Rhodesian government in 1975. Irrespective of what the forces did, as long as it was deemed to 'preserve national security' the prosecution of anyone in the security forces was prevented. There was a state of emergency in place at the time because of the troubles. As soon as this law was enforced, reports of people being systematically detained, searched or abused increased.

After that meeting I wanted to know more about the massacres and what Mugabe had really been doing with his power. There were no textbooks that told us Mugabe was a dictator, no local documentaries or newspaper articles, but many websites I discovered on the Internet suggested so. And when I discovered that world I soaked it up like a sponge. I found it hard to believe at first because it was so shocking but the evidence just kept mounting up. There were many websites that painted a true picture, the best probably being the now defunct ZimToday.com. This was the one that piqued my interest the most because, until I stumbled across it, I had always thought that the president really was a revolutionary hero.

There are some good things that can never be taken away from Robert Mugabe. He was instrumental in dismantling a racist system that most of the people of the world today would agree was unacceptable. But Mugabe was much more than just a former liberation hero now. He couldn't live off that achievement for the rest of his life. He had crossed a line in my mind and shown himself to be a murdering tyrant.

ZimToday and some other sites had the most harrowing images of people killed by the forces in Zimbabwe in the early 1980s. Just thinking of those images makes me feel sick even now. They were just about the most horrific things I had ever seen. I began to feel cheated.

CHAPTER EIGHTEEN: TIME FOR CHANGE

All this turmoil affected every sphere of life in Zimbabwe and cricket was no exception. As Mugabe raged against the evil white man, the newspapers began to talk about racism in the game, suggesting it was a reason for our poor form.

By the beginning of the new millennium Zimbabwe was in an economic and political mess.

In the mid-1990s the International Monetary Fund (IMF) had given loans to Zimbabwe as part of a globalisation measure called the Economic Structural Adjustment Programme. These loans had some serious interest rates and it wasn't long before the IMF repayments were crippling the country.

Then in the late 1990s Mugabe and his government became involved in the plunder of resources in the Democratic Republic of the Congo (DRC). In a nutshell the regime chose to support the Congo's rebel leader Laurent Kabila and help him defend various parts of his country being attacked by his former Ugandan and Rwandan allies. In return, Kabila allowed Mugabe a share of the DRC's vast resources, including diamonds.

So it appeared Mugabe and his cohorts were making millions on the back of mining concessions, as well as siphoning off vast wealth from the people of Zimbabwe in an ill-advised war. At one point the civil war in the Congo was costing Zimbabwe upwards of US$1 million a day. Figures suggest that at its peak it was costing US$30 million per month in 1998 or 0.6 per cent of the country's gross national product. Sadly, that money was forever lost to the economy. None of the 'blood diamond' money, as it became known, ever made its way back into the local economy, either, to help ordinary Zimbabweans.

The year 2000 was a watershed year for Zimbabwe when the political landscape changed for ever. There was a referendum in February, with one of the key amendments that the people were asked to vote on being the empowerment of the government to seize white-owned farms, without compensation, and give them to landless black farmers. This would later grow into the land reform program that completely destabilised the farming community.

The referendum also sought to allow Robert Mugabe the ability to enjoy another two uncontested terms in power and some felt this was one measure too far. Many in the country had become weary of his rule. Thanks to our involvement in the Congo the bottom had fallen out of the economy, with inflation starting to soar and with that the inevitable loss of jobs. The referendum went to the vote in the country's constituencies and much to the chagrin of the government it was resoundingly defeated thanks to the 'No' campaign which had been spearheaded by the emerging opposition party, the Movement for Democratic Change (MDC).

It was totally unexpected and President Robert Mugabe was personally insulted while the MDC had emerged as a true political contender. It wasn't long then before the political problems began to polarise people. The MDC was viewed as a party for educated urbanites and white people, funded by the West, while ZANU-PF was the party for those loyal to Mugabe.

In the midst of this economic and political turmoil, stories continued to circulate that there was widespread corruption within the government, and the majority of the population felt it was about time that Mugabe and his regime were held accountable. Mugabe sensed the disgruntlement of the people and he needed a scapegoat – the most common of these being the white man, Britain (the former colonial master before the Unilateral Declaration of Independence in 1965) and the West.

Zimbabwe's history is littered with colonialism, subjugation, land inequity and segregation. These were systems that were patently wrong and immoral, so it is no surprise that many will never be able to see the bad that Mugabe has done simply because in their eyes the injustices of the past outstrip any evil he has committed. I can understand that viewpoint because the system in the former Rhodesia was not a fair state of affairs. But according to Mugabe 20 years on, the colonial masters of the past were still ruling in the shadows because white people still owned much of the country's land.

All this turmoil affected every sphere of life in Zimbabwe and cricket was no exception. As Mugabe raged against the evil white man, the newspapers began to talk about racism in the game, suggesting it was a reason for our poor form. I personally believed Muralitharan, Vaas and Attapatu had more to do with our bad results against Sri Lanka but to be fair to them, the media was asking a pertinent question. They wanted to know why there weren't more black players in the team. It was now around five years since I had made my debut and there were only myself, Pommie Mbangwa and Everton Matambanadzo plus a couple of others getting anywhere near selection.

This difficult and controversial question raised some serious debate in the team and undoubtedly made a few players a little nervous. South Africa had already begun to talk about enforcing a quota of non-white players in their team and some people believed that Zimbabwe was lagging in this area despite becoming an independent country before apartheid ended in South Africa. They had seen more non-white players than us come through the ranks, too, such as Paul Adams, Roger Telemachus, Victor Mpitsang,

Justin Ontong, Makhaya Ntini, Henry Williams, Omar Henry, Herschelle Gibbs and Mfuneko Ngam.

Some quarters in Zimbabwe were becoming impatient, and it was reflective of the way that the country was starting to grow impatient in general.

In January 2000 we went to South Africa for a triangular tournament that also involved England. The first match was against South Africa in Johannesburg and I wasn't selected. We batted first and scored 226, a total that South Africa passed with the minimum of fuss.

The day before the second match, against England in Cape Town, we received a visit from Hylton Ackerman from the Plascon Cricket Academy. He gave us a pep talk that reminded me of one of Mel Gibson's pre-battle speeches in *Braveheart,* and we were all pumped up and inspired by what he said. He told us that he loved the way Zimbabweans took pride in playing for their nation.

When we got to the ground I bumped into the Englishman Grant Shepperd, another man who uses sport to preach. We had first met in a duty-free shop in Dubai of all places, where he had come up to me, told me what he did and said we must keep in touch. When he saw me he told me that he was going to pray that I would have a good game. We struggled to 211, so it looked like Grant's prayers had gone unanswered.

Now, Newlands is notorious for doing strange things in the evening. Apparently very few teams can chase totals over 200 there but I was still sceptical. Locals say it was something to do with the tide coming in; it supposedly makes the ball swing more. Anyway, as I prepared to deliver my first ball I said a wee prayer and with Hylton's words ringing in my head and the thought of Grant's prayer I felt as relaxed as I have ever been on a cricket field. And so it was that as I charged in for the next hour I swung the ball both ways and took wickets cheaply and consistently – Nasser Hussain, Nick Knight, Graeme Hick, Vikram Solanki, Chris Adams and Chris Read. I finished with figures of 6 for 19 and England were dismissed for 107. I only bowled one bad ball all day, which for me was unheard of. It was as if I had developed a skill that I never knew I had and it was really a day when absolutely everything clicked for me as a bowler.

They were the best limited-over international bowling figures ever set by a Zimbabwean and at the time the best figures by an international cricketer in South Africa. I was interviewed by the very suave Mark Nicholas after the match, a man whom I would get the opportunity to work with in the commentary box many years later.

We came crashing back to earth when we played England again in our next match at Kimberley. Kimberly is an area rich in diamonds exploited by the De Beers company and the open pit 'hole in the ground' can be seen from the air. England were clearly intent on extracting revenge and bowled us out for 161 before reaching their target with 107 balls remaining. The outstanding statistic from this match was the fact that Mark Ealham took five wickets and all of them were LBWs, a world record.

But we weren't finished yet. We beat South Africa at Kingsmead in Durban, restricting them to 227 for 7. I got the wickets of Herschelle Gibbs and Louis Koen and to round off another momentous upset we reached our victory target off the last ball of the match.

South Africa then turned us over pretty easily in Port Elizabeth and the annoying thing about that match is that our management again failed to do the maths. I was last man going out to bat and asked the coaching team if it mattered how many runs we scored – we knew that we were going to lose the match, but there was always the matter of the net run rate. I was told that it didn't matter and that I should just go out and swing the bat so that's what I did, and I was duly bowled by Paul Adams without scoring. It later transpired that again had we scored a few more runs then we would have made it to the final. I guess that second time round I should have known better.

South Africa went on to beat England by 38 runs in the final thanks to some fabulous bowling by Shaun Pollock, who took five wickets. England then arrived in Zimbabwe for four One Day Internationals. I bowled well enough but we lost the first three games, and the fourth was rained off.

At this time we began to hear about the first white-owned Zimbabwean farms being invaded by war veterans led by a violent leader called Chenjerai 'Hitler' Hunzvi. He was a self-declared leader of the veterans although there was some doubt surrounding the validity of his war credentials – records suggest he was training in Poland as a medical practitioner at the time of the war. Basically, Hunzi and his followers were unhappy that after years of independence the impoverished black masses still did not have their own land: most of the farmland was still largely white-owned and managed.

Initially their fight was with the government after the failure of the referendum to ratify the seizure of white farms, so the regime appeased them by giving them huge pensions and gratuity payments. This brought them on side but it didn't take long for Mugabe to see how, in light of the growing unrest in the country, these invasions could play into his hands. He could force through the land reforms he wanted by the back door if the invaders forced their way onto the farms independently. So, despite numerous court cases brought to expel the farm usurpers, the government effectively condoned their actions by doing nothing about it.

From this point the real madness in Zimbabwe began, and to this day it has not abated, with many people ultimately being dispossessed of their land. The police would often side with the invaders and it appeared that instructions were coming from higher up the chain, that the invasions were well co-ordinated and not just being carried out by a bunch of random fringe rebels.

Not for the first time in Zimbabwe, the country as a whole paid a heavy price as farm production was devastated and the historic description of Zimbabwe as "the breadbasket of Africa" came under threat. This time it was not because of drought but some disastrous policies. Years later Zimbabwe is still reeling from the invasions and has ended up requiring food aid from the United Nations on numerous occasions.

The government soon jumped officially onto the bandwagon and, with the presence of the militant invaders, legislation was put in place to formally force through the desired objectives of Mugabe. Many white farmers retained their land, initially at least, but the government vowed to reclaim every single farm in a land reform program that would take years to complete. All of this troubled me deeply. Where would it lead to? Civil war? Most Zimbabweans dreaded going back to the days of guerrilla warfare: we just wanted peace.

On 4th March we escaped the tension by flying to the West Indies for our first ever tour of the Caribbean. For the first time in years I had a bowling coach. Carl Rackemann, the former Australian fast bowler, had been employed for the brief tour to come and assist the fast bowlers. We played a couple of warm-up matches before we were due to face the West Indies in two Tests, and in the second match we took on the West Indies Board's President's XI. I trapped Sarwan stone dead leg before when he had only scored four or five runs, but the local umpire refused to give him out. Sarwan had been struggling for form and they knew he needed time in the middle ahead of the Tests, so they simply ignored a perfectly good appeal and he went on to make a century. It was another blatant example of unfair play by officials.

Prior to the first Test I saw my first ever carnival – I went out to dinner with a teammate, Trevor Gripper, and was mesmerised by the loud music, parades and flamboyant regalia. It was an incredibly colourful experience.

The first Test was played at Port-of-Spain and it turned out to be memorable for all the wrong reasons. They batted first and we bowled them out for 187, Heath Streak taking four cheap wickets amidst the intermittent rain. Andy Flower then hit 113 in our reply of 236 and when we bowled them for 147 the match was there for the taking. Streaky was relishing the conditions, taking five more wickets in the second innings and I chipped in with a couple.

We woke up the next day knowing that all we needed to do was crawl our way to fewer than 100 runs to set up a Test win that would have been truly and stupendously historic. The West Indian team was packed with legendary bowlers and before the final day's play Jimmy Adams, the West Indies captain, had brashly said that he felt that his bowlers were capable of getting us out before we reached our target. We thought he was just being bullish but at the back of our minds we were aware that 100 runs on this low-scoring wicket would be a challenge. The cracks were widening, there was inconsistent bounce and England had succumbed on this same track for 46 in 1994. I am sure that Walsh and Ambrose, who had both been playing in that match, looked back on that occasion and believed it was possible to repeat it.

What happened next was a case of performance anxiety and paralysis on our part. The star of the day wasn't any of the decorated West Indian veterans but a young upstart called Franklin Rose. With each falling wicket the panic began to spread through our ranks and we were like deer in headlights, we simply couldn't get any sort of consistency. In fact the only thing that was consistent was the fall of wickets. Grant Flower was the only Zimbabwe batsman to get into double figures as we succumbed for a miserable total of 63. It was horrendous and Rose was the pick of the bowlers, taking a five-wicket haul to destroy our ambitions. Curtly Ambrose bowled 11 overs, six of which were maidens, and he took three wickets while conceding just eight runs. It was an embarrassing rout, and perhaps the saddest day of my playing career because of what could have been. Adams had the last laugh and annoyingly he is a man who is always smiling anyway.

The second Test was played in Jamaica, where before the match we went for a bus trip into Kingston town which passed the house where reggae legend Bob Marley grew up. We had a disastrous start when Heath Streak pulled a muscle in the warm-up and was unable to play. Honours were just about even after both teams had completed their first innings. We made 308 and the West Indies scored 339 with me taking three more wickets. But their bowlers then massacred us again, this time for 102. This was the match during which Courtney Walsh became the leading wicket-taker in Test cricket and guess whom his record-breaking victim was? The celebrations were extraordinary as the game came to a halt while his achievement was hailed. It didn't take long for them to chase down our humble total and they coasted to victory by ten wickets.

Jimmy Adams has his home in Jamaica and after the Test he invited a number of the Zimbabwe players, including myself, to have dinner with him. He made a huge impression on me as a truly wonderful man and a true gentleman on the pitch. Who would have thought that 15 years or so after first watching this man play with the young West Indians on tour to Zimbabwe, I would be playing against him in a Test and then having dinner with him in his home?

We then played a few One Day Internationals with the addition of Pakistan but didn't do too well in those so overall it was a tour that had promised so much and yet only delivered much disappointment.

And another one lay around the corner. Prior to departure for home at the end of the tour, a number of senior players decided that we could no longer work with David Houghton and felt it was time for a change. Apart from anything else, most felt that he had become demotivated, very grumpy, stressed out and was taking things out on the players. There were also the slight miscalculations we had experienced over a couple of years that had cost us in two tournaments. So with all the team members present we had a show of hands and passed a vote of no confidence in him in a team meeting. Not everyone voted but it was more or less unanimous. Andy Flower was the captain and he was against it, but the rest of the players were adamant. The feeling was that the situation had become untenable. Perhaps coaches have a shelf life and, after being in charge for about five years, we thought that the relationship between the team and this coach had run its course. The manager of the tour was then officially informed of the players' feelings and on hearing the news, which I am sure was very difficult for him, David handed in his resignation.

This moment was a turning point in the short history of Zimbabwean cricket because it pitted the management against the players. It was a sad chapter but it was the only option the players felt they had. The losses had hurt over time and we needed a coach who did not have the trauma of the previous years to contend with. Unfortunately, one of the consequences of that fateful team meeting is that cliques began to form and in my opinion it ironically bred a culture of selfishness among players as player power became an increasing force in the game.

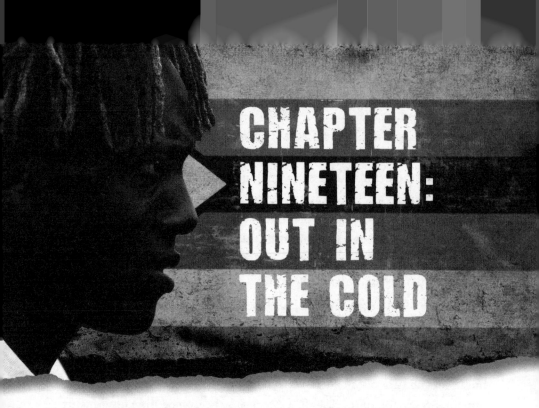

CHAPTER NINETEEN: OUT IN THE COLD

I felt that this was bang out of order so I let the player understand my feelings. I turned round and said, "Hang on, some of us might find that offensive: you can't just say that."

Back home in Zimbabwe the situation was becoming pretty tense and Martin Olds, an old Plumtree schoolboy from before my time, became the first white farmer to be killed as Mugabe allowed the land invasions to continue. White people (and their labourers) were being thrown off their land left, right and centre and the violence began to escalate.

We had a tour of England coming up and some of the players flew directly to England from the West Indies. But I needed to go home to deal with some personal issues so I went back for a couple of weeks and got a first-hand sense of the tense, troubled mood of the nation. I had a sick feeling in my stomach as all the talk was of war and revolutionary struggle or 'Chimurenga' as it is called in Shona.

I flew to England at the end of April 2000 for a three-month tour that would leave its mark on both my teammates and me. After David Houghton's departure we had been given a stand-in coach, Andy Pycroft, the former Zimbabwean batsman, and our new manager was a man called Dan Stannard, a former officer with the Central Intelligence Organisation. He was going to stand for no nonsense, the forced resignation of Houghton having pitted the players firmly against the Zimbabwean cricketing establishment.

There was a warm-up match in Kent at the start of the tour. The weather was freezing but it wouldn't have mattered if it had been a glorious summer's day because our focus was not on cricket. Emboldened by our discovery that we could effectively hold the management to ransom we figured we might as well go for something we had all hoped of achieving throughout our careers, financial security. We felt in a position of strength because we were a relatively small pool of players which now had a good core of seasoned pros and we were capable, on our day, of beating the best.

For many years, despite Zimbabwe cricket being in a relatively healthy state, we had been playing international cricket against players who were doing the same work as us but earning up to ten times what we earned. Zimbabwe cricket had the money but was still being run by old-school management who felt that the honour of playing for your country should be reward enough. It wasn't that we were getting paid a pittance, because we were well paid compared to the rest of the Zimbabwe population. It's just that some of the senior players felt that they had very little time left in the game and most of them could have earned more playing club or county cricket in England. Few would be able to retire comfortably after ten years of international cricket. Compare that with India where we had heard that if a player played for India for just two years he would be set for life. Boy, were we miffed. The Zimbabwean Cricket Union had very healthy coffers and there was no reason not to pay the players better.

We kept being told by the board that all the money we were generating was being ploughed straight back into the game for development, but the evidence of this was sorely lacking. Yes there was development but it didn't cost millions. I will admit that we didn't go through the accounts in detail but we knew there was a lot of leeway between going broke and paying the players a fair wage. Neil Johnson, who was one of the best players we have ever fielded, was to later walk away from cricket in Zimbabwe because he found he could earn more money elsewhere playing provincial cricket.

So, unsurprisingly, when we informed Stannard at some point during the match that we were considering strike action, he was not at all happy. He made it clear that he was disgusted that money had taken priority on the tour. It was not long before a stalemate ensued and a mediator was sent to England to talk to the players and we were told that it would be dealt with when we got home. In the course of time it was, but never again did the board trust the players. For that brief time, however, the players were united, all speaking with one voice.

Prior to the first Test and after the second warm-up game I began to feel a sharp pain in my left leg when I ran in to bowl. "Oh no," I thought, "what now?" I told the physiotherapist and it was all systems go for a few days because we thought it would be a rush to get me fit to play. I had X-rays and MRI scans but they revealed nothing. "Great," I thought, but my leg felt like it was about to explode if I placed any weight on it.

However, in the light of the X-rays and scans showing nothing, some of my teammates were very unsympathetic. It was crazy how the team reacted to different players being injured. I didn't remember this kind of response when Streaky was injured in the Windies. I suppose he was the heart and soul of the team. He was the mickey-taker, the joker if you will, though normally at another's expense. He was indispensible and perhaps I wasn't, or at least that is the vibe I got. I was on crutches for a few days and in the end I couldn't take part in the first Test at Lord's. This is easily the biggest regret I have in terms of my career. I had played a One Day International at this wonderful ground but never a Test match and it was especially disappointing because I had been bowling pretty well leading up to my injury.

The match was a disaster for us. England bowled us out for 83 with a new bowler called Ed Giddins taking five wickets and then they scored 415 in their first innings. Heath Streak got his name on the boards in the famous pavilion by taking six wickets but in our second innings we subsided to 123, to lose by an innings and 209 runs. It was not our finest hour.

Before the second Test we had a match against Yorkshire at Headingley. For the record, we won by 32 runs, with Pommie Mbangwa taking ten wickets in the match. But many things were about to change. Still feeling the effects of my injury, I was not playing, but I was in the dressing room and I took serious exception to a comment made by one of the white players to Mluleki Mkala, a junior black player, when he told him, "You are so black, you are like charcoal."

I felt that this was bang out of order so I let the player understand my feelings. I turned round and said, "Hang on, some of us might find that offensive: you can't just say that." Not much in it, just a gentle rebuke.

A few other white players chipped into the conversation and it deteriorated and several things were said that shouldn't have been. I was on my own with the other black players remaining silent. Some in the team said I had a chip on my shoulder and that I needed to get over myself. They basically ganged up on me and I ended up saying something like, "I don't agree with these land invasions, but I tell you what they will knock some of you guys off your high horses."

Some of the white players in the team didn't like this one bit. It struck a nerve but, surprisingly, they couldn't see their own prejudice so I went on. "Some of you guys own farms, and I bet you don't treat the black servants as equals." "Oh yes I do," one of the guys retorted. I had to smile because I would love to have believed him. The looks in their eyes spoke volumes. They were saying, "Who the hell are you to lecture us, Olonga?" From that day on my life in the dressing room was never the same as clear venom emanated from some of them.

Hindsight is a wonderful thing and I admit now that what I said about the land invasions was offensive. I have always attempted to be man enough to admit when I have screwed up and so I later apologised to a few of the players involved, individually and also generically in a letter to the then captain Andy Flower. But I had also been right in a way. There were some arrogant white people who never saw even me as being equal enough to correct their prejudice. Interestingly, only one of them said sorry back to me for the things that they had said, a gentleman called Gary Brent.

Here is what the players I was arguing with never understood. As much as there are wicked black men in Zimbabwe, who have done horrific things, there are equally some evil white folk who had done their fair share, way back in the past and up to the present day. I felt it was my responsibility as the senior black man in the team to stand up for the junior member of the team who could not stand up for himself. It's just my way.

The argument carried on for quite some time and it ended up with my being ostracised by my mainly white teammates. The management were informed that I had started it and that, "Olonga was talking some racist stuff". When asked to give my side of the story the manager was unsympathetic: it appeared that he had already made up his mind. An already dramatic tour, due to the strike, had become even more heated.

I was disappointed that I was accused of having a chip on my shoulder because nothing could have been further from the truth. I hope that I have made it clear in this book that white people have played a huge part in my life and the influence that most of them have had has been incredibly positive. Ironically, I was living in a flat in Harare with three white guys at the time who had the highest levels of integrity and I loved them as brothers. To this day they have remained some of my closest friends.

It was the start of a miserable time for me and if you look at my career from late 2000 to 2002, there was a clear slump in form, where I was very average. Make no mistake, I was no world-beater anyway and I had an average career. But I am happy to admit that I was more average after that. On an emotional level I had been bruised.

I was injured and, because in their eyes I had caused this nonsense, the team made it clear that I was better off going home to recover. There was definitely no sympathy now. I remember climbing up a flight of stairs, barely able to walk, and when I got into the changing room a player said, "What the **** is wrong with you? The X-rays have found nothing wrong."

I was put on a train and then flew back home, but the ZCU said they wanted me to return for the One Day Internationals. The CEO called me to his office in Zimbabwe. "How long do you need to be fit?" he asked. "I really don't know," I replied. "Well, we need you back in England, so let's call it a month. Yes? A month, that will be long enough." I returned to

England and tried to play but it wasn't right. The atmosphere in the team was still a little ice cold towards me. Nobody believed that I was genuinely injured. No matter what had been said between us, how could they think that I was making this up?

If I was expecting any sympathy then I was going to be bitterly disappointed. I had to accept I was viewed as a troublemaker within the team. It felt like if a group of players were going out for a drink I wouldn't be asked to join them, and if there was any banter going on around the table during a team meal then I would be excluded from the conversation. If I made a joke no one laughed.

By the end of the tour I was pretty down and considering my options. I wasn't sure what to do but I felt so rotten after the Headingley incident that I was considering taking an indefinite break from cricket. Andy Pycroft got wind of this and spoke to me prior to leaving the squad and told me to think long and hard about it. He said that I really was an integral part of things and that I ought to reconsider. It was really good, solid advice and I think I could always count on his very sober opinion on matters. Besides, it's not often you get free advice from a lawyer.

The only bright spot of my time in England came when I was asked to appear on John Inverdale's sports TV show, and I got to sing and answer the constant question concerning the morality of our tour to the UK in the light of what was going on in Zimbabwe. I had never been made more aware of the moral argument against our tours and yet although I had all the cute answers, a part of me realised that the questions had validity.

I also made an appearance on Channel 4 where I got another opportunity to sing and many people bizarrely still tell me they remember this episode of the cricket show. I became aware of how critics in the UK can be ruthless, too. I got some terrible write-ups in the British press about that. Naturally I thought it was all rather over the top because I hadn't deliberately set out to ruin anybody's evening.

After these performances I was approached by a BBC producer called Martin Smith, who was interested in my music and, from there, I met Sir Tim Rice, who is not only a wonderful lyricist but is also a cricket fanatic. He was at a Lord's Taverners match and he was gracious in giving me some of his time to chat. For a kid who had grown up singing this man's songs it was an amazing experience. I was then told that somebody knew somebody who knew Charlotte Church's manager and they would put me in touch – the usual promises but nothing came of it.

Before returning home I spent some time with my stepmother, who by now was living in Ealing on the outskirts of London. I just wanted to take stock and decide what the next chapter of my life would be. While I was with her I stumbled across a poem we had learnt in school, *If* by Rudyard Kipling, and I printed myself a copy,

If you can keep your head when all about you
Are losing theirs and blaming it on you,
If you can trust yourself when all men doubt you,
But make allowance for their doubting too;
If you can wait and not be tired by waiting,
Or being lied about, don't deal in lies,
Or being hated, don't give way to hating,
And yet don't look too good, nor talk too wise,

If you can dream – and not make dreams your master;
If you can think – and not make thoughts your aim;
If you can meet with Triumph and Disaster
And treat those two impostors just the same;
If you can bear to hear the truth you've spoken
Twisted by knaves to make a trap for fools,
Or watch the things you gave your life to, broken,
And stoop and build 'em up with worn-out tools,

If you can make one heap of all your winnings
And risk it on one turn of pitch-and-toss,
And lose, and start again at your beginnings
And never breathe a word about your loss;
If you can force your heart and nerve and sinew
To serve your turn long after they are gone,
And so hold on when there is nothing in you
Except the Will which says to them, "Hold on!"

If you can talk with crowds and keep your virtue,
Or walk with Kings — nor lose the common touch,
If neither foes nor loving friends can hurt you,
If all men count with you, but none too much;
If you can fill the unforgiving minute
With sixty seconds' worth of distance run,
Yours is the Earth and everything that's in it,
And — which is more — you'll be a Man, my son.

At that moment in my life this poem spoke volumes to me, and I decided to keep my head up high and soldier on.

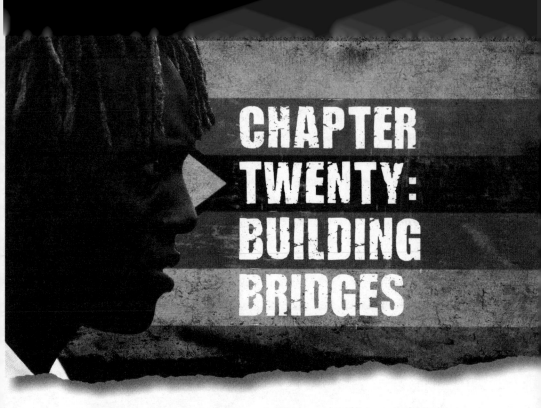

CHAPTER TWENTY: BUILDING BRIDGES

They said that they had formed a body called the Campaign to Eradicate Racism in Zimbabwean Cricket. I didn't like how militant it sounded but I was willing to listen.

In the spring of 2000 New Zealand arrived in Zimbabwe. I was returning from injury and had been chosen to play for the A team and on 7th September we began a three-day match against the tourists. As soon as we looked at the wicket we were mortified. It was the deadest, flattest wicket imaginable. I bowled 20 overs that cost 120 runs and Mark Richardson, the Kiwi batsman, scored a personal best 306 out of a total of 677 before they bowled us out for 168 with Daniel Vettori taking six wickets. Boy, did I hate warm-up matches like this. We managed to get a draw, but only because they ran out of time.

Entering the Test series a few changes in personnel had occurred. Andy

Flower had been replaced as captain without being consulted by the board. Clearly Andy was paying the penalty for his part in the players' strike in England. His replacement was announced as Heath Streak but some in the team felt that he really should have turned the offer down in support of Andy, and also for the sake of player unity.

At the same time, Carl Rackemann was elevated from bowling coach to full-time coach. Carl was an affable, easy-going guy and would go on to become a very much-loved coach.

I missed the first Test because I was still not fully fit or bowling well. I was replaced in the squad by David Mutendera, a tall, promising fast bowler. David came from an urban community and was the first black player to genuinely progress through the Zimbabwean cricket development system so the story that he might make his Test debut was perhaps as significant as mine had been. He had made his international debut in a one day series in Kenya in the 1999/2000 season and was a nice, softly-spoken guy with very little animosity. I would have given anything for Mutendera's height, by the way, as he was over six foot tall, which would help him produce some serious bounce off a good length. At this point in his life he was probably bowling better than he had ever done and he expected to be a shoo-in for the first Test, especially since I wasn't selected.

Anyway, the team was announced and he wasn't in it. He was down to be twelfth man, but he was so upset, literally crying and crying about it, that in the end Guy Whittal pulled out of the side so that Mutendera could make his Test debut. We lost and he didn't get any reward with figures of 14-4-29-0 in the first innings. He didn't bowl at all in the second innings and, on top of that, Grant Flower was called for throwing, which caught us all by surprise. I mean if you compared his action to that of other dubious players out there his was squeaky clean.

Before the next game I was asked to sing at the Miss Zimbabwe beauty pageant. I was starting to sing more and more and I was really enjoying being back on stage as other areas of my life were taking a blow.

I was then, to my surprise, picked for the second Test in Harare and although I was bowling fast we lost that too. This time New Zealand only scored 465 and Richardson fell on 99. I bowled 27 overs and took three wickets but for plenty of runs. I should have had one more wicket because

I was convinced that I had Chris Cairns, caught nicking down the leg side to Andy Flower. The umpire gave him not out, and I wasn't best pleased, especially when Cairns went on to take the game away from us.

I believe that the technology of today would have proved that he was out. I mean that's my job, right, to get batsmen out, isn't it? So why should I be denied my rewards when I have done everything right? I am a big fan of the referral system because on a couple of occasions it could have enabled us to stay competitive in a Test. We were then made to follow on after collapsing to 166 all out. In our second innings, Guy Whittal scored a magnificent 188 and Andy Flower got 65, but it still wasn't enough to save the match and we lost by eight wickets.

It was many months before I was on cordial speaking terms with my teammates. After the dressing room row in England, whenever I was selected I would often be dropped straight away if I didn't return an amazing performance. I began to struggle with my form. Strangely it was never a level playing field when some players underperformed. Certain players took ages to put in a match-winning performance and yet they were picked consistently; although I cannot definitively say why, I know that some were favoured over others and it wasn't always about performance. It seemed to be a question of not what you did but who you knew. There was a core group dubbed the royal family by the media in Zimbabwe because they never ever got dropped, irrespective of performance.

By now there was a policy that there would be a minimum number of black players in the side, to try to integrate the team even more. It wasn't called a quota system back then but a target. They earmarked a certain number of players they wanted in the side and because of my experience I was still one of them.

The thing was this actually made matters worse for me, as you can imagine, because the people who had a problem with me now had an excuse to ostracise me even more. Now they were convinced that I wasn't even good enough to be in the side, that I was just there to make up the number of black players.

In October I was included in the squad for the ICC Knockout Trophy, which was played in Nairobi. Basically, like before, if you lost your first match you were on your way home. As such it proved to be a short and not terribly sweet trip as we lost our first match, again against New Zealand. Even though I bowled well enough and took three wickets we were out of the tournament and on our way home.

I was selected for the return tri-nations tournament of Sharjah in the UAE but didn't play a match. Then, despite my prevailing poor form, I was picked for the tour of India, where we lost the Delhi Test very heavily although the match produced some interesting surprises. We won the toss and, batting first, we declared our first innings for 422. We were going well, so much so that Andy Flower and I made a Zimbabwean record partnership for the tenth wicket. We battled for 40 overs, scoring 97 runs (of which I scored a handsome 11 and Andy ended the innings on 183 not out), to take the score from 325 to 422. Then we inexplicably declared. Carl had suggested to Heath that we declare our first innings to give us enough time in the match to bowl the Indians out twice. In my humble opinion this was a mistake and few teams ever do this unless they have world-class bowlers. Who knows how many runs Andy would have scored in the end? All that I had to do was hang around and I was glad to do that.

India then made 458 declared in their first innings before our second innings came apart and we were all out for 225. I was the victim of a shocking decision when the umpire gave me out to a ball that everyone else except for him felt was going down leg. They were not going to allow me to hang around again. Then India chased the 190 they required without too much of a problem.

We then played the second Test in Nagpur. India scored 609, mainly off the back of a smashing double century by Sachin, and managed to enforce the follow-on. But Andy Flower's form was just impeccable and in our second innings he scored 232 runs not out to save the match. Thus began his purple patch of form and his ascent to becoming the world number-one batsman. And after playing for eight seasons of international cricket we were all relieved to see Alistair Campbell score his first Test hundred – the monkey was off his back.

From my point of view, this trip was awful because I bowled with little reward and got murdered by the Indians on low, slow wickets. In truth, apart from Andy we all struggled. I was working closely with Carl Rackemann on my action and perhaps I was too technically focused. I remembered how I had bemoaned the lack of a coach who had bowling experience and now in a paradoxical twist I was ruing it. Carl is a wonderful person and he brought the best out of some of our players like Andy. But to be honest I struggled a little with his particular focusing on my technique. I would be in the middle of a spell and the twelfth man would bring a bottle of water at fine leg and tell me, "Coach says your left arm is too low." It wasn't always helpful when done to excess. But to his credit, he truly believed in me and believed I could be a top-ten bowler. But I was never going to be that good. I was a wild bowler at best who had good days. The problem was that now I was caught between bowling fast for wickets and slow for accuracy and perfect technique. In a word, I bowled rubbish on the whole of that tour and beyond because of my double-minded approach.

Carl's cultured side saw us going for a memorable trip to the Taj Mahal on a day off. There had been initial resistance but it became a team activity and I am really glad I went.

During the five game one day series we managed to win just one match. I was dropped for the last few games but not after a few disappointments including having Tendulkar dropped for nothing off my bowling. He went on to make a big score and it was at a time when I couldn't buy a wicket if I tried. That was a bitterly disappointing time because I needed a few things to go my way and they simply didn't. Ever since Headingley it seemed that more than the usual number of catches were going down off my bowling and I am sure I never imagined it – although I admit that I was very sensitive at the time.

When I got back from India I was approached by Ozias Bvute, who would later become the chief executive of the Zimbabwe Cricket Union, and he asked me to come to a meeting with another associate called Maxhood Ebrahim. His father was a judge, who loved cricket and had been instrumental in organising for me to go to the various academies I had attended. Max also ran a cricket club called Sunrise which was a mainly Asian club and I met him and Ozias in Harare. We met at a popular coffee shop and, in the parking lot where they could not be overheard, they told me that they felt there was a culture of racism in Zimbabwe cricket. They said that they had formed a body called the Campaign to Eradicate Racism in Zimbabwean Cricket. I didn't like how militant it sounded but I was willing to listen as it seemed they knew something that I had had to deal with head on.

They brought up the case of a really promising contemporary of mine, a lad called Everton Matambanadzo. Everton played at Sunrise and was close to Max. He had progressed through the schools cricket structure with me and could easily have been the one to make his debut before I did. He had been picked for a Test match and was then dropped after an average performance and it had not gone down well with the black community. They argued that there was no logical cricketing reason for dropping him and the selection favouritism that was extended to white players was not given to black players. In addition, they argued that very few Asian players had ever been considered for selection. In light of all this they wanted me to join the body but my initial reaction was I wanted nothing to do with it because I thought they were quite radical in their approach. I am, believe it or not, a mostly moderate character.

They informed me that every other black player in the Zimbabwe squad had already signed up and that I was the last to be considered. I wasn't a natural activist and they had put me in a very difficult position. If I didn't sign up I would be seen as working against the cause of the other black players but I felt that if I did join them that I would be regarded as even more of a troublemaker by the establishment and team. I was caught in the middle.

I eventually decided that I had no option but to throw my hat in the ring with them, but I told them that I wasn't prepared to be a spokesman or to be seen as the ringleader. I didn't want them to use my name or to put statements in my mouth. I wasn't militant and I sensed that they were and that as the first black player for the country they would have loved to use me as a pawn to get their wishes. It made me very nervous. Yes, I was aware that the political situation in the country left a lot to be desired; yes, I knew there was corruption at the highest level; and yes, I knew that there was some racism within the game I loved.

There was segregation in all facets of life in Zimbabwe. It was endemic because many of the systems and infrastructures that had been in place for decades were still there. Cricket clubs in particular were hard to integrate. The national selection committees were mainly white, as were the squads and the administrators. In spite of that as a player my view was that if Zimbabwe were going to compete in international cricket then we had to do so with a team that was capable of competing, period. Having had a taste of success with the team I didn't share their radical approach. I felt that their view was tunnel-visioned simply to get more black players in the team and I felt that fast-tracking the process may not be in our interests or those players' either.

There was little time to digest all of this before we were off again, this time on tour to New Zealand, and when we arrived in the country the newspapers were full of stories that I was going to be sent home due to poor form. I don't know where those stories came from but perhaps members of the management had been saying things in some interviews. I was glad to be in New Zealand where the wickets at least had a little bit of grass on them after slaving on dust bowls in India, but now apparently I was going home?

Carl Rackemann said he would fight my corner and he did as I was allowed to continue on the tour. Carl really stuck by my side but what he didn't realise is that mentally I was just not there at this time. He was such an approachable, likeable fellow and I so wanted to tell him how I felt, that I was effectively on the outside of the team but I just thought he would never understand. It wasn't that my teammates and I were not civil with each other. It's just that cliques had formed and I wasn't in any of them.

We played a warm-up match at the Jade Stadium in Christchurch prior to the Test series. The pitch had been dropped into place, having been prepared elsewhere, and it had a lot of grass on it so the fast bowlers were licking their lips. We won the toss and bowled. It was nothing like we expected and the ball didn't seam about as much as we thought it would. However, I was bowling with a wonderful rhythm that I had not enjoyed for a long time. I picked up a bucket-load of wickets and was feeling I was ready for the Test series. A young bowler bowling for the province was bowling extremely quickly and we were stunned by his deliveries as he went on to pick up a five-wicket haul. He hadn't played for the Kiwis but he would soon. His name was Shane Bond.

We played a one-off Test in Wellington on a wicket that was a batsman's dream. My 30 wicketless overs cost 105 runs and the match was going nowhere, heading towards a draw. I didn't bowl nearly as well as I had done in the warm-up game and part of that may have been to do with the fact that I was bowling upwind at the Basin Reserve cricket ground and the pitch was criticised for being lifeless. I won't call it an excuse but if you have bowled there you will know what a challenge it is to bowl into a 20-mile-an-hour headwind. It was hard work getting any wickets.

Anyway, at the start of the final day's play Trevor Madondo was on 44 not out and quite possibly on the way towards becoming the first black Zimbabwean to score a Test century. Trevor was not popular with everyone in the squad because he was not afraid to say what he thought, and he often did. This was a man who would have no qualms about using colourful language to tell his teammates where to go if they disagreed on something. He enjoyed the odd smoke and also enjoyed the odd drink and in all things he was a free spirit, or a rebel depending on your viewpoint. Trevor was also a bit more confident about speaking his mind because he was quite close to Peter Chingoka, the president of Zimbabwe cricket.

I had played both with and against Trevor since junior school and I had no real issue with him. He was very talented and we got on well. I often used to give him throw-downs as he warmed up to bat and we would sometimes go out for meals together. Anyway, the night before day five we had had a team talk and Carl and Heath spoke about the possibility of contriving a result.

As we had already lost some time in the match due to rain, the thinking was that if we declared our first innings at around 340, perhaps New Zealand would make a game of it by setting us a run chase. However, in my opinion, on a slow pitch with an even slower outfield, there was virtually no chance of a result in the match.

As Trevor batted on in the morning session, it looked like we were watching history in the making. I was thinking, "This Test is heading nowhere: let the man get his century", but then Heath declared with Trevor on 74 not out.

To make matters worse, from ball one in their innings the New Zealanders were mocking us, telling us that they weren't going to give us a sniff of a chance of getting a result. They told us we should have batted all day. In the end the target of about 300 they set us was unachievable and the game was called off early.

As you can imagine, Trevor was gutted as were some of us for him. Many cricket lovers back home could not understand why the innings was declared with Madondo so close to such an historic landmark. This was the kind of ammunition that the campaign needed and it may be that it was lost on most of the players in the squad, but not on the black players. We saw that it was an opportunity lost and we were surprised that it seemed we were the only ones thinking that way.

Next were the one dayers. During one of the one day matches in New Zealand I was twelfth man and after running onto the field during one of the games I felt the familiar pain in my lower leg left again. "Oh no,'" I thought, "not again". Nothing seemed to be going right for me, and there seemed to be no end to the resentment about my presence in the team. I just bit my tongue most of the time. I helped when I was asked for help: I carried drinks faithfully, I gave players throw-downs and I even helped them with their computer problems. But I was beginning to fall out of love with what I was doing and my passion for the great game was drying up. It wasn't all bad, though, and there are some players I still got on with on a friendship level like Guy Whittal, Trevor Madondo, Mluleki Nkala, Doug Marillier, Gavin Rennie and Brian Murphy. Most had not been in the Headingley dressing room so took me at face value. It was just a small clique of the senior players who appeared to continue to resent me.

I played no part in the one day series, which we won after a thriller that went down to the wire at Eden Park in Auckland. Streaky smashed a magnificent 79 not out and hit the last ball for six to hand Zimbabwe their first ever ODI away-series win.

After the series I was told that I was being sent home and would not be staying long when the team moved on to Australia. They replaced me with a bowler called Gus Mackay, another ex-Plumtree pupil. I had no problem with Gus being included in the squad. I think I frustrated Carl because he could see tremendous potential in me but couldn't understand why I wasn't able to fulfil it more consistently. But I was having all these problems with my leg and the truth is I had a huge amount on my mind. My on/off relationship back home, my fitness and form, and what was happening in my country. More and more farmers were being thrown off their land, and there was increasing unrest and racism as a whole, and all this put cricket in perspective for me.

When I got home my dad told me that he was worried about my injury and announced that he was going to get it X-rayed properly and they were going to get to the root of the problem and sort it out for me. It turned out I had suffered from a stress fracture, twice, both in England and New Zealand. I was told that the problem with a stress fracture is that it will not show up on an X-ray until the area has begun to heal and then a bump shows up. When I had gone to see the team physio in New Zealand and told him I was struggling again, all the time he had been convinced that it was a soft tissue problem.

One of the treatment techniques to use for soft tissue is ultrasound but that is not the way to treat a stress fracture and if anything is likely to make the pain worse. It had never had the chance to heal properly because it was misdiagnosed and it was only when I visited a shoe specialist that I discovered that the boots I had been wearing were the cause. I was told that to recover from a stress fracture you need six weeks' complete rest, but I had been hobbling around trying to play while my teammates muttered about there being nothing wrong with me. I had really wanted to do well for the team so this had been extremely hurtful.

I had been pretty devastated when I was told that they would not be needing me in Australia because in addition to playing there for the first time I had really wanted to meet up with Tara Read again, the girl I had met in Adelaide in 1996. I needed a friendly face in my life at that moment. There were no romantic notions, but we got along well and had stayed in touch with one another and I wanted to see her again, but that did not happen after all.

Of all the flights I had taken on my own due to various injuries, the one from Melbourne to Johannesburg was the longest. I had had lots of time to think and I reflected on the last few years and realised that the months of built-up stress and being ostracised by some in the team had begun to take their toll on me mentally and emotionally. I had tried to man up and take it on the chin, to never reveal the true extent of my depression. But behind the brave face a certain regression had taken place, back to the child I had been in junior school. I had become unsmiling and introspective and I hated it. This was not me. I was not that kind of depressed, morbid guy any more.

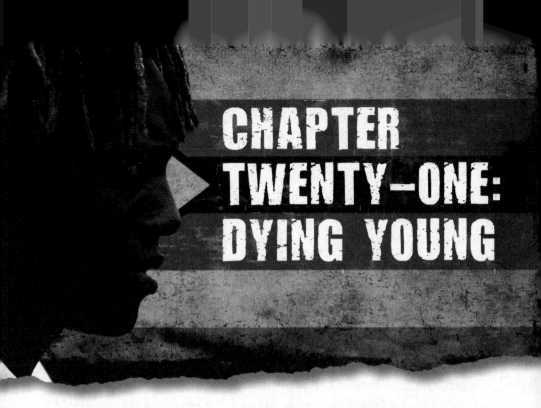

CHAPTER TWENTY-ONE: DYING YOUNG

**Now flies the flag our nation's glory
We'll live with pride, inside our hearts
As we all stand to build our nation
This our land, our Zimbabwe**

When I arrived back in Zimbabwe I wrote a letter of resignation and handed it to the Zimbabwe Cricket Board. The dressing room incident in England should have been a distant memory but clearly it still lingered in the back of some of my teammates' minds. So I basically decided, for the sake of self-preservation and for the peace of a team who clearly would rather have other players to play alongside, that I'd had enough. I told them I wanted to be released from my contract. I didn't want to cause a scene, but I just felt I needed to get away to clear my head.

I didn't discuss it with too many people and I didn't have the foggiest idea what I would do next, but I knew that I was being eaten up inside. I know what it is like to have an inner battle raging away, so I can empathise with what Marcus Trescothick went through when he had to confront his inner demons. I wasn't bitter or angry or vengeful. My faith had sustained me in it all but I just wanted a little respite, just a little peace. I do not know the true extent of my depression but I know that it was very unhealthy when I was at my lowest point.

I was immediately summoned by the president of Zimbabwe cricket, the chief executive officer and the convenor of selectors and they asked me to explain myself. They had a copy of my letter with bits underlined in red. "Great," I thought, "they are treating me like a naughty schoolboy now." I told them what had happened in England and how I had felt victimised ever since. They said they didn't think it was right for me to resign, that I was an important part of Zimbabwe cricket. "Don't worry, we will sort it out. We have invested a lot in you and we don't want to lose you," they said.

After telling them what had happened and how I felt, it was as if a huge weight had been lifted from my shoulders. I just felt better that I had told someone in the establishment and had been heard. Someone had bothered to listen to my side of the story. They asked me if I still wanted to resign and I said, "No, actually, I feel fine." With that, I picked up my letter of resignation and I tore it up. We all agreed that we would not say a word to anyone about it.

However, within days the media had got wind of the story and the headline "Olonga Hands in Resignation over Allegations of Racism" was emblazoned on the back page of the biggest daily, *The Herald*. The team were still in Australia but I was absolutely livid.

It hadn't come from me, so one of the three wise men who were in that meeting must have leaked the story. I have always suspected that it was the president, Peter Chingoka, because he had begun to develop some opponents within the sport. There were people who regarded him as a dinosaur and perhaps he saw this as an opportunity to get rid of a few of them. Zimbabwean sport now mirrored its politics. I admit that this is just conjecture, but someone in that room spilt the beans and only one of them had everything to gain from it. But I felt used and I wasn't impressed one bit.

A little while later the Zimbabwe Cricket Board established a task force charged with assessing, once and for all, whether there was racism in Zimbabwean cricket. The whole process was overseen by an American man working for an independent conflict resolution consultancy firm, the idea being that people would trust that it was being handled properly. We were all called to Harare Sports Club – players, umpires, administrators, curators, just about anybody who was a major stakeholder in the game – and a questionnaire was handed out containing about 20 questions. There were many multiple-choice questions such as 'Do you think there is plenty, some, little or no racism in Zimbabwe cricket? Answer A, B, C or D'. They asked around 140 people and accumulated huge amounts of data.

A few weeks later we were summoned to hear the results and you will probably not be surprised to learn that the black and white people saw things completely differently. Almost all of the white people said no, there is no racism in the game, while the black players were just as adamant that there was. On the one hand you had a group of people saying, "There's no racism in Zimbabwe cricket. People are just overreacting." And on the other you had "Of course there is racism in Zimbabwe cricket. It is rampant. I was a victim. So-and-so swore at me on the field, using a derogatory term."

When presenting his final assessment the man running the whole process said, "I believe that Zimbabwe cricket is like a powder keg about to explode. We asked, 'Is racism a problem in Zimbabwe cricket?' 80 per cent of the black respondents said yes; 80 per cent of white respondents said no." *Quelle surprise*! And so it continued. At the very least it proved that there was conflict and that there was no real consensus.

Some very extreme racist views emerged from the process. It was an anonymous survey so people were free to speak their minds. One person wrote, "You can't give black people anything to run in Africa because they will run it into the ground." Another wrote, "These black people have ****ed up our country, they have ****ed up our hockey, they have ****ed up our farms, they have ****ed up everything and now they want to **** up our cricket." Somebody else wrote, "Black people will never be good at batting because they are physiologically incapable of timing the batting stroke, although they might be good bowlers." What about

Brian Lara? Or Viv Richards? It was like being at a Ku Klux Klan meeting.

Some of the comments that had been recorded clearly revealed the animosity some of the white people held towards their black counterparts and it was all down in black and white, if you'll excuse the pun. Whether we like to admit it or not, most people have their prejudices, but this was malicious and much of it was blatantly offensive.

The result was that the ZCU set up a task force charged with ensuring that there was proper integration within the sport and that black players got a fair crack of the whip. This task force introduced an official quota system, whereby they set a target for the minimum number of black players in the national squad for each level of the game by January 2004. It also demanded equity within the board, with equal numbers of black and white secretaries and the like. Naturally, it made a lot of white people feel very uncomfortable.

It wasn't a perfect solution, but at least it brought things out into the open. The problem was that a lot of white people – players and officials alike – somehow blamed me. I hadn't been looking for a fight when I came back from New Zealand: all I had wanted to do was resign. To this day I resent the fact that my resignation was leaked to the press and I had been used as a pawn in someone else's game. They didn't consider that the finger would be pointed at me when it all hit the fan. But I suppose for them the cause was greater than one man. Certainly I never again felt integrated into the team so none of this benefited me personally in any way.

While all of this was going on I also had to deal with the news that two of my good friends had been killed in a car crash. The vehicle in which they had been travelling had been sandwiched between two lorries on the motorway and they didn't stand a chance. It was a tough time for me. I was coming to the inevitable conclusion that there was something seriously wrong with my country. I hadn't lost my sense of patriotism or my love for Zimbabwe but I knew it could not be right that we were at loggerheads with each other. I was taking stock again and tired of fighting with people I was supposed to be working together with. How did we get here? We were fighting over just about everything including who played cricket for the country on the basis of their skin colour. Equally, I was becoming more outraged that farmers – black and white – were being kicked off their land illegally and that the country as a whole was being affected. I asked myself who was winning in all of this. The answer of course was that nobody was. At least not any of the common people.

In 2001 I got together with my flatmates and friends and told them that I wanted to write a song to attempt to unite the country. I suggested that we ought to be a voice that goes against the tide of conflict and hatred. I was hoping that it would be an anthem of sorts and they all agreed that it was a good idea. We had a listen to a few songs including *Anthem* from *Chess*. We felt it needed to be rousing. In England, when the football team plays in a tournament the whole country gets behind them, but that didn't happen in Zimbabwe and I hoped to try to do something that might change things, even if only in some small way. I had also been touched on my travels to India by how patriotic the fans were when the team played against us.

We decided to call the song *Our Zimbabwe* and it was designed to get every Zimbabwean to look at the country as being theirs, irrespective of race, colour or creed. It was in the midst of the troubles so we wanted to speak prophetically into the situation. Bruce, Andrew and I sat down around the piano for a few hours and duly produced the words. We also wrote a song called *Someone for Me* about an orphan child. We released *Our Zimbabwe* as a single, got it to some DJs and they decided that they loved it.

It received huge amounts of airplay and we ended up filming an amateur video for it, which you can still see on YouTube. While we were doing so, the director decided that she wanted to do a shot from a microlight, but ended up crashing it into a tree, so halfway through filming we had to rush her and the pilot to hospital and then come back and carry on with the video.

It was so well received that it ended up going to number one briefly in the Zimbabwe charts. In the end we did five versions, including an instrumental and a dance version. The lyrics may not mean a lot unless you have experienced what we did. At the time, I found myself being accused of racism against white people, which was just plain daft. Again, I lived with three white guys for goodness' sake. So this was what we came up with:

BLOOD, SWEAT AND TREASON

Our Zimbabwe

This land our land, is our Zimbabwe
A land of peace for you and me
Once born in pain and segregation
But now we live in harmony
Now flies the flag our nation's glory
We'll live with pride, inside our hearts
As we all stand to build our nation
This our land, our Zimbabwe

Though I may go to distant borders
My soul will yearn for this my home
For time and space may separate us
And yet she holds my heart alone
Now flies the flag my nation's glory
I live with pride, inside my heart
I'll make a stand to build this nation
This my land, my Zimbabwe
Now flies the flag our nation's glory
We'll live with pride, inside our hearts
As we all stand to build our nation
This our land, our Zimbabwe

We've been through it all
We've had our days
We've had our falls
Now the time has come for us to stand
To stand as one

The night has gone and with the morning
Come rays of hope that lead us on
So we will strive to give our children
A brighter day where they belong
Now flies the flag our nation's glory

We'll live with pride, inside our hearts
As we all stand to build our nation
This our land, our Zimbabwe
Now flies the flag our nation's glory
We'll live with pride, inside our hearts
As we all stand to build our nation
This our land, our Zimbabwe

During my lowest moments the words have spoken volumes to me and now that I am actually living in exile it means even more.

The ironic thing is that the song wasn't really being played on national radio to start with until a free press journalist called Leo Hatugari wrote a disparaging article suggesting that the song was some sort of propaganda by the government. After that the then Minister of Information, Jonathan Moyo, jumped on it and before long you couldn't turn the radio on without hearing it. The truth is that if Leo had actually listened to the words he would have realised that the things being said were anything but the kind of drivel the government spin doctors spouted.

At around the same time I was invited to sing at the Harare International Festival of the Arts (HIFA). This was a big deal for me because although I was a Test cricketer, I got a huge kick out of singing. It balanced my life out. HIFA is Zimbabwe's equivalent of the Edinburgh Festival and I loved every second of it. I performed early on in the evening singing a Duke Ellington piece backed up by a choir. Later on an awesome Portuguese singer called Sara Tavares headlined the night. I also did a recital concert accompanied by Bruce Izzett, my flatmate, and it was well received although there weren't many people in the audience.

Music became a hugely important outlet for me, and I would go on to perform in quite a few concerts. I also started drawing and painting again, things I had loved doing when I was at school. People were telling me that I could go further with my singing, so I got together with a voice coach called Lorna Kelly and it helped a great deal. A man called Graham Nish asked me to put on a concert in a city called Masvingo . The evening was the first of the now typical *An Evening with Henry Olonga and Friends*, and I also sang with some schoolchildren.

After all the traumas and controversies of the last few years I also decided that if I got another chance to play for Zimbabwe then I was going to try to enjoy every minute of it. I had no idea how much longer my cricket career would last and I didn't know whether they would pick me again.

It was one thing to vow to enjoy myself, but it wasn't quite as simple as that. When the squad would get together for net sessions it was clear that some of the white players now really blamed me for everything that had happened so far. When I would bowl to one or two of them they would try to smash me as hard and far as they possibly could, and leave me to go and collect the ball. The disappointing thing was that the senior players were the worst culprits. If I had thought that the past was going to be laid to rest, clearly I was wrong.

They did this to another exceptional black bowler called Brighton Watambwa as well. Brighton became a close friend and he introduced me to the game of golf. Most cricketers are good golfers but I was a late starter so he taught me all about the rules and a little bit about technique. He was to leave in 2002 with the increasing politicisation of the game in Zimbabwe and the lack of appreciation given to his talents when contracts were handed out. Both of us would find ourselves getting smashed all the time at nets.

If Gary Brent ran up and bowled his medium-pace deliveries he was treated with respect but good luck to some of the black bowlers. I wish I was making this up but I was experiencing it first hand. You would probably only bowl a few balls a session because for most of the time you would be recovering your ball from deep in the outfield. People can be so cruel and sadly not even the coach would step in to deal with this behaviour. Zimbabwean politics had left everyone treading on eggshells. But I had decided I was going to just count my blessings and enjoy my cricket: my attitude had changed and I vowed that I was going to be bigger than them. So I took it on the chin once again.

In June 2001 we had some time off and Trevor Madondo decided to go on holiday to the Victoria Falls, where he contracted malaria. Everton Matambanadzo bumped into me one day and said that Trevor was staying with him and was really ill with malaria. He had been suffering from a fever but wasn't improving. A few days later we were devastated to hear that he had succumbed to cerebral malaria. He was only 24, and that's too young to die. Sadly, Trevor's brother Tafadzwa would also die young at the age of 27 in a motorbike accident.

Most of the team attended his funeral and as I looked at him in the casket I saw that he had a familiar smirk frozen on his face. I had been to a few funerals in my time, but this one really had an impact on me. Trevor was the real deal as far as talent was concerned and I am convinced that he would have gone a long way in cricket.

At one point during the funeral one of the white players turned to me and said, "Well, it's not as if anybody is going to miss him because nobody liked him." Myself and one or two of the other black players looked at each other in disbelief. Had we really just heard that? We shook our heads and I have never been so close to smacking someone. This was a teammate's funeral, for Pete's sake. It was almost as if this white player was glad that Trevor was dead. This was a sad day, perhaps the saddest for Trevor's family, for me and for most in Zimbabwe cricket. But not for everyone evidently and that was disturbing.

The last time I had seen Trevor had been at a players' meeting with a man called John Jameson, the players' representative. Trevor was drunk – he had problems with drink throughout his short life and few could reason with him when he was in this state. On this occasion it was entirely inappropriate for him to be drunk and I regret that this was my last memory of the guy. You never know when your last conversation will be with someone and it's at moments like this that remind us how fragile we all are.

After Trevor's death we had to try to pick ourselves up for the visit of India, who arrived to play two Tests. There were all sorts of things going on, not the least of which being the fact that Heath Streak decided to resign as captain. Two of my friends had also announced they were getting married and that got me thinking that perhaps it was about time I did the same.

I was selected for the opening Test in Bulawayo, but for the umpteenth time we didn't make enough runs in our first innings. We scored 173 and it would have been much worse had Andy Flower not hit yet another half century. We did pretty well to dismiss a full-strength India for 318, but the deficit was too big and although we managed 328 in the second innings, with Andy scoring 83 this time, it was never going to be enough. India duly scored 184 for 2 to beat us by eight wickets and I picked up a hamstring injury and was unable to bowl a ball in their second innings.

I still wasn't fit for the second Test and neither was Andy, who had injured his thumb and required an operation but, wouldn't you just know it, this time we beat India by four wickets thanks to Streak, who took seven wickets, Grant Flower, who made 86, and Stuart Carlisle's 62.

Hot on India's heels were the West Indies. I had to sit out the two Tests with my injury. In Bulawayo they massacred us by an innings and 176 runs. We were dismissed for 155 and 228, and that was despite Alistair Campbell scoring 103 in our second innings. They scored 559 with Chris Gayle contributing 175 and Carl Hooper 149. It was horrible. Poor Ray Price's 44 overs cost him 157 runs and three other bowlers also went for more than 100.

When they all moved to Harare for the second Test and the West Indies bowled us out for a pitiful 131 it looked like a repeat was on the cards, but the lads fought back magnificently to secure a draw. West Indies made 347, a lead of more than 200, but Hamilton Masakadza dropped anchor and made 119, to historically achieve the first Test century by a black Zimbabwean. He was just 17 years old at the time. He was ably supported by Craig Wishart with 99, Heath Streak 83 and Andy Blignaut 92 in a total of 563.

There was also a one day triangular series featuring Zimbabwe, India and the West Indies, but we lost every match and the West Indies won the final after dismissing Sachin Tendulkar for a duck.

While I was on the sidelines I was asked to do some TV commentary work and after I'd got a taste for it and realised that it came fairly naturally I figured that this might be something else that I could turn my hand to later on in life. I wasn't afraid of the microphone and I wasn't bothered about making mistakes, which is probably just as well. My first gaffe involved Ridley Jacobs, the West Indies wicketkeeper. He failed to take a return over the stumps cleanly, bashing his finger and swearing loudly. The microphones had picked it up so I said, "To all the young children watching at home, just ignore that." The next thing was that I heard the director screaming in my ear, "Don't draw attention to it, Henry, just leave it!" It was quite embarrassing because I really didn't know what to do, but I quickly learnt that I was there to simply support the main commentators.

DYING YOUNG

Our Zimbabwe was still getting airplay in the charts and we were being inundated with requests from people who wanted to know where they could get a copy and if we were going to perform it. Lots of people around the country wanted to be associated with the song. I felt it was time that I set up a website, and so henryolonga.com was born. A lot of people thought it was weird, but I wanted people to find out about the song and more importantly what the motive behind it was. It also meant that I could get feedback from the outside world. I had entered cyberspace.

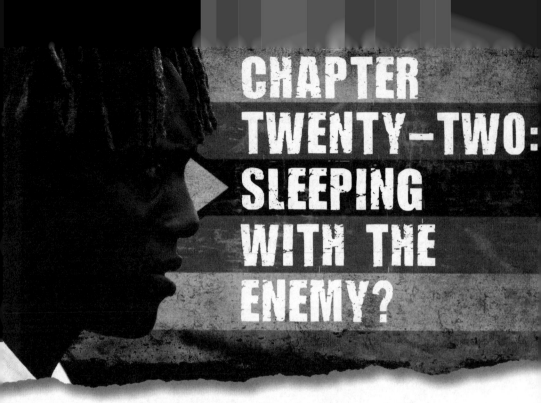

CHAPTER TWENTY-TWO: SLEEPING WITH THE ENEMY?

I wanted to sense what made him tick. Was there good behind his eyes or evil? Yet I saw nothing. I felt no malice as he puffed on an expensive Cuban cigar and listened, but I couldn't help feeling uneasy.

One of the recurring themes throughout my time as an international was our battle for better pay. The Zimbabwe Cricket Union had begun a policy of dividing and ruling and were not paying much attention to our player representative. So we made a very dangerous turn to get the balance of power shifted back into our court.

One afternoon, after a practice session, Alistair Campbell wandered over to a group of us and asked if we wanted to fly to Harare from Bulawayo with him and some of the other guys for a meeting with a businessman. He asked me and Pommie if we would go and we said OK, although we didn't really know what it was about.

We got to the airport and a private jet was waiting for us. It was the last word in luxury – leather seats, chocolates, free drinks. I have never been one to think that I could get used to the high life because the way I look at it is if there is a high life then often there is usually mischief not too far behind it. But I was impressed either way.

As I've explained I wasn't absolutely sure why we were going to Harare, but I'd heard that we were going to meet a tycoon with political clout, and if the private plane was anything to go by this man was clearly pretty wealthy. It turned out that the man we were going to meet was John Bredenkamp, a prominent Zimbabwean businessman and former international rugby player. Rumours abound concerning how this tycoon procured his wealth but make no mistake about this: he was very powerfully connected in political circles.

We met him and he was very pleasant. Throughout his life he had established himself as something of a philanthropist and he listened patiently as we aired our grievances. This was familiar territory for him as he had set up a sports management company called Masters International and had represented players such as Nick Price the Zimbabwean golfer. We told him that we didn't feel we had enough political power or clout to get things out in the open with the Zimbabwe Cricket Board. We hoped that if we could get somebody of Bredenkamp's standing onside then the board would have no option but to listen to us. Right from the off, as soon as I heard the level of person we were getting involved with, I thought it was a big mistake. I thought this could go either way and quickly escalate because the board could then appeal to a higher power, the patron of Zimbabwe cricket, His Excellency the President of Zimbabwe, Robert Mugabe.

I often attempt to read people's vibes and the eyes hold the key. It has been said that the eyes are the window to the soul. Yet while I looked into Bredenkamp's eyes I was unsure. I wanted to sense what made him tick. Was there good behind them or evil? Yet I saw nothing. I felt no malice as he puffed on an expensive Cuban cigar and listened, but I couldn't help feeling uneasy about the fact that we were making money this important, that we were happy to wander into the murky world of African political powerhouses. Should we be trying to make these kinds of deals? Would we be selling our souls?

In my career I have fraternised with powerful people – presidents and people of all backgrounds with varying power and I just wasn't sure what to make of this meeting. The boys played him *Our Zimbabwe* from the speakers of a small laptop and it seemed to move him somewhat. He brought our meeting to an end by telling us that he would see what he could do for us. He had no specific influence within Zimbabwe cricket, but he had plenty of influence within Zimbabwe politics and there was a sense among the senior players that if we got this man on our side then we would get what we wanted.

Our own player representative had been attempting to negotiate for better overall treatment of the players: more wholesome pensions, health-care plans, sponsorship car deals, single rooms, wives and girlfriends being brought on tours and so on. But often he found himself coming against a disinterested management board who felt that the cricketers had cushy enough lives already. But a few national players had played county cricket and knew that Zimbabwe lagged far behind in basic player care.

Perhaps what we really wanted was a shift in power between the players and the management of the game. We also wanted fairness. Surely we were Zimbabwean cricket's greatest asset but were often taken for granted. The balance just needed to move a little more to the centre. A trite example was how for years the team often flew in economy on long-haul flights while the executive board members travelled business class and had access to business class lounges while the players didn't. The board members would also often bring their wives on expenses-paid tours and limit the players in this regard. It's not as if there was a lack of money and the players were not greedy for the most part. But this was a drastic way to have our grievances heard.

I haven't a clue what transpired behind the scenes after our meeting but it did get us what we wanted in the short term and things even improved for us in most respects for a while. But in the long term all that was achieved was to further alienate the cricket board, who vowed that no group of players would ever have so much power again. They set about dismantling the power base of senior players, whom they blamed. The board used contracts to control players. In truth the power was truly with them and many players found themselves demoted, excluded from selection or forced to take pay cuts. This saw many players leaving the sport in the years to come

In September 2001 South Africa arrived in Harare for the first Test, for which I wasn't picked, scoring 600 for 3 declared. Herschelle Gibbs made 157, Gary Kirsten a fabulous 224 and Jacques Kallis 147. Kallis was not dismissed once in the two-Test series. The Proteas then dismissed Zimbabwe for 286 and enforced the follow-on. Andy Flower scored two back to back centuries with the second score of 199 not out in a total of 397 before the tourists knocked off the required runs to record a nine-wicket victory.

I didn't play in the second Test either but I was there to bring on drinks. It ended in a high-scoring draw with Kallis recording another huge score, 189 this time. They rubbed our noses in it with a whitewash, winning all three One Day Internationals. Flower's heroics saw him elevated to a very well earned number one in the world batting rankings. His fortitude and focus had enabled him to enjoy a string of extraordinary success that lasted for more than a year. From my view in the bunker I suspect that one possible source of that focus was the simmering anger he had about what was happening in Zimbabwe as a whole and also in the cricketing fraternity.

Then England flew out for five One Day Internationals. They won all five and I bowled really poorly in the two games for which I was picked.

We were back in Sharjah in October, facing Pakistan and Sri Lanka in a triangular tournament but they might as well have left me at home. We didn't play well and I only got picked when we already knew that we couldn't reach the final. While we were in Sharjah, the players started arguing about money again. Even though we didn't progress we still had a prize fund to distribute for coming third. Some didn't want any share of the prize money going to the backroom staff, that is the coach, physiotherapist, fitness instructor and so on. Others insisted that any prize money be split equally among the entire party on a proportional basis as we were all a team and this is the way we had always done it.

I had been twelfth man for most of the games so contributed little to the discussion but I made it known that I thought we ought to share. That was what happened in the end but it left a bad taste in the mouth and didn't improve the atmosphere in the dressing room. Greed had begun to truly manifest itself and it appeared that some players were just focused on what they could get out of the system now. The unity that had bound players together in a common cause was now disintegrating.

If your confidence is fragile, in international cricket there is only one thing to do – take on Bangladesh. On 8th November 2001 in the first Test in Dhaka we bowled them out for 107. I took three wickets and Travis Friend grabbed five. This was more like it. We replied with 431 and then set about bowling them out for the second time. We had them at 125 for 3 but then the weather intervened, we lost two full days and they somehow escaped with a draw. That's also when I accidently broke the hand of our skipper, Brian Murphy, practising before the start of play. Sorry Brian.

There was to be no escape for Bangladesh at Chittagong, of which Heath Streak said, "If I never go back there again it will be too soon." It is a sad place with far too many of the population living in poverty. Again, though, the local people were great human beings who smiled a lot. We piled up 542 for 7 declared (Andy Flower scored another century), and then bowled them out for 251 and 301. I only took a couple of wickets, but Grant Flower helped himself to eight. Trevor Gripper scored the 11 runs we needed for victory. We also beat them 3-0 in the one day series, but I played no part in that.

Unfortunately, our bubble was burst shortly afterwards, courtesy of a tour to Sri Lanka. The first Test in Colombo was a massacre, with the home side making 586 for 6 without breaking sweat, which is more than can be said for my fellow bowlers and I. My 23 overs cost 103 runs and I was wicketless. Streak went for 113 but at least he got three wickets, while Friend went for 102 runs and, like me, didn't pick up any wickets either. They then dismissed us for 184 and 236 to beat us by an innings and 166 runs. It wasn't much fun.

I wish I could tell you that we picked ourselves up off the floor, went to Kandy and got our own back in the second Test, but it simply wouldn't be true. This time we batted first and made a measly 236. I scored 18 runs! Those annoying Sri Lankan batsmen then put us to the sword yet again, racing to 505, with Jayasuriya scoring a flawless 139. If I had bowled poorly in Colombo, it was nothing compared with what happened this time. I sent down 24 overs that cost 131 runs. Ouch! Demoralised, we were bowled out once more, this time for 175 runs. Muttiah Muralitharan took 13 wickets in the match – in our first innings he was on for all ten wickets until Chaminda Vaas spoilt the party by taking the wicket of Henry Olonga. This time we lost by an innings and 94 runs. There were a few dropped catches off my bowling which was very disappointing. I am sure no one drops a catch in international cricket on purpose, though I had a few Sri Lankans like Marvan Attapatu come up to me and say it was clear that something looked very odd. From the sidelines, to them it appeared like a few easy catches off my bowling were being uncharacteristically dropped. I gave my team the benefit of the doubt: they wouldn't go that far, would they? But it is a serious and sobering thing when your opponents make such an allegation.

Surely things had to get better in the final Test in Galle. You could argue that there was an improvement because at least we stopped them from reaching 500 in their first innings. They made 418 and this time I only went for 52 runs, again without a wicket. In reply we made 236 yet again. The Sri Lankans declared at 212 for 2 from just 41 overs, with Marvin Atapattu making a quick-fire hundred before they wiped us out for 79. Muralitharan took nine wickets in the match. He had also managed to grab eight in the first Test, which meant that in a three-match series he picked up a quite astonishing 30 wickets. I was his 400th wicket in Test cricket. Why was I always the victim when these records were being set?

Worse was to come. After the Tests, the West Indies arrived for the LG Abans triangular series. In the opening match in Colombo we were humiliated. Sri Lanka bowled us out for 38, with only Stuart Carlisle reaching double figures. Five of us were dismissed without troubling the scorers, including myself. Somehow we picked ourselves up off the floor to beat the West Indies in the second match, during which I bowled pretty well but only took one wicket. Sri Lanka hammered us again, although this time we did at least manage to put a few runs on the board and the West Indies thrashed us by eight wickets with 96 balls remaining in our final match after they had got us out for 154 – at one stage we had been 9 for 3 so that did represent something of a fightback.

We were turning into international cricketing cannon fodder, and so it proved when the team went to India in February and March 2002, losing both Tests. At least we made a contest of the one day series, going down 3-2. I was not picked for the tour but I received an invitation asking me if I wanted to commentate, so I watched it from the sidelines. By now, the chief executive of Zimbabwe Cricket was Vince Hogg and I had to ask his permission. He said yes and I found myself flying out to India in business class while the team were travelling cattle class. I must say that it felt weird because I wasn't actually a part of the team and yet here I was with them. Nevertheless, it was an invaluable experience for my development as a commentator.

When I got home I was made captain of Manicaland and there was a match against my former province, Matebeleland, when I got to the crease with us needing 50 runs to win. The fact that I was batting meant that we were down to our last-wicket partnership, you understand. We reached the stage where we only wanted one more run to win and the bowler delivered a wide. I walked out of my crease to celebrate with my teammate at the other end when the keeper caught the ball and ran me out. There was some controversy but eventually it was agreed that I should never have been run out off the no ball so we had won in the most dramatic fashion. I was proud of that and really felt that I had led from the front as we were the clear underdogs.

At around this time I recorded a duet with a singer by the name of Bonnie Deuschle, which got to number one. This bizarrely caused some resentment in cricket circles: it was almost as if I were not allowed to do more than one thing with my life. I had made a point of ensuring that my singing did not affect my cricket in any way so why the fuss? And in those tough years it had turned out to be a tremendous outlet for me.

I was then asked by one of the selectors, Steven Mangongo, to join a club called Takashinga. This was great news for me because it meant that I was going to be given the opportunity to mentor some of the most promising young black cricketers in Zimbabwe who were graduates of the development program. It was an all-black club that had formerly been known as Old Winstonians. Andy Flower and his dad Bill Flower had been instrumental in its formation and had already produced some world-class cricketers like Tatenda Taibu, Hamilton Masakadza and Elton Chigumbura. But the Flowers had long gone now and the atmosphere when I arrived was more militant than I expected. It was going to be an interesting mentoring experience that I both loved and despised.

CHAPTER TWENTY-THREE: YOUR MONEY OR YOUR LIFE

"Olonga, you are going to know what it is to die tonight."

Although as a team we often felt we were not adequately rewarded by the ZCU, there were some perks. I suppose that my biggest as a contracted Zimbabwe international came in 2001 when I was given a car, a Nissan hard-body twincab to be precise, as part of a sponsorship deal. They were tremendous utility vehicles and were extremely popular throughout the country because they could carry four passengers in comfort and were also capable of transporting heavy loads in the back. I was delighted when I received my set of keys although I did have some serious concerns as well.

Life was becoming cheap in Zimbabwe: there was an air of lawlessness and too many innocent people were falling victim to opportunistic criminals. I joked with Heath Streak that I was worried our Nissans might make us targets for carjacking, a crime that was on the increase in Zimbabwe. These vehicles were expensive, well-built and incredibly sturdy and were the same as those used by both safari operators and farmers.

What would normally happen is that they would identify a car and follow it to a secluded spot, whereupon they would leap from their own vehicle, haul the driver out into the road and drive off. If the driver chose to fight back he or she would be beaten up and sometimes even murdered.

The gangs were fearless and very often they would be high on drugs or drunk. They didn't care whether it was day or night. All that mattered to them was getting the car and fleeing the scene. They would then take the vehicle back to their paymaster, who would give them a cash bonus. Within days the vehicle would be transported out of the country and shipped to countries in central Africa. There is little doubt in my mind that crime syndicates with connections in very high places were involved in this seedy underworld.

I was in a good place, having being picked as captain for the Zimbabwe A team. It wasn't quite the same as being named as captain of the full national side, of course, but it was a pretty close second and was extra special for me because it was to be my first experience of captaincy at a senior level. We were due to go to Namibia to take part in an ICC tournament over two weeks.

It meant that somebody in the Zimbabwe hierarchy had seen some leadership skills in me. I was selected to be the first black player to captain the B team but, as usual, the initial weight of significance of all of this was slow to sink in. I just wanted to play cricket, get as many wickets as I could and hopefully be a good leader in doing that. Even when one of the senior white players said that it would be the first time in his career that he had ever been captained by a black cricketer it didn't really sink in at first. He had made light of it but then I sat down and considered the position I was in and it finally dawned on me that I was entering uncharted territory.

In truth, I was brimming with excitement. This was such an honour. I had been asked to captain the team because I had obviously made a good impression somewhere, perhaps not just as a bowler but as a leader. It was a good thing to feel that the selectors obviously felt I was good enough to lead this well-balanced team with a good mix of young and mature players. Perhaps they even saw me as a future captain of the senior side. I knew that I had to do the job properly.

I was brought back to earth with a bump on 4th April 2002. Having been to the movie premiere of *Vanilla Sky*, starring Tom Cruise, with my girlfriend I drove her home. At that time we only lived about 100 metres from one another, so I stopped the Nissan outside her gate. The plan was to see her safely to her home and then drive the car to mine and park it up for the night. It was our last evening together before I was due to fly to Namibia with the A team, so we sat and spoke for a while.

When we had finished she switched on the interior light to help her find her keys. I don't know why, but something about her doing this unnerved me. I then kissed her goodbye and she got out of the car but she didn't even close the door before turning round and climbing back in. "I don't like this," she said.

Another car had pulled up and parked right behind us. When she had gone to leave the Nissan she saw the occupants of the other vehicle walking towards us. They came to the side of the car and, as I started the engine – I was going to try to make a run for it – one of them shouted, "Stop or I'll shoot."

Realising that he meant business, I switched off the engine without a second thought. He then ordered me to get out of the vehicle and I did so without protest. There was a great deal of shouting and swearing going on by now and one of the guys had gone to my girlfriend's side of the vehicle. She got out of the car and, as she did so, he hit her in the side and grabbed her handbag. A real hero. I was livid, but there was nothing I could do. When somebody is pointing a gun at you it tends to focus your mind and persuade you that it is not, perhaps, the time to pretend to be Jean-Claude Van Damme or Steven Seagal.

They wanted to know if the car was fitted with an anti-hijacking device and I told them it wasn't. The next thing I knew was that one of them jumped into the driver's seat and started the engine. I could smell alcohol on his breath. I didn't know if they were simply going to drive off and leave us there, which is what I was hoping would happen, or if they planned to bundle us into the car and take us with them, but I had already made up my mind that I would co-operate fully with them. These were clearly not men you wanted to upset.

By this stage I had worked out that there were four of them – carjackers, thieves, thugs, call them what you will. Once they got the Nissan started they tried to get me into the back seat but they couldn't figure out how to unlock the door. To an outsider it must have looked like a slapstick scene but to me it was anything but. I was vaguely aware that, having grabbed my girlfriend's handbag, they had lost interest in her and pushed her to one side. But they clearly hadn't believed me when I had told them there was no anti-carjacking device so it soon became clear they were going to take me with them. Having failed to get me back into my car, they forced me into their vehicle, a clapped-out pick-up truck that I later discovered they had also stolen earlier in the day – it had wind howling through the ventilation system and air rushing down from the back.

As we drove off, one of the men gave me a back-hander to the face. It was unprovoked and totally unnecessary. Blood started to pour from my nose. I felt no pain but my blood poured everywhere. To my utter astonishment, the driver gave me some tissues for my nose, which seemed an especially odd thing to do bearing in mind what was happening. Meanwhile, the guy who had hit me held me down by my hair. I found this quite reassuring because I reasoned that if they didn't want me to see their faces, the chances were that they were not going to kill me.

I had no idea where we going, but I sensed we were driving out of town. All the while, I was subjected to a volley of abuse. For some strange reason, they seemed to derive great enjoyment from the word 'bitch'.

There was something extremely amateurish about all of this. We had been led to believe that the carjacking gangs were well organised and that they planned their operations meticulously. These guys were anything but well organised. Perhaps they were simply opportunists. There had been no indication that they knew who I was either.

Bizarre as this may sound, I found myself blaming Mugabe for my plight. Perhaps these guys had been forced into this desperate course of action because they had lost their jobs. Zimbabwe as a country was in a mess because of a series of disastrous economic policies and the corruption that was rampant within the government. Maybe these men were just victims of that situation. Or maybe they were not and were just really evil people.

I didn't want to antagonise them. Addressing one of them as 'sir' certainly hadn't worked as he had responded by getting very angry and delivering several powerful blows to my head. They had been drinking, so trying to reason with them was out of the question. Besides, one of them had a sharp object pressed firmly against my back. They wanted me to think it was a knife and it might well have been, although I began to seriously doubt that this was the case, perhaps it was a broken bottle. I thought it was best not to find out for sure.

It occurred to me that I could die that night, but I was ready to meet God if that was what fate had in store for me. I mean that I was ready in the sense that death may spring up on any of us when we least expect or invite it. I didn't want to die just yet though. I had things that I wanted to do with my life. I knew that I would have to be smart and there might even come a time during the hours that followed when I would have to be brave.

They asked how much fuel was in the tank, and I told them I'd filled up the tank earlier that same day and done very few miles since then – remember that we were not in my vehicle so they didn't know what the fuel gauge was registering. Then they tried to mislead me. One minute they pretended to be foreigners, the next they spoke to one another in Shona. They said that within 24 hours they would be across the border. No, these guys were definitely not part of an organised crime syndicate, of that I was now 100 per cent certain.

The verbal abuse continued until they asked me my name. I had a choice – I could either make up a name or I could tell them who I was. I decided to tell them the truth and, thankfully, it seemed to soften them up a bit.

"Are you that guy, the one who sang *My Zimbabwe*?" one of them asked.

"Yes. Yes I am," I replied, deciding it was probably not a good idea to tell him it was actually called *Our Zimbabwe*.

Now that they knew who I was, I thought they might treat me with some respect but, no, I couldn't have been more wrong. "Olonga, you are going to know what it is to die tonight," I was informed. I remember thinking that I couldn't die that night, I just couldn't. Strangely, it registered with me that both of the men in the car with me were wearing similar footwear – blue on the bottom, white on the top, basketball-style trainers. How odd that with all this going on I should zone in on their shoes.

Even with all the detours they were taking, the many turns this way, then the other, we finally arrived somewhere I recognised. It was Houghton Park, a suburb in Harare. There could be no doubt about it because not only did it seem familiar but there was the sign on a lamppost. These guys really weren't very bright. Mind you, what good did it do me to know where I was when I was being held captive?

We went over lots of speed bumps and each time we did so, the object in my back dug in just a little deeper.

I was asked how much money I had on me. Oddly, they hadn't taken my wallet or gone through my pockets earlier. I replied that I had Z$20,000 but realised as soon as I'd said it, that I was wrong. I'd gone to an ATM earlier that evening intending to withdraw that sum, but the bank had been offline so I hadn't been able to withdraw anything. I now had to tell them I'd got it wrong. They were not amused, and proved it by raining another series of blows down on me.

Then they decided it was high time that they did search me and they took my wallet, my watch, my mobile phone and the rest of my possessions. Fortunately I was not wearing trainers because if I had been I am pretty certain that I would have been relieved of those too, which would have meant that when they finally decided to dump me, without any money or phone, I would have had to have walked barefoot. Mind you, dumping me seemed to be the last thing on their minds at present.

No more than ten minutes after the first guy had asked me for my name, the driver asked me the same question. I laughed quietly, until his partner once again informed me that this was going to be my last night on earth, that I would never play cricket again. I truly didn't know how serious they were but I was prepared to do whatever it might take to get them on my side so I announced that I was the first black player chosen to captain the Zimbabwe A side in a major tournament. It seemed to have the desired effect. They were clearly quite impressed with this information. Not sufficiently impressed to let me go, mind you. Instead they wanted to know how much money I had in the bank so I told them that I could give them whatever they wanted. I had to play along with them because one of them had said that he knew international cricketers had lots of money and I knew that it wasn't going to be a good idea to dissuade him of that notion.

I said that I had a UK bank account and that I could get them plenty of foreign currency, but I would need to make a few phone calls to sort things out.

Next, they asked me where Andy Flower lived and I told them the first place that came into my head because they were clearly living in fantasy land by this stage. Then they wanted my address and I gave it to them. There was no point in lying because it would have been easy enough for them to check through the documents in my wallet to get my address. I was happy for them to have the car and if they wanted me to hand over some money then they could have that too. I was coping with all of this but I was filled with dread when they told me that they wanted to keep hold of me until after midnight so that they could get to the ATM with me. They would be able to get two lots of money if they withdrew just before midnight and then just after midnight as every day has a maximum withdrawal limit. It was 11 pm and I wasn't sure that I could manage another hour in their company.

Both cars stopped and the guy in the passenger seat got out to take a leak. Then the other guys joined them and I could hear them discussing how much money I had in my wallet. The driver held the knife or broken bottle or whatever it was very firmly to my back and told me not to get any bright ideas. He said if I tried anything he would kill me. I considered trying to make a dash for it but I came to the conclusion that I didn't want to be shot in the back.

I was staring at the floor of the car and started to quietly pray. One of them heard me and asked me what I was saying so I told him that I was cold. This was true. I was wearing a thin shirt and the temperature had plummeted. I continued to pray under my breath, somehow resisting the urge to say that if I got out of this alive I would never tell dirty jokes again or something like that. I was determined that, as difficult as this situation was, I would not make a vow to God that I could not keep, although I was already certain that what I was going through was going to be a life-changing experience.

At one stage, and for no reason whatsoever, the guy in the passenger seat cut my back with whatever it was that he was holding. I got the distinct impression that he was toying with me and that he was loving every moment of my suffering. I later wondered if he had given me a dose of HIV tainted blood: the youth militia in Zimbabwe are taught to do some pretty evil things so it wasn't as far-fetched as it might sound.

We started to drive around again, bouncing over another series of speed humps before we reached a dusty road in the middle of nowhere and they stopped again. Both men got out, together with one of the men from my Nissan. This man opened the door of the car and pulled my feet out. He was clearly intent on removing my footwear – until he realised that I was wearing a pair of boring moccasins. He wacked me on the head and said, "Olonga, next time we will sort you out."

Then they turned their attention to their old vehicle, the one in which I had been travelling, and one of them went over and slashed all of the tyres. They returned my wallet with my driver's licence and ID card and then, without a word, they climbed into my Nissan and drove off, taking my bank card with them. They also had my PIN. When they had asked for it, I gave it without thinking because it just seemed to be the most sensible thing to do. Banks tell you to never divulge it but in a life-and-death situation like that, perhaps a few dollars are worth ditching to stay alive.

I was in the middle of nowhere and there was nothing for miles around apart from a few cows in fields and there was nothing left to do but to walk. In the distance I saw a light, and I headed for it. It turned out to be a school. By now it was probably about 1 am and I managed to rouse a security guard and explain to him what had happened. He gave me his phone and I called an anti-car jacking service that had been set up. They knew what to do, to let my flatmates know I was all right and to give them an idea of where I was. Phoning the police was not a priority because they are absolutely useless in cases like this, "We have no fuel," being the usual excuse.

I was told that my friends had sent out a search party to look for me, although how on earth they ever thought that they would find me I will never know. Anyway, I got in touch with them, told them where I was and they arrived to pick me up. There was the pastor from my church driving the car with one of the elders, and when I saw them I had this huge outpouring of emotion and relief. It was at this point that I also realised that the injury to my back was extremely painful and that it was bleeding badly.

I was told that the protocol in Zimbabwe is that when you have been a victim of a crime such as this, you are meant to go to the police and tell them, and then go to the hospital. So we thought, anyway. I knew that I wasn't seriously hurt so I told the guys that we should try to find a police station. As we were driving around looking for one, a car overtook us. Unbelievably, it was my Nissan 4x4, and there was only one guy in it at this stage.

"Hey guys, that's my car," I shouted. I couldn't believe it!

The church elder got very excited, chased my car and caught up with it. He followed at very close range, trying to slow the driver down by getting in front of him and gesturing with his arm to stop. Both myself and the pastor were mortified. I had simply wanted to follow him at a safe distance to see where he went. Now we had surely upset him and he wouldn't have had a clue who we were. In fact, it's possible that he thought we were another gang of carjackers.

Anyway, at this point he stopped, turned around, put his foot down and drove off at high speed in the opposite direction. The next thing was that I heard the elder telling the pastor to pass him his gun. As he did so I was yelling at him, telling him that it was only a car, and that it wasn't worth it, but the elder would have none of it. He was on a mission. He leant out of the window and fired off a couple of shots. It was like being in a bad movie. I was screaming at him to stop shooting. One shot hit the rear of my car and, by this stage; I was beginning to feel pity for the car thief.

Suddenly, he brought my Nissan to a halt again and turned it round to face us. For a few nervous seconds it was a classic stand-off and, again, I had to tell the elder not to think about firing the gun. I did not want this night to end in death. Thankfully, the elder eventually saw sense and we allowed the thief to drive off into what was left of the night.

I was then taken to hospital, where my friends were waiting for me. My back injury needed four or five stitches but what hurt most of all was the fact that I obviously wasn't fit to go on the tour of Namibia with the A team, and I was never again mentioned as a possible captain.

The next day, I got a call to tell me that the Nissan had been found.

They'd abandoned it, probably terrified that it was going to cost them their lives after being chased and shot at. They had damaged the dashboard when trying to remove the radio with a crowbar. If they'd used the screwdriver in the toolkit they would have been able to remove it easily without any trouble!

At this point, I had another brainwave when I saw several beer bottles lying on the floor. They were unopened but I had watched the police drama CSI on TV and I knew that there must be fingerprints on the bottles. I gingerly removed the bottles, being careful not to smudge the fingerprints. We then found a police station, where I told my story in full before triumphantly producing a bag full of said bottles. The police officer thanked me, dipped his hand into the bag and pulled out the bottles one at a time, putting his grubby pawprints all over them. There is not the slightest doubt in my mind that he and his colleagues washed down their lunch that day with free beer. They certainly didn't ever have them brushed for fingerprints. I should have known better.

The car was taken away for a couple of days and when I got it back it was as good as new. The thieves had used my bank card to get their hands on Z$20,000 before we were able to put a block on the account. They were never brought to justice; well, not for that crime anyway.

For me, this whole sordid incident was another clear sign that my beloved Zimbabwe was starting to fall apart. When I had been in Singapore with the team I had been struck by what a clean, safe and family-orientated society they had there. My country was completely different. All that I was hearing in Zimbabwe was vitriol, mainly by the government against the white population. It seemed to be such a waste of effort and energy to me. Why should we regard white people as being enemies of the state? Hatred achieved nothing.

Up until the point where my car was taken I had been happy to mind my own business, to play cricket, mentor young players and to bury my head in the sand if you will. But that changed everything for me. I also became rather paranoid about travelling at night.

Apart from the carjacking, the big news in 2002 was that Australia cancelled their tour of Zimbabwe, citing safety and security concerns. There had been an election which Mugabe won, of course, amidst widespread allegations of vote-fixing and corruption, with many citizens being terrorised and told not to vote for the MDC.

The eyes of the world were now more and more focusing on Zimbabwe and because of international pressure Mugabe suspended us from the Commonwealth, encouraging him to even further vent his anger on the British government.

CHAPTER TWENTY-FOUR: TENSIONS BREWING

I remember one black player almost having a fight with a white opponent on the field, and the most disturbing thing of all was that this kind of behaviour was not discouraged.

Over the next few months the situation in the country deteriorated. I remember reading an interview with Heath Streak in an independent newspaper called *The Daily News*, where he had been asked whether or not he thought it was safe to tour Zimbabwe. Streak said that it was OK for people to tour Zimbabwe, and what I guess he meant by that was that from a safety point of view it was really no more dangerous than anywhere else in the world. When we toured other countries and were asked if it was right that we should be doing so we were coached to tell the foreign media that we were in their country as ambassadors and that we were not there to get involved in politics.

When it all started to hit the fan I began to realise that I could no longer churn out the party line. People who had seen the disintegration of their lives in Zimbabwe were not too impressed with Streak's point of view, and neither were the victims of brutality. I remember somebody writing a letter to *The Daily News* in response, which pretty much said, "How dare Heath Streak say this? Cricketers have a cushy life and are paid lots of money and have access to foreign currency. They tour the world and spend most of their time away from home, so they haven't a clue what is going on. They don't have to deal with all the stuff we do."

That letter had a deep impact on me because it made me realise that many ordinary Zimbabweans thought we were a bunch of *prima donnas* who were out of touch with reality. I started to feel that I needed to do something to show that I had solidarity with my fellow citizens.

The corruption within the government was affecting the most vulnerable members of our society. Some corrupt government officials were prepared to splash out countless millions on new Mercedes-Benz cars for themselves, presidential birthday parties and new mansions while the ordinary people suffered in abject poverty. I had a growing feeling that as high-profile sportsmen we should stand up and be counted, that we needed to tell the population that we did know what they were going through or at least that we cared about their fate. We were living in the same country and although we were not affected by poverty, we were experiencing other issues that were unpleasant. I was ready to do something, even though I had no idea what it might be at that point. This was the country I had grown up in and had come to love. A core group of people and their cronies were oppressing the rank and file, and it was wrong.

There were other problems within the cricket squad too. I had lived with being left out in the cold but many players also had issues with Heath Streak, captain now after Andy Flower had effectively been sacked as a scapegoat over the pay row that had flared while we were in England. Some in the team believed that if Heath had turned down the captaincy it would have been seen as an act of solidarity and it would have strengthened the squad.

Some Zimbabweans even went as far as suggesting that Streaky took on the captaincy to keep on the right side of the authorities and preserve his farm but I felt that was overly cynical. It was not long before he would threaten to resign a number of times, citing grievances over selection and also captaincy affecting his own game. Make no mistake about it, though: despite his troubled captaincy Heath Streak was Zimbabwe's finest all-rounder of his generation and Zimbabwe's talisman who single-handedly won many games for us.

In November 2002 there was a home Test series against Pakistan and I wasn't considered for the original squad of 30 players. It was a body blow but I took it in my stride, even though I was bowling well. Sportsmen and women go through periods where luck is either with them or it isn't and during this spell I had a run of three provincial games where I only picked up four wickets. To the outsider, it may have seemed that I was bowling really poorly but the reality was rather different.

The problem was that I was bowling quick again and my provincial teammates were not reacting quickly enough to take the chances I was creating. I lost count of the number of edges that should have been taken but were being put down. You try not to get too frustrated or upset because you know your teammates are not deliberately dropping the ball, but it can be the difference between claiming five or six wickets in an innings or none at all.

I felt I was bowling well but everybody was giving me grief – coaches, players, selectors and even the media. I am happy to admit that I was never a great cricketer. I was inconsistent, I was injury-prone and I lost form very quickly but on my day I was a match-winner. I felt the overt criticism was rather harsh. I still have the best and third best bowling figures for Zimbabwe in One Day International cricket, and during my career I guess that I bowled maybe five match-winning performances for my country. When I was good I was international standard but when I was bad, which was most of the time . . . well, you know.

We had other players who never set the world alight but for reasons that I could never quite fathom they didn't get the criticism I received. There was added pressure on me to perform because I had broken into the team at such a young age and because I had been the first black player to be chosen but I never felt that held me back and I could never believe it was a reason for singling me out. Perhaps it's because the selectors saw the potential I possessed but I am here to tell you right now that I never walked onto a cricket field and told myself that today I was going to bowl badly. I always gave it everything that I had. I was as frustrated by my inconsistency and struggles with injury as anybody was – more so. I am a slight guy. I don't possess the height and build of the likes of Glenn McGrath or Curtly Ambrose, and that meant that I always had to give every single delivery 100 per cent. Inevitably, that took its toll on my body and I did suffer. The human body is not designed to hurl a cricket ball at 90 mph.

I don't mind admitting that I grew restless at the realisation that none of my international teammates were ever subjected to the amount of scrutiny and criticism that seemed to come my way. It took a lot of restraint, but I never cried foul in public, I just got on with it.

In the warm-up matches, Pakistan obliterated every side they faced so, lo and behold, I suddenly got the call-up and was told that I would be playing in the first Test after all. I guess they decided that they needed pace and I was one of the few optioins on that front. But it wasn't as simple as that. With me it seemed that it never was. It didn't help that I had now gone from an A grade contract to a C grade, which obviously meant a cut in pay.

They kept referring to me as a senior player but treated me like a kid. I could stand to be corrected but I am pretty certain that no other Zimbabwe cricketer has ever been demoted from an A grade to C grade contract in one season. Before the match the selectors called me in and said basically, "Listen, Henry, this is your last chance. You've got to get out there and take lots of wickets or else we won't look at you again." One selector, Terry Nicholls, was the only person who heard me out when I tried to say why I had had a torrid couple of years.

Another thing that happened at this time was a very good friend of mine was diagnosed with a terminal illness. I hadn't told anyone about it and when I told them I had been struggling with some private issues they were having none of it. I felt like the most misunderstood man in cricket. I didn't have a victim mentality as if the whole world was against me. No. I just had issues that I could never share with selectors. To them I was a fast bowler who should just go out there and punish his body for his country and they didn't give a damn about what else was going on in my life. Perhaps that's not their job: they aren't psychologists but a little bit of empathy would have gone a long way.

Steven Mangongo was one of those national selectors, and he was also part of Takashinga, the club where I played for perhaps a season and a bit. As I mentioned before, Takashinga was an all-black club which had been established by Andy Flower and his father, who used to run coaching schools and try to identify promising talent. They would also provide scholarships in conjunction with Churchill High School to enable gifted kids to further their cricketing skills.

I had been asked to play for the club and to mentor some of the younger players, which I was happy to do as I saw it as my responsibility as the first black player for Zimbabwe. The club was an amazing hotbed of talent and players like Taibu, Masakadza, Chigumbura, Utseya and Matsikenyeri all came through this development scheme. On the one hand this club has been a great blessing to Zimbabwe cricket because it allowed young kids from underprivileged backgrounds to have opportunities previously closed to them. For the most part I enjoyed building with the club but it had some underlying issues.

Mangongo, I felt, was a power-hungry man on the rise, a man who had patiently worked his way up through the cricketing system. He had never played the game himself but had qualified as a coach. Underneath, he was quite a militant individual, highly politicised and surrounded by like-minded individuals. With the likes of Mangongo in the background, I never enjoyed my time at Takashinga. There were others, too, like the manager Givemore Makoni who said things that made me cringe. He did not have tact or diplomacy when speaking to his teammates or opponents. He was an unsavoury character. It was rumoured that some of the people at the club were demanding a percentage of the earnings of all the international players at the club to be pumped back into the club. I cannot vouch for where the money went and they didn't dare ask me, but they did exploit the youngsters.

We were constantly being told by them that racism existed in our country and of course I knew that: I had experienced it myself. They went on and on about it as if it was the only important thing, but what they failed to see is that racism can work both ways. The black players in our team would swear at their white opponents and verbally abuse them, and this was something with which I felt incredibly uncomfortable.

I am sure you can understand how this was a dilemma for me. Firstly, I don't believe that racism is right whichever direction it goes. Secondly, I never felt they accepted me as part of their team because of my middle-class background, Kenyan heritage and having friends from diverse backgrounds. Talk about feeling like you're in the middle of the crossfire.

I remember one black player almost having a fight with a white opponent on the field, and the most disturbing thing of all was that this kind of behaviour was not discouraged. I remember one player turning up to nets wearing a ZANU-PF T-shirt, and nobody said a word. It would be like a white player warming up to play for England while wearing a swastika T-shirt. Bizarrely, after my protest some of the people at Takashinga were the first ones to tell me that sport and politics shouldn't mix.

We had a small hardcore in the team who were focused on cricket, but the rest weren't so much. All the players who had played international cricket, like Taibu and Masakadza, Chigumbura, Matsikenyeri and a few others, were really nice guys who were moderate in their outlook and just wanted to keep performing. Some of them had travelled abroad and knew what it was to be tolerant of people from different cultures. But it was the guys on the periphery that were the most rabid, the ones who needed to prove a point. The guys who were running the show were bad news and they did nothing to quell what I considered then and still consider as being blatant racism. And of course, a lot of other teams did not enjoy playing Takashinga and I know this because of all the comments I got at national team net sessions. These games very often weren't cricket: they were more like war.

Anyway, with the ringing endorsement of the selectors fresh in my mind, I went out to face Pakistan, who were then and still remain one of the most entertaining and unpredictable sides in world cricket, capable of brilliance one moment, utter incompetence the next. But they possessed many world-class players.

We lost the first Test in Harare by 119 runs but we did actually make a game of it. We bowled them out for 285 and managed 225 in reply. I bowled well when it was their turn to bat again, taking five wickets. Pakistan made 369 and left us with too much to do, but we batted pretty well to get to 310, and we might well have been closer had it not been for the bowling of Shoaib Akhtar. We then headed for Bulawayo, where normal service was resumed. They sent us back to the pavilion for 178, made 403 themselves and bowled us out again, this time for 281. I picked up a couple of wickets in that match. It took them 8.3 overs to knock off the required runs and beat us by ten wickets.

The one day series that followed was a disaster. We played them five times and they won the lot. I played the first and final matches and my personal highlight turned out to be my batting performance in the fifth match, when I scored 31 as we were bowled out for 230 chasing 301. I just smashed the part-time spinner for a few sixes in one over. Then the skipper brought Sami back on and that was the end of my fun. This was my highest score in One Day International cricket.

At the end of 2002 we played three One Day Internationals against Kenya. Two of them were affected by the weather, but the third match was the one that I will always remember. It was played at Bulawayo and we bowled them out for 133 in 29 overs. I took six wickets for just 28 runs. It was one of those days when everything you try comes off. We reached our target for the loss of one wicket in only 16 overs. We had done to Kenya what so many teams had been doing to us. Strangely nobody came up to me and said a heartfelt "Well done, Henry." Only Bvute said to me I had just "bowled my way into the World Cup squad".

I was over the moon to be back in the fold and was told that I would be attending a pre-World Cup training camp in Bulawayo over Christmas. My girlfriend was not best pleased that I would be away and threatened to end the relationship just before Christmas. Little did I know that my relationship would soon be the least of my worries. My life would take on a whole new direction.

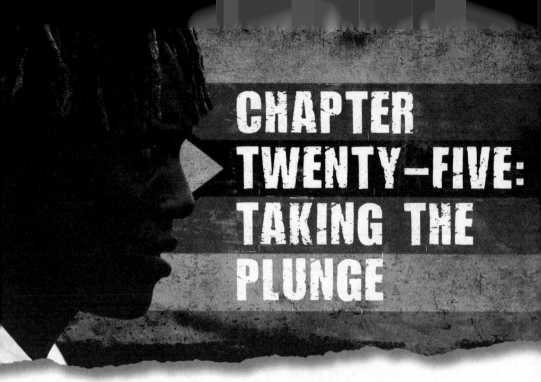

CHAPTER TWENTY-FIVE: TAKING THE PLUNGE

I agreed to meet Andy in a shopping mall where he dropped his bombshell.

In late 2002 I was selected in the 14-man squad for the 2003 World Cup and my date with destiny. We would be competing against the finest sides on the planet and the best thing of all was that we would be playing our opening-pool matches in Zimbabwe. What an incredible opportunity and what a buzz to be playing at home and once again in front of billions all over the world.

Some weeks before the World Cup got under way, Andy Flower spoke to me after a net session and asked if we could meet. I was surprised because, as you know, we hadn't been getting along too well for many months now due to the dressing-room row and the racism inquiry and when we spoke to one another generally the only thing on the agenda was cricket. Mind you, even before I was ostracised I had never engaged in too much friendly banter with Andy or the other senior players beyond a certain level. That's just the way it was and just the way we related. His laptop breaks down I help him fix it. He needs some throw-downs I help him out with that. He had a world-class cricket career to focus on and it often seemed to me that nothing was allowed to get in the way of that, so clear was his mindset.

During the difficult times in our country, Andy channelled the anger that he felt about what was happening in Zimbabwe into his cricket and turned himself into the best batsman in the world, which was no mean feat for a man playing in such a comparatively weak side. It was amazing to watch him smash the best bowlers in the world to all parts of the ground. He was a great batsman, of course he was, but he was also very angry at the way the game he had helped to develop was being ruined by some nefarious people and in a funny kind of way that definitely helped his game.

But now I couldn't figure out why this guy who hadn't been prepared to give me the time of day for so long would want to talk to me now. Andy may well disagree that we got on badly. Maybe he didn't mean to come across in that way. But it was intriguing that he suddenly wanted to talk away from the cricketing environment which, as far as I was concerned, was the only thing we now had in common. Besides, we were in the squad together preparing for the World Cup, so why couldn't he talk to me then?

However, I agreed to meet Andy in a shopping mall, where we sat outside a restaurant drinking coffee before he dropped his bombshell, "Henry, there's a gentleman who has come to see me. His name is Nigel Huff and he thinks it's high time that somebody should take a stance against what's happening in the country. He believes that what is going on here should be challenged."

This gentleman was a Christian with a strong conscience, and he was an old friend of Andy's. I believe that he had told him that the cricketers of Zimbabwe had a God-given responsibility to challenge what was going on. He described cricket in Zimbabwe as a normal sport being played in an abnormal society, copying the mantra of the ANC in the apartheid era. Countries had stopped sending sports teams to tour South Africa in protest at the regime. And now, here was a fellow countryman of mine suggesting to Zimbabwe's finest ever cricketer that our homeland was no better. It was food for thought.

Huff wanted the whole Zimbabwean cricket team to boycott the forth-coming World Cup and I was being asked to come on board because they thought I could persuade the black players to refuse to play. It was a hell of a thing to ask anybody to do and initially I thought, "You cheeky so and so. And Andy, after all the treatment you know I have been subjected to, you come and ask me to consider this. What are you playing at?"

And who was this Huff, anyway? The greatest honour a sportsman can receive is to be asked to represent his country. Now here was this person asking the country's finest player of his generation to give up the opportunity of playing in the sport's greatest competition, a competition that was to be played in front of his fellow countrymen and a competition that would be Andy's final opportunity to play on the biggest stage – he had already announced that the tournament was going to be his swansong. Not only that but he was proposing that we get the whole team on board as well: young, old, white and black.

As far as Huff was concerned it was the right thing to do, but I thought, "It's easy for him to say." Andy agreed with Huff but he didn't think that he could get the black players on his side on his own without the boycott seeming to be a white conspiracy. He had clearly realised that if Henry Olonga could be persuaded to talk to the black players then that would be a different kettle of fish.

Initially I was non-committal at the meeting, although what was being suggested had the ring of being right to me. How could it be wrong to stand up for other people less fortunate than you who would never be heard? But this was some heavy stuff to sift through and so I needed some time to assimilate it all. I told Andy I would think about it and I promised to keep it to myself. He suggested that we meet again sooner rather than later.

I did think about it, and then I looked at the young black and coloured guys during the next net session, players at the start of their careers, players who were desperate to play in this prestigious tournament, and I realised that not only did I think I wouldn't be able to get them on board, but I knew that I didn't want to.

It would be one thing for me to do something, but why would I want to put these young men at risk? Even at this stage I was also worried about the consequences of any action that we took.

Andy and I met again, and this time Huff was present. He announced that it was the right and Godly thing to do, which was a stance I had no problem with, and he reiterated his views about us living in an abnormal society. He insisted that standing up to Mugabe was the right thing to do. "You need to get the whole team to boycott the World Cup," he said. "I am sure you guys can do it." I still wasn't sure what to make of him but the bigger picture in my mind was beginning to take shape slowly. I felt that it was probably right to do something, but I didn't know what. However, I was absolutely convinced that getting the whole team involved would be a mistake, for all sorts of reasons, and probably impossible. There had to be another way.

Of course, seeing the discord in the country and the team had brought me to this place already. I had reached the conclusion on my own that someone had to speak out. I was now fully aware of the corruption at the heart of the Zimbabwean government, and the tortures and murders that had taken place in their name, but I also felt that my conscience or, dare I say it, God was guiding me in this direction.

Several years earlier I had been asked to get involved with the Mumvuri project, which was an orphanage in a town called Banket north of Harare. It was run by a woman called Felicity Ferriman who took it upon herself to look after children who had lost their parents – mostly through AIDS – and she would try to rehabilitate them and get them placed with extended family so that they could lead normal lives. Instead of leaving those families to their own devices, the project would source funding to pay for school uniforms, food and suchlike.

I was asked to be a patron and was quite happy to do so, a position I still hold to this day. My main efforts revolved around trying to raise money and at one stage we put on a fund-raising concert that made around Z\$100,000, which was a half decent amount of money at the time. Now it wouldn't buy you a loaf of bread.

I went to the orphanage two or three times and met the children who, naturally enough, had a profound effect on me. My heart went out to them and I wrote a song, *Someone for Me*, about the plight of an orphan which was inspired by my experiences there. The song is featured on my first album *Aurelia*. I couldn't get them out of my mind and I actually felt a pretty strong sense of injustice. These children had not asked to be born, and they certainly hadn't asked to be left all alone in the world, depending on the decency of a single white woman and a wonderful team around her for their survival, but that is what their lives amounted to.

One day I was reading the Book of Isaiah chapter 1 verse 17: "Learn to do good, seek justice, rebuke the oppressor, defend the fatherless, plead for the widow."

It is important to look after orphans, but what struck me was that it tied everything in with an oppressor. I found myself asking, "Hey, wait a minute. Robert Mugabe, how much does he do for orphans?" Here he is running this autocratic society, this tyrannical, dictatorial regime; every month we see his ministers enriching themselves, buying new cars, building new houses and flaunting it. But nobody thinks about these orphans apart from a few caring people with little means.

They have taken the initiative and are trying to ensure these young kids get some kind of chance in life. At the time it was estimated that there were over a million street children in Zimbabwe. Meanwhile, the leaders had built an empire based on corrupt fortunes for themselves that ran into millions of pounds but they didn't lift a finger to help the most vulnerable people in society. It has since transpired that Zimbabwe's elite have again shown their lack of compassion for the masses by plundering an area of the country rich in diamonds for their own ends. The area, called Marange, apparently has enough diamonds in it to pay off all the nation's debts. But it's not for the poor, the widows or orphans, just the fat cats.

Seeing the lack of transparency was one of many episodes that drove home the fact that my homeland was not in good hands. There was a problem of broken lives, and there still is a problem. We had government ministers who didn't give a second thought about their people and that could not be right, but who would keep them accountable? The media? There was only one legal daily newspaper, one viable TV channel and a few government radio shows and they weren't about to be too critical.

So I was in a place where I was feeling righteous indignation, and I was asking myself, "What does 'rebuke the oppressor' actually mean?" I came to the conclusion that, for me, it was all about standing up and saying, "Come on, this is just wrong. You can't just oppress people because you feel like it or because you can. Learn to do good."

So when Andy Flower came to me and spoke about something that I felt so passionately about, even though I was very cautious and didn't commit to anything I was pretty much on board soon after our chat. And when I did I made it clear that we needed to find the right way to make our protest.

A number of meetings followed and at one of those I told Andy that I didn't think we could get the rest of the team on board, and that I didn't think it was right or fair that we even tried. We were also concerned that anything we did was going to be misinterpreted by the media as the white majority within the squad influencing the black minority and it was very important to me that it wasn't seen to be that way. I also felt that boycotting the tournament didn't feel like the right thing to do either.

Andy was retiring, as was Alistair Campbell, and Guy Whittall was considering it. Why would we want to deprive our teammates, and yes, even ourselves, of that final opportunity to say goodbye with dignity? There had to be a different way of making our stance, so we agreed that the two of us would go away and think about what we could do that would have the maximum impact but would not affect the rest of our team.

We concluded that Huff was right about the need for a protest but not the method. We later agreed on a framework. Firstly, it would just be the two of us and we would stand up in unity, showing solidarity. I would represent the black people in the team and beyond, and Andy the white people. Our message would suggest that, "We are together, we are Zimbabweans, we are proud of it and we disagree with what's going on in this country." However, at this stage we still hadn't a clue what that protest might be. We just knew that we had an opportunity that we couldn't afford to miss. We didn't want to live in regret for the rest of our lives knowing that we had an opportunity to stand up and be counted and wasted it.

While we were at the training camp in Bulawayo I suggested to Andy that we go and see David Coltart and ask for his advice. As well as being a human rights lawyer, David was a founding member of the Movement for Democratic Change and he was now an MP who opposed everything that Mugabe and his regime stood for.

So a meeting was scheduled and we were invited around to David's for a meal, with security staff stationed outside. Well, just the one guy at the gate actually, with a stick.

Naturally we exchanged stories of our different experiences of life under Mugabe. He told us of the time he was followed by a car that tried to run him off the road and about various death threats he had received. We met his wife and his kids and then, after we had eaten, we got down to business and started talking about politics.

David told us again about the letter he had received from Mugabe when he first came to power and his famous speech about wanting to create a thriving economy with whites and blacks living in harmony. He said that he had been mesmerising and promised from the bottom of his heart that it was his intention to rebuild Zimbabwe and to do that he needed the best brains to remain in the country.

Mugabe said, "If you were my enemy, you are now my friend. If you hated me, you cannot avoid the love that binds me to you and you to me. It could never be a correct justification that, because the whites oppressed us yesterday when they had power, that the blacks must oppress them today because they have power."

"If yesterday I fought you as an enemy, today you have become a friend and an ally with the same national interest, loyalty, rights and duties as myself."

It was what people had been waiting to hear and, as a direct result of that speech, many white Zimbabweans who had been intent on leaving the country and even had suitcases packed decided to stay. Many others who had been living in South Africa also decided to come home.

Coltart showed Andy a copy of the report on the Matebeleland massacres compiled by the Catholic Commission for Justice in Zimbabwe, which he had shown me some years before. As I've said, it is horrific reading – the evidence of the brutality by Mugabe's Fifth Brigade or 'Red Berets'.

I told them both of another story that a GP-turned-sports doctor had once told me about people being brought in to him who had been beaten so horribly that he had had to cut off their buttocks to save their lives. Their flesh had been so badly mashed that the cell walls and connective tissues had been destroyed and their bodies would begin to poison themselves with toxic enzymes. Removing what was left of the flesh was the only way of giving these people a chance to live. There were hundreds of such victims, and they were the lucky ones. A lot of people died of kidney failure after being beaten.

After Andy had briefly read the dossier we again discussed the idea of a protest, and David came up with the idea of wearing a black armband. He said that people wore them to mourn the death of icons, so why couldn't we do something similar to mourn the death of democracy in our country? It would be peaceful and it would be effective. Nigel Huff's idea had been that we would go to the opening ceremony in South Africa and then announce that we weren't going to take part in the World Cup but we rejected that because we felt it was too disruptive. Besides, they could simply have picked another team, and then what would have happened to us?

So we always knew that his idea was a non-starter but a black armband, now that had some potential. When we told Huff he disagreed. He still wanted us to get the whole team to withdraw, but we'd made up our minds. In our naivety we thought that we would be able to wear black armbands in every game of the World Cup. It seemed like the perfect solution.

However, we knew that the armbands alone wouldn't be enough. We decided that we needed to put out a statement as well, so we went back to see David Coltart and asked for his help in drafting it. We knew that his legal background would be crucial in helping to ensure that we got the wording right. The last thing we wanted to do was to defame Mugabe – we didn't want to end up in court being unable to defend ourselves – and David would make sure the statement was legally sound.

We had to explain our stance and our reasons for taking it. We also had to make it clear that it was down to us, that the rest of the team knew nothing about it. So we sat down around a table, discussed all the points that we wanted to include and batted things back and forth. Then we went home, e-mailed ideas backwards and forwards, discussed it further until we got it right, until we knew that the wording was perfect.

We then had a meeting with some well-connected people whom Andy had sought advice from. This involved driving to a golf club, parking the car, getting out, climbing into the back of somebody else's car and being advised by somebody who used to work for the secret police.

"What you guys are planning to do, it's incredibly brave and very danger-ous," we were told. "You need to know that when these guys react it's never pretty. You guys need to weigh this up. The worst-case scenario is that you will have to go into exile. If you are ready and willing to do that, good luck to you both. You'd better be sure you want to do this."

These guys seriously didn't recommend what we were planning to do. Suddenly, it was like we were starring in our own spy movie but we knew that if any bullets started flying around, the blood would be real, and there would be no chance of doing a second take.

The conversation left us in no doubt about the seriousness of the situa-tion we were about to find ourselves in, and it also got us thinking deeply for the first time that there might be serious consequences for ourselves and our families too.

CHAPTER TWENTY-SIX: THE DEATH OF DEMOCRACY

I remember how we had both been tossing things back and forth and agreeing that the worst thing in life was to have an opportunity to effect change, a chance to do something meaningful, and choosing to do nothing.

We had decided that we were going to give our statement to Geoffrey Dean of *The Daily Telegraph* on the morning of our opening World Cup match against Namibia. He was somebody we felt that we could trust. The wonderful article he had written about me as a teenager who stood on the verge of becoming the youngest player to represent his country, and the first black player to do so, had gone over my head at the time. I really hadn't understood the significance of what I was about to do back then, but I did understand the significance of what I was about to do now.

The agreement was that I would print the statements out and give them to Andy, who would hand them over to Geoffrey at his hotel. We decided that we would embargo it until 9:30 am for the simple reason that, by then, the teams would have been named, the toss would have taken place and it would be impossible for the Zimbabwe Cricket Union to withdraw Andy or I from the side.

I knew the dangers. I was aware of the risks. I knew that I had to speak to my dad about it because he would be drawn into it but I didn't have the guts to tell him that I was going to stand up to Mugabe and ostensibly call him a wicked dictator. Somehow I just couldn't imagine my dad giving me his blessing and telling me to go ahead, that it was a fantastic idea. Instead I did it in code. I had dinner with him one day shortly before the World Cup and said, "Dad, do you think it would be a good idea if somebody stood up against the president and told him what they thought?" Unsurprisingly, he said, "Yes, of course, somebody should do precisely that." "Wouldn't it be great if somebody did something, if somebody did some kind of public protest, if we had somebody who would be brave enough to stand up and be counted?" He was agreeing with me, over and over. "Yes son, definitely, it would be wonderful if somebody were to do that because people are suffering here."

So, as far as I was concerned I had his approval, however tacit. I could turn round to him afterwards and say that he had agreed with my view that somebody should take a stance. Of course, I didn't reveal that the somebody was going to be me.

Our plan was now in place but before the tournament started we travelled to South Africa for the opening ceremony at Newlands in Cape Town and while we were there we met the England team. They were in the same pool as us and were due to play us in Zimbabwe. We were asked to go to a secret meeting which was attended by Nasser Hussain, the England captain, Duncan Fletcher, the coach, and David Morgan of the ECB. Representing Zimbabwe were myself, Andy Flower and David Coltart. Fletcher is from Zimbabwe, of course, and announced at the start of the meeting that he didn't want to be part of any decision. He said this was because he loved his country, even though he understood why the England team might feel uneasy about playing there.

The reason for the meeting was that Hussain and his players wanted to know whether or not it was a good idea for them to play us. They wondered how they would be perceived by the people of Zimbabwe if the match went ahead, how the safety and security issues stood in our opinion and also whether there was a moral case for staying away. We decided to tell them what Andy and myself were going to do and I guess that answered most of their questions. If two of Zimbabwe's more experienced cricketers were taking a stance against their political regime, how on earth could England justify playing cricket in the country? I thought it was fantastic that they should ask us if we felt it was morally right to play. Most of the other countries didn't care two hoots about the moral issue.

I sympathised with Hussain when he said, "You guys don't understand what our media is like. They will crucify us if we play." In fact in my humble opinion, they would have crucified the players no matter what they had decided to do. Damned if they did and damned if they didn't. Andy and I felt that boycotting the match was the right thing to do, but Coltart disagreed. He said it would do more good to get the English media into Zimbabwe so that they could witness for themselves what was going on, but of course as it turned out the press came anyway.

We left that meeting not knowing what England would do.

The night before the Namibia match at home I gathered my flatmates around and told them what I planned to do and asked them to pray for me. "I want you guys to know because you are living with me and I don't know what's going to happen, but it could get scary," I said. They were all very supportive, but my girlfriend was distraught and begged me to reconsider.

That evening before our opening match I spent most of it watching *Gladiator* starring Russell Crowe. It is one of my favourite films and if ever anything was going to get me in the mood for what was to come then it was this movie. I paused and rewound the arena scene when he unveils his mask. I felt pumped up and ready to take my stance.

I was excited about what we were going to do but also apprehensive about what the aftermath might be. I believed that during the World Cup we would be safe because of our profiles, and that would at least give me a certain amount of time. Andy, who is married to an Englishwoman and has children, knew that he would be heading off to Great Britain to see out his playing career. Even without the protest he was leaving Zimbabwe anyway. Henry Olonga? I hadn't thought that far ahead, in fact I hadn't a clue. Yes, I had been warned of the dangers of the action we were about to take but in my optimism I naively still expected to live out the rest of my life in Zimbabwe.

I remember how we had both been tossing things back and forth and agreeing that the worst thing in life was to have an opportunity to effect change, a chance to do something meaningful, and choosing to do nothing.

I am not going to speak for Andy because I don't know precisely what got him to that place. In addition to having a good conscience, I believe that Nigel Huff may have also taken him to a defunct farm to see with his own eyes the devastation that was happening there. Andy has wonderful God-fearing parents and that he cared about his fellow man did not surprise me.

I will never deny that there were balances that needed to be redressed in Zimbabwe after years of colonial rule, but there is a right way to go about it and a wrong way, and violence is the wrong way. When you realise that your leaders who are crying foul against the West for their imperialism are themselves racist, it hits you right between the eyes. This is a concept lost on a lot of people. There does exist a black racism against white people in Zimbabwe.

These were the thoughts that were running through my head when the morning of the match finally arrived. This was it. I got in the car and drove to the ground, heart thumping, knowing that there was no way back now. I knew what it was like to play in a Test match against Australia, I knew what it was like to face Shoaib Akhtar, but this had me more nervous than any of that. It was an exhilarating feeling, tinged with uncertainty about what the aftermath would be.

When the team was assembled at the ground we did all our usual warm-ups and exercises. As far as every other member of the Zimbabwe team was concerned this was just another game of cricket – an important game, yes, but just a game. It was an odd feeling to look around at my teammates, knowing they hadn't the foggiest idea what was about to happen.

We knew that having given Geoffrey Dean the statements there was no way back. We had asked him to distribute the statement to everybody else who was in the press room once 9:30 kicked in.

Heath Streak went out to the middle and won the toss. When he returned to the dressing room Andy and I looked at each other, knowing that our moment of destiny had arrived.

And so it was that at 9:30 am on 10th February 2003, at the start of our opening World Cup match against Namibia, the following statement was released on our behalf:

It is a great honour for us to take the field today to play for Zimbabwe in the World Cup. We feel privileged and proud to have been able to represent our country. We are however deeply distressed about what is taking place in Zimbabwe in the midst of the World Cup and do not feel that we can take the field without indicating our feelings in a dignified manner and in keeping with the spirit of cricket.

We cannot in good conscience take to the field and ignore the fact that millions of our compatriots are starving, unemployed and oppressed. We are aware that hundreds of thousands of Zimbabweans may even die in the coming months through a combination of starvation, poverty and AIDS. We are aware that many people have been unjustly imprisoned and tortured simply for expressing their opinions about what is happening in the country. We have heard a torrent of racist hate speech directed at minority groups. We are aware that thousands of Zimbabweans are routinely denied their right to freedom of expression. We are aware that people have been murdered, raped, beaten and had their homes destroyed because of their beliefs and that many of those responsible have not been prosecuted. We are also aware that many patriotic Zimbabweans oppose us even playing in the World Cup because of what is happening.

It is impossible to ignore what is happening in Zimbabwe. Although we are just professional cricketers, we do have a conscience and feelings. We believe that if we remain silent that will be taken as a sign that either we do not care or we condone what is happening in Zimbabwe. We believe that it is important to stand up for what is right.

We have struggled to think of an action that would be appropriate and that would not demean the game we love so much. We have decided that we should act alone without other members of the team being involved because our decision is deeply personal and we did not want to use our senior status to unfairly influence more junior members of the squad. We would like to stress that we greatly respect the ICC and are grateful for all the hard work it has done in bringing the World Cup to Zimbabwe.

In all the circumstances we have decided that we will each wear a black armband for the duration of the World Cup. In doing so we are mourning the death of democracy in our beloved Zimbabwe. In doing so we are making a silent plea to those responsible to stop the abuse of human rights in Zimbabwe. In doing so we pray that our small action may help to restore sanity and dignity to our Nation.

Andy called the whole team together and said, "Henry and I have done something. There is a coffin [a big box used to transport cricket kit] in the corner and if anybody wants to have a look and read what is in there please feel free."

We stood back as members of the team wandered over, picked up copies of the statement and started to read. The look in their eyes told us everything we wanted to know. There was no negative reaction, but it was clear that nobody had expected this. One or two of the guys told us that we were very brave, that it was something they would have liked to do but didn't have the guts.

Geoff Marsh, our coach, was not happy and neither was the manager, Babu Meman, an Indian gentleman who had been in charge of the team for a few years now. Babu was the one most unimpressed. "Henry and Andy, I have just heard what you have done. You have to come and speak to the CEO downstairs right away."

The CEO at that stage was a gentleman called Vince Hogg. He was a good businessman and a good guy and I respected him but he wasn't as independent as his predecessor. Hogg sat us down and said, "I cannot believe what you have done. You guys cannot do this. You can't let this get out. The outside world can't know you have done this. You guys are too precious to Zimbabwe cricket. We can't let you go ahead with it, so I have to tell you to withdraw it."

He appeared to be genuinely concerned about our safety, which was good to know, but I truly believed in this so there was no going back.

"I am sorry, sir, but it's too late. It's done," I said. "We embargoed it until 9:30; the moment 9:30 came the whole world got it."

"Guys, I have to insist and tell you again that you can't do it."

We repeated that it was too late, and he then asked if we fully understood the consequences of what we had just done. Naturally we told him that we did. Unusually, I remember that on this occasion I did a lot of the talking.

In exasperation, Hogg brought the conversation to an end by informing us that we would have to live with it.

Considering the detail of our preparations, ironically we hadn't been able to get hold of proper cloth armbands. Neither of us had a clue where you would go to get such a thing, so we improvised with black insulating tape. I helped Andy put his on, and he strapped mine to my arm. As armbands went, they weren't particularly impressive, but when I sat down to consider what they stood for the hairs on the back of my neck stood on end.

We went out and flayed the Namibian bowlers all over the park, smashing 350 for 2 off our 50 overs. Craig Wishart played a career-best innings with an unbeaten 172 off 151 balls. When Andy went out to bat he had his black insulating tape wrapped around his arm. To be honest as I watched from the pavilion balcony I found it pretty difficult to make it out. At one stage I looked down and saw Howard Burditt, the Reuters photographer. By now he knew what was going on and had clearly been asked to take a picture of me, so I looked directly into his camera lens and gave him the thumbs up, making sure that my black tape was on show for all to see. His pictures are the best known from that day.

Andy made a bright and breezy 39 and then we managed to bowl 25.1 overs before the rain fell. Namibia scored 104 – and we beat them quite comfortably using the Duckworth-Lewis method. I had my insulating tape on my arm as I sent down my three overs for eight runs. I have looked at pictures since then, struggling to make out the armband, and have found myself chuckling and thinking, "I got into so much trouble for *that!*"

At the time we had no idea that word of our stance had quickly spread throughout the spectators and that some among the crowd of 4,000 had made their own armbands. "We support Andy and Henry. They have made a brave stand and they have said it like it is," one cricket fan was quoted as saying on satellite TV, sporting a hastily made armband. "They have acted like true sportsmen and have stood up for fair play. I am only sorry that Heath Streak is not doing the same thing."

I discovered later that Mike Carter, a Zimbabwean businessman, was arrested at the ground for wearing a black armband. "Five police took me to Harare Central and really abused me verbally," he said later. "It was frightening. Eventually they charged me with conduct likely to cause a breach of the peace. I paid a small fine and was released."

I also learnt later of a quote from an unnamed teammate who said, "The team is 100 per cent behind Andy and Henry. They think what they did takes a lot of balls and that it was the right thing to do." But at the time we didn't know much about the support we were being pledged far and wide. It was quite strange, like being in the eye of the storm.

Even after the game, none of our teammates said anything, maybe just "See you tomorrow at training" or whatever. The management didn't talk to us. I just went home. In England, there would have been endless media interviews, but here there was nothing. I switched on the television but was not surprised to find that Zimbabwean TV had decided to ignore our actions. I couldn't get the BBC and there was nothing in the following morning's papers either, which was not surprising really, considering they were all state-controlled.

In one sense I felt that it was finished now, that we'd done it, and yet I knew it wasn't over. One minute I was exhilarated thinking about what we had done, the next I was fearful about what would happen next. On the one hand brimming with excitement at what we had done and a sense that this is going to change the world, and on the other hand there was this feeling of trepidation because of course there was this ever-present sense of possible doom. We knew Mugabe; we knew his henchmen, his youth militia. We knew what they had done to other activists or opponents and now all we could do was wait to see what they would do.

The first thing that happened was that it was reported that my club were suspending me. Givemore Makoni, the chairman of Takashinga, was quoted as saying, "It is disgraceful what Henry Olonga and Andy Flower have done. Taking politics onto the playing field is a thing the International Cricket Council and all sports organisations have been trying to avoid. It is disappointing because Olonga was a hero and a role model to black cricketing communities. By taking politics onto the field and bring-ing the game into disrepute, Henry appears to have breached Takashinga's code of conduct. The code of conduct is non-political and it is quite clear that all its members must refrain from making public statements that are political."

Makoni said that I would be hauled before a disciplinary committee to explain my actions and that my most likely punishment was that I would be expelled from the club. Steven Mangongo was a key provincial and national selector and, as a member of the club, was in a position to ensure I was not picked again which would effectively end both my domestic and international cricket career.

Nobody from the club got in touch with me directly to tell me that I had been suspended, however, so I contacted my lawyer who informed me that Takashinga had broken their own rules. I wasn't just a player: I was also a club member and according to the constitution of the club they could not suspend me for having a political view.

In the meantime, the whole England thing was still rumbling on. Would they come? Would they boycott the match? If they chose not to play, would they be docked the points? Would Zimbabwe be awarded the points? Would the game be classed as a draw? The whole thing was a complete shambles. The International Cricket Council insisted that all was OK, that it was safe for England to play in Zimbabwe. In the end, England didn't play us and the official reason was that they were concerned about their safety. It is my personal conjecture, based on the meeting we had, that they boycotted the game against Zimbabwe for moral reasons, and I still believe more good would have come from them announcing that this was why they were not coming. What a powerful message it would have sent to Mugabe if the official England statement said that. But I suppose they weren't allowed to.

I later described Nasser Hussain and his team as 'heroes' and although he refuted the fact that they had boycotted the game in protest and said that I was wrong to describe them as such, I believed it then and I still believe it now. The England team had the guts to stand up for what was right. They may never be thanked as they should have been but I describe them in the very least as having good conscience. The upshot of all this was that Zimbabwe were awarded the match which gave us full points for a victory that we hadn't actually achieved.

A few days later Takashinga held a disciplinary meeting at the club headquarters. We had a showdown and they were surprised and put on the back foot when I arrived with a lawyer. The meeting was going nowhere while they were stumbling over their words. When asked where exactly in the constitution the rules had been broken they were speechless: they simply could not say.

In the end I said to Makoni, "We both know what we want here. I know that you don't want me to be part of your club any more; you have made that pretty obvious. So just let me go. But you cannot legally expel me, so how about we just go our own ways and never have anything to do with each other ever again?"

He had been ready to fine me and suspend me, but he knew that technically I had actually done nothing wrong. Ironically, the statement the club put out bemoaning my bringing politics into cricket was blatantly political. My career with Takashinga was over, but that was hardly the biggest disappointment of my life. Things were heating up.

The next thing was that we heard that the International Cricket Council had convened a meeting of their disciplinary committee to decide if Andy and I had broken any rules. It took them about a week to deliberate and Dave Richardson, the former South African wicketkeeper, lawyer and also the General Manager for the ICC, wrote us a letter telling us that they didn't think we had broken any rules. But they did say that we should adhere to any guidelines that our local board imposed upon us. In other words, cricket's governing body had batted the ball straight back to the Zimbabwean authorities. The irony of all this for me was the ICC had taken a week to decide that we hadn't brought the game into disrepute but my club had taken a day to decide that I had. Even now, that still makes me laugh. They were a rabid, politicised club and they couldn't stand by and let me get away with what I had done.

I have to admit that I had some sympathy for the ICC. They couldn't outlaw black armbands and nothing that we had said in our statement could have been considered to be inflammatory, so how could they condemn us when the rest of the world was saying that we had done the right thing? I knew this because both Andy and I had begun to receive e-mails from all around the world, with people telling us that they supported the action we had taken and they hoped it might actually lead to some changes in Zimbabwe.

Before our next match, against India, Andy and I were called in by Vince Hogg again and this time his attitude was very different. There was no

compromise; there was no sympathy or understanding. "Guys, you diso-
beyed a direct order," he said. "You must not wear black armbands again."
We agreed, but that didn't mean that we couldn't wear red armbands, black
wristbands or whatever, did it?

I had been dropped from the team but all the white players had made it
clear that if Andy Flower was dropped then none of them would take to the
pitch either. Well, he was the best batsman in the world at this time. And so
it was that Andy wore a black wristband against India. I was twelfth man and
I had my black wristband too. We just about got away with that, but the red
sweatbands we wore for the next match against Australia were the final straw.

All around the ground were members of the youth militia. Known as
the Green Bombers because of the colour of their uniforms, they are almost
all teenagers. They are forced to shave off their hair; they are indoctrinated
from a very young age, being consistently tortured until they accept without question that they must follow orders and do Mugabe's bidding. They
also pick girls for the militia, and they are treated even more brutally, with
gang rapes being part and parcel of their 'training'. I have heard that part
of the Green Bombers' initiation ceremony involves going home and beating up members of their own family to prove their devotion to the president.
It is like the Hitler Youth movement was. These are the guys who do all
the dirty work for the regime. They make people disappear; they throw
white farmers off their land; they beat up innocent people.

Anyway, I was taking the drinks onto the field when one of these thugs
came up to me and said, "Hey Olonga, you're a sell-out, we're gonna get you.
You're a sell-out." They are so indoctrinated that anybody who stands up
against the regime is a traitor. This was how one-sided politics in Zimbabwe
had become: "You're either for us or you're against us."

After the match against Australia we were called in again. "You are not
allowed to wear anything that is not part of the official team kit," said
Hogg. By now, he had completely lost patience with us, was unsmiling and
I realised that I was running out of friends very quickly, at least as far as
the cricket administrators were concerned. Irrespective of people's personal
beliefs, they weren't sharing them with me, even if they believed that what
we did was right. I should have been scared, but feeling like everyone else
has abandoned you focuses your mind.

For our next match against Holland, in Bulawayo, I wasn't in the team but I had been named as twelfth man again. And again I took no meaningful part in the game. But then a wicket fell and I was about to take some drinks out on the field when I got a message from the team manager saying that I wasn't allowed to be seen anywhere on the field and was to stay on the balcony for the rest of the duration of the match. I was effectively banned from taking any part in the game including taking drinks to my teammates. It was disappointing and also sinister. Where were these instructions coming from? Were they coming from a higher authority than the ZCU?

Apart from not being able to continue the protest, the frustrating thing about all this for me was that I had come into the tournament bowling as well as I had done in a while and I wasn't being given the opportunity to prove it. I had been clicking well with our bowling coach Kevin Curran and I could have been making a positive contribution to the team. Instead, I was effectively an outcast. But any thoughts of bowling and cricket would soon pale into insignificance.

I was starting to get a little worried now. Every day things seemed to get worse. I began to get some nasty e-mails and suspected that my phone was being bugged. The thing with the secret police in Zimbabwe is that they aren't very secret. I was literally on the phone one day and a third voice came on the line. After that I began seeing cars following me every time I looked in my rear-view mirror and people lurking on street corners and in doorways. It's possible that I was imagining things, but it illustrates what was going through my mind at this time. I knew that while the eyes of the world were on Zimbabwe there was no chance that they would do anything to me, but what would happen when the World Cup was over and I was on my own?

I think I very quickly realised that they had more power than we did. I was dropped from the team, they stopped us from wearing the armbands or wristbands and finally the concrete threats came. You have to remember I had always been a law-abiding citizen. I had no idea, really, how to be defiant, to stand up to these people. I was just a cricket player. Perhaps if there was any flaw in the whole black armband thing it was the naivety of not having a plan B. Andy had his but what do I do next? If the world responds positively, great, but what if they don't? What if these guys do follow through with their evil plans to destroy me, what then? There were enough examples of people who had stood up against the government who had been tortured, but there were plenty who had been left alone as well. At this stage I knew it could go either way.

The thing is, Mugabe's government had got to the point where they weren't even pretending to be a democratic regime any more. I remember being incredibly shocked by an incident in 2001 involving Job Sikhala. Job was an MP in Zimbabwe for the Movement for Democratic Change and one day in the early hours of the morning about 50 members of the army arrived and he and his pregnant wife were physically assaulted. There was no attempt to cover it up. It was quite outstanding in its audacity. This was an MP! That had quite a profound impact on me because it's one thing to hear about villagers being tortured in the wilds of the countryside, but it's another thing when an elected MP is assaulted this way. And this affected Andy as well: I remember him expressing his disgust about it during a nets session.

By now I was carrying a gun whenever I went out at night, which I had bought after the carjacking. It was all legal and above board. Carrying around a weapon that could end somebody's life escalates things to a whole new level. I found myself asking, "What am I doing with a gun? Is this how I want to live my life?" It most certainly was not. How on earth had it come to this? I was a cricketer, for goodness' sake.

A few days before our final group match against Pakistan, I received a phone call from my dad. "Listen, I want to have dinner with you," he said. I went to his house and he told me that he'd received a message from someone he knew who had contacts high up in the central intelligence organisation or secret police. The message had been simple and to the point. It was a warning. It said, "Tell your son to get out of Zimbabwe, now!"

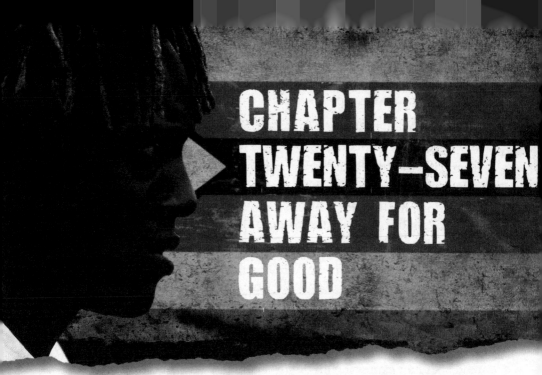

CHAPTER TWENTY-SEVEN
AWAY FOR GOOD

"You are on your own now." He turned to Babu Meman, the manager, and spouted, "Give this man his air ticket."

And so to that fateful final group match against Pakistan, when the rain came from nowhere to wash away my fears – at least for the duration of the World Cup. What would I have done if we had lost the match and been knocked out of the tournament? To be perfectly honest I do not know. But that hadn't happened. My prayers had been answered and the rain had come.

A very short while after play in the match against Pakistan had been called off, the clouds disappeared and the sun shone through. Pakistan may have felt they had been cheated, but not me. The feeling was one of elation; it was a huge and absolute sense of relief at having quite literally got out of jail, in my mind at least. Now I had my ticket out. I felt so full of joy. We were still in the World Cup and the authorities couldn't touch us in full view of a watching world that appeared to be begging the question, "What next for these two rebels?"

I felt sorry for Pakistan to a degree, and I also felt sorry for England, who were also eliminated, who deserved more after the stance they had taken. Had they played us they would probably have beaten us and qualified for the Super Sixes. I am reminded every day that I owe a latent debt of gratitude to so many people who don't even know that their loss was my gain.

I went home to Harare, not knowing if it would be the last time I would ever see my home. It was a certainly a possibility that I would never be back but I also had strong reasons to return to Zimbabwe after the World Cup was over. In a funny kind of way I still hoped I might be able to go back without too many recriminations. I still had a home and a girlfriend I was engaged to. I had family and friends and I had always envisaged a future in the country I grew up in, represented at international level and had been shaped by. I had always believed that I would naturally move back into cricket to give something back to the people that had made me what I had become.

A few days later I got on a plane to fly to Johannesburg in South Africa with the rest of my teammates. I left knowing that I had my ticket out of potential danger but trying to reconcile that I had so much left behind. I hadn't yet quite let go and for most of the trip over my heart was still in Zimbabwe. Beyond that, I hadn't a clue what was to become of me, but at least I had escaped the clutches of Mugabe's murderous regime.

After the improbable no-result against Pakistan, we still had three matches to play in the Super Sixes. We batted reasonably well against New Zealand, scoring 252, with Heath Streak hitting an impressive 72, but they reached their target with a couple of overs in hand. Next up were Kenya and, to my utter astonishment, I was told that I would be playing despite not having bowled a ball in anger for three weeks. I scored three runs as we were skittled out for 133 and I took what would turn out to be my last wicket in international cricket when I had Kennedy Otieno leg before for 19. In total I bowled four overs, costing 21 runs, as Kenya thrashed us, requiring just 26 overs to do so.

But a few days before our final match against Sri Lanka I received an e-mail in which my ex-girlfriend ended our relationship, saying that she wanted to remove herself from my life and move on. I took the decision in my stride because everything else was collapsing around me anyway. It's like when you get caught in the rain and you get wet – eventually you reach the point where it doesn't matter if it keeps pouring down because you are saturated and cannot possibly get any wetter than you already are. But it still hurt.

She had been the main reason to risk returning home to face the music and now that reason had gone. I sat down in silence on my own staring at that e-mail for a while. Now even if I did risk going back, what on earth did I have to go back to? Yes, I had some investments, but not enough to keep me going for long. My cricket career was effectively over, certainly in Zimbabwe, and although I had some family and friends in the country many had left for overseas as well.

I spoke to a few people about what I should do next and they all told me that I should remain in South Africa. My mind was made up for me the day before the game with Sri Lanka when I received an anonymous e-mail. It said, "You stupid n*****r, I wish that Mugabe had killed you, but don't worry you will be dead soon." So here was another threat. It wasn't the first, but it was very unnerving to keep getting these things. I spoke to the team's security man and even he told me that he thought I should remain in South Africa, that it would be foolish to go home. I had a visa that entitled me to remain there for a few more months, which was long enough to decide what I was going to do.

I started to put things in place. The night before the Sri Lanka match I told the coach and skipper not to pick me. "Mentally I am not there, guys. I have too much else going on in my mind. There is no point selecting me," I said. So they left me out.

I went to the ground the next day and the same security guard who had advised me to remain in South Africa approached me and told me that he'd heard that there were six Zimbabwean policemen in the ground at East London in the special VIP box. "What?" I said. "Six Zimbabwean policemen in the VIP box? Zimbabwean policemen don't even know what a leg bye is. They don't really follow cricket. Why on earth would they be here?"

The conclusion I came to was that they can only have been there to make sure that I got back to Zimbabwe and to arrest me when I stepped off the plane. True or false, all my fears crystallised in that instant. There was no way that I was going home, but I decided that if I was going to go down, then I was going to go down fighting, so I released a statement announcing my retirement from international cricket because of the threats that had been made upon my life. I sat down with Alistair Campbell while we were batting and told him what had transpired over the last few days. I said I needed some help to write another quick statement so we got some paper and scrawled a few rough copies before settling on the following:

It is with great sadness that I am officially announcing my retirement from international cricket. My continued involvement with the Zimbabwean team has become untenable for the following reasons.

The stand I took earlier in the World Cup has undoubtedly had repercussions that have affected both my career and my personal life. I have received threatening e-mails, which, I believe, make it dangerous for me to return to Zimbabwe.

I was never under the illusion that my stand would have no consequences, but I believe that one should have the courage of one's convictions in life and do all one can to uphold them.

I believe that if I were to continue to play for Zimbabwe in the midst of the prevailing crisis, I would only be neglecting the voice of my conscience.

I would be condoning the grotesque human rights violations that have been perpetrated against my fellow countrymen.

To my fellow Zimbabweans, the Zimbabwe we dream of must not merely remain in our hearts. We must be strong, stand united and strive to give our children the brighter day in which they belong.

We knew of a journalist that may be sympathetic to my cause, the cricket writer Neil Manthorp, and we smuggled a copy out to him.

A few hours later, when word got out, I was summoned again. During one of the disciplinary meetings the Zimbabwe Cricket Board had ordered us not to make any other political statements so, as far as they were concerned, I had overstepped the mark again. Bvute was fuming. I could see the anger in his eyes and he was almost shaking. He said, "Olonga, we are guests in this country. We gave them assurances that this would not happen again. We told you not to make any statement."

It wasn't pleasant, but I suppose that it was what I had expected. Then he said, "You are on your own now." He turned to Babu Meman, the manager, and spouted, "Give this man his air ticket." He handed me my plane ticket home and made it quite clear I no longer had anything to do with the Zimbabwean cricket team. Bvute was now clearly the man in charge of Zimbabwe cricket. I couldn't help remembering his sugar-coated words from a few years earlier as he tried to enlist me to join the Campaign to Eradicate Racism in Zimbabwean Cricket. Now he was showing his true colours. No doubt I had brought this upon myself but my, how much he had changed in such a short space of time.

I returned to the dressing room feeling like a schoolboy who had been lectured by the headmaster. A few minutes later the drugs testing agency came around to take urine samples from two players in the team and guess who the team manager chose? Perhaps they hoped that I had ingested something I shouldn't have to discredit me but I never played that game so I was clean.

That night, a guy came to my hotel room and knocked on the door. He'd been sent by Channel 4's producer, Gary Francis, and said, "I'd like to talk to you. I'm with Channel 4 in England. What are your plans for the summer?" Of course I had no idea what I was going to do with my life. And he said, "We'd very much like you to come to England and do some commentary for us because Zimbabwe are on tour."

I said I couldn't give him an answer as my head was all over the place, but we exchanged e-mail addresses and it didn't take me long to realise that this was the best offer I had. OK, it was the only offer I had, not that I had the faintest idea how I was going to get to England.

The night before we were due to return to Zimbabwe, I was told that as I wasn't part of the squad any more I would not be allowed to travel to the airport on the team coach and that I would have to pay my own hotel bill. I said that this was ridiculous and, thankfully, I got some support from a couple of teammates, so I didn't have to pay the bill in the end. The vindictiveness was amazing. I had played cricket for my country for eight seasons and this is how I ended up being treated. But there was precious little time to sulk: I had to get to safety.

Through all of this I believe it is fair to say that out of Andy and I, it was undoubtedly me who received the harshest treatment. I suppose the authorities saw what I had done as the greater betrayal because I was black. The very people who purported to be vying for the integration of Zimbabwe cricket had reserved their worst ire for me, one of their own and the first black player to play for them. Or perhaps that's why it was seen as the worst betrayal of all.

During this difficult time I was shown kindness in the most unlikely of places when one of the South African security men told me not to worry about going to the airport because I could go with them in their car if I wanted. I figured staying in the spotlight for as long as possible was probably the safest thing to do so I said yes, and it turned out that this guy had been the bodyguard of one of my icons, Nelson 'Madiba' Mandela, so we had a wonderful conversation on the way there.

At the airport I asked a teammate, Douglas Hondo, if he would take my cricket kit back to Harare and give it to my flatmates, and he graciously agreed to do so. I went to the airport with the security men and said goodbye to everyone and made it clear that I would not be returning to Zimbabwe. The wife of Babu Memen, the team manager, broke down, gave me a brief embrace, began to weep and wished me luck for the future. I managed to hold it together but that was a very rare show of positive emotion toward me by anyone involved in the team during that time.

I am sure some involved in the game thought, "Good riddance". But after the reaction at Trevor Madondo's funeral I didn't care what some of them thought. Saying goodbye was never going to be easy but in the end it was all matter of fact.

The future? I hadn't the foggiest idea what that held for me. I contacted a good Christian friend, a pastor called Bill Bennott and told him that I had decided not to return to Zimbabwe. So he organised for a couple, the Webbs, to take me in. They lived in a fabulous house in a good part of Johannesburg with seven or eight rooms and a pool table and they were incredibly kind to me considering that I was a complete stranger to them.

I stayed with them for a month or so, but I knew that I did not want to remain in South Africa for the rest of my life. It is a beautiful country, but life is cheap. This is a place where you can be murdered for your car and with my previous carjacking experience I didn't fancy staying a day longer than I needed to.

While I was with the Webbs a woman called Charlene Huntergault interviewed me for CNN. I was very impressed that she had tracked me down, although if I had sat down and thought about it I would have realised that if she could find me so easily then so could anybody else – and that included my enemies. I told Charlene my story and I didn't think much more about it until a few days later when a guy called David Folb, who owned a cricket club called the Lashings World XI, based in England, got in touch. I had also been contacted by Kathleen O'Dea, a woman who had experience of what Mugabe was capable of – she had been held hostage at the farm of former Zimbabwe MP Roy Bennett as his farm workers were beaten up. She had fled Zimbabwe and was living in England and she offered to help me. She kept telling me that she was going to get me out of South Africa. Suddenly I didn't feel quite so alone in the world: there were people out there who really wanted to help me.

Anyway, Folb told me he wanted me to play for his club. He said that he had a big house in England and that I could live with him while I was looking for somewhere more permanent. He would also pay me to play for Lashings. This was a team of former world superstars – the likes of Richie Richardson, Chris Harris, Brian Lara, Gordon Greenidge, Devon Malcolm and Graeme Hick have all played for Folb and here he was telling me that he was certain I would fit right in. I decided to go for his offer – it was a no-brainer.

"All you have to do is get to England, and I will look after you when you arrive here," he said.

I had also been in touch with Channel 4 and told them that I was interested in their proposal, all of which was well and good, but at this stage I hadn't been paid by the Zimbabwe Cricket Board so paying for a flight to Europe was easier said than done. All I had was a bank card, but it would only allow me to withdraw a few hundred rand a day. There was a cash machine about a mile or so away so this meant that I would have to go to this ATM perhaps more than 15 times to get enough cash to buy my ticket.

With not a lot to do I had plenty of time to visit the British High Commission in Johannesburg to get all my paperwork sorted out. I was adamant that I did not want to apply for asylum, but that was fine thanks to David Folb who acted as a kind of sponsor – without him, who knows how many hoops I would have had to jump through?

I still had doubts about Folb as I didn't know whether or not to trust him. It was nothing personal at all, it was just I didn't know who to trust. I guess that I just couldn't understand why he wanted to go out of his way to help me. You know what they say – if it sounds too good to be true, it probably is. Only this was different. By now I was getting daily phone calls from both Dave and Kathleen: it was almost like they were in a wrestling match to get me over to England. I was extremely flattered. David Folb had told the MP Anne Widdecombe about my predicament and had managed to get her on side as well. On top of that, a keen cricket follower called Tony Brennan who worked at the Foreign Office was doing a lot of work on my behalf behind the scenes. So it transpired that I had many powerful friends working to help me, even though they were all complete strangers to me. Clearly I had struck some sort of a chord in the UK and soon I had a work permit.

Meanwhile, back at the ATM, it was about day seven and I was gradually accumulating my ticket money. I was desperate to get it all sorted out, not least because the ATM was over a mile from where I was staying and I hate walking long distances. It occurred to me that by the time I had completed my mission I would have completed a marathon, and then some. I remember standing at the ATM one day thinking, "Crumbs, it would be much easier if somebody just bought me an air ticket," and when I got home there was a voicemail message on my mobile phone from a South African gentleman called Vernon. He said he had seen my interview on CNN and he wanted to help me. I didn't know who this guy was from a bar of soap. I didn't even know how he had got hold of my number or again whether I could trust him.

The message said that he would send his chauffeur to pick me up. OK, it could have been a trap, but I had a good feeling about this so I decided to call back and arrange a meeting. After everything I had been through, it was heart-warming to suddenly discover that so many people wanted to assist me.

A chauffeur-driven Mercedes was sent to pick me up a few days later and I was taken to offices on the outskirts of the city and shown into the boardroom, where I met Vernon. "We saw your interview on CNN and we really want to help," he said. "The boss is quite busy just now but he will be along soon," said Vernon. So this guy wasn't the head honcho.

I was offered coffee, told to relax and make myself at home and I started looking at the photos on the wall. There was one featuring a man with slicked-back hair and a goatee shaking the hand of George Bush Sr. There was another, identical to the first, but this time he was with George W Bush. These were official-looking photos with the American flag in the background, perhaps taken in the Oval Office. O Lord, whoever this person was he had some serious connections and he wanted to speak to little old me. In another photo he was pictured in the cockpit of a fighter jet. I turned round and looked at Vernon, who informed me that this was something his boss flew for fun at weekends. We're talking about a plane that must have cost a few million dollars. I was pleased to see there were no pictures of the man with Mugabe, if I had I might not have been quite so relaxed.

Then he walked in, a big, powerful man. He had a thick American accent. "Ah," he said, "so you're the guy who ticked off Mugabe."

"Yes, sir, that's me."

"I've seen your interview. You are a very brave man. Let me tell you a story. When I was younger I was very successful but then I did one bad deal and I lost everything. I was at rock bottom, but then a man gave me a loan. He gave me $5,000. It was a loan that helped me get back on my feet. But it turned out that it wasn't a loan, it was a gift. He said he didn't want it back, but that he wanted me to remember the gesture and if I ever saw anybody else in trouble then I was to help them by passing it along.

"I got back on my feet, started another business and now I am doing really well. Then another time I was in Zambia and the president said he wanted half of my company but I told him I wasn't prepared to do that so he told me that he would throw me in jail. I had to flee for my life, so I know exactly what it feels like: I know what you are going through.

"Today what I do is I fly planes. I have an airline and I know that you need to get out of the country and I want to fly you wherever you want to go, at my expense, and give you whatever money you need to make a fresh start. And when you see someone else in need just pass it along."

My jaw hit the floor. Just a few days earlier I had thought wouldn't it be easier if someone just bought me an air ticket and out of the blue a total stranger offers me just that. Surely this was a divine hand at work.

It was a short meeting because he was a very busy man but I told him that I would love to take him up on his offer. That was all he needed to hear. The meeting concluded with him rising to his feet, shaking me by the hand and saying, "It has been very nice to meet you. I wish you luck. If you come back on Tuesday, Vernon, my assistant, will fly you to England."

And that, believe it or not, is exactly what happened, except that Vernon wasn't my pilot – he sorted out a ticket on a commercial flight for me, and I was soon on my way to my new life.

CHAPTER TWENTY-EIGHT: THE START OF A NEW LIFE

So we shook hands and I said, "Hey, thanks for getting me over", and he was like, "Hey, no problem, man".

can't remember what airline I flew to England: it was something like Angolan Airlines, which had to land somewhere else in Africa on the way, the Congo or Angola or somewhere. We all had to get off the plane for an hour or so and I remember being really nervous. I was thinking, "I'm still in Africa; Mugabe is a very powerful guy." I didn't feel that I was out of danger. I wouldn't say I was looking over my shoulder, but ever since I'd heard that the secret police were waiting for me in East London, I had been watchful, imagining them round every street corner, in every parked car, in every check-in queue or toilet cubicle. I wasn't quite a paranoid schizophrenic but I was on my guard. I wasn't going to breathe easy until that plane was back in the air and we were on our way to London.

Once the plane took off again and we were only eight hours away from

England, there was a feeling of elation. I had got out of jail in Zimbabwe with the rain coming and I had got out of jail in South Africa with this ticket. Now finally I felt I could get some rest. Just chill out for a week or two and think of life again, because when something so tumultuous and life-changing comes your way you run on adrenaline. My emotions had shifted from the elation of making the protest to fear then paranoia, but I had always been running on adrenaline, knowing I needed to keep my wits about me to survive. Then all of a sudden I was sitting on this plane leaving all this behind and I was finally able to exhale. I was safe and my mind flooded with peace.

All I had with me at this stage was a laptop, a change of clothing and a few hundred pounds.

So anyway, I landed at Heathrow Airport. David had said that he would be there to pick me up. He said he knew what I looked like so he'd find me. I'd never even seen a photo of the guy but I knew his voice because I'd spoken to him for hours on the phone. He's a very forceful guy; he had said he was a man who gets things done and has made a lot of money in business. From this impression over the phone I assumed he would be a tall guy, a biggish guy. This was a guy who was effectively my saviour, so perhaps I'd built him up in my own mind as this masculine monster of a man. So I walked through customs and into the airport and this guy walked up to me and introduced himself. He was short, stocky, round, with short podgy fingers, absolutely nothing like I'd pictured.

So we shook hands and I said, "Hey, thanks for getting me over", and he was like, "Hey, no problem, man". And the first thing I noticed was that he loves to put on his West Indian accent. "Man, it was seeeerious," he would say. This is a white guy from Kent who normally speaks with an immaculate English accent. It was so funny. So anyway we got into his car which was a little sports Jaguar; the boot was barely big enough for my bags, completely impractical, and on the back seat was his dog Buddy. So I was sitting there in this tiny sports car, thinking, "I'm sitting here in a car with a guy whose best friend is a dog," the dog licking my ear.

It was unusual to see how much he loved his dog. Buddy is a really cool dog and grew on me over the next couple of years, but it really brought home to me how much my life had been turned upside down. Suddenly I found myself in a country where people die and leave a million pounds to their cats.

David had said that he would put me up, but I didn't know where he lived. I guess I was thinking he would live in London, but he said he lived in Maidstone: I had no idea where that was. So we arrived at his very nice home – he lived in a group of townhouses in a riverside complex – and I instantly became the talk of the local community. I soon noticed how sensitive relationships with neighbours can be in England. There were many arguments about noise, garbage, over-parking and so on. It was a different world for me as in Africa people care less about such things. But on the whole I loved how welcoming people were and how slick everything was.

Anyway, David put me up for two years and we became great friends. We had a few bust-ups along the way but in a funny way they made us closer, which was lucky because where else would I have gone? I think it was just a culture clash. I can't help but have an affinity for this guy who got me into this country, gave me a chance for a new life here and allowed me to be part of the furniture at his home and his cricket club. He's had a recent bout with cancer and has overcome that, and I have a hell of a lot of affection and respect for him. David didn't have to help me, and I've seen him help countless other people who were in trouble.

So much had happened and changed in such a short time that I think I was in mild shock for a while. It was all so surreal. In a space of two months my whole world had been turned upside down. I had had to leave everything behind at the drop of a hat. Here I was in England with no money, no home, no friends. At least some of my family were here – Victor, who was playing rugby down in Cornwall; Lionel, Yolande and Judith, who had been here for a while – but this was a very sobering time for me and as you can imagine it caused me to ponder. What was I to do with my life now?

It was also unusual for me to see this happy-go-lucky attitude, because there are relatively few problems here compared to Africa. Bizarrely, one thing I really noticed was the lack of maids: that to me was weird. Everyone in Africa has a maid, even middle-class and lower-class people, because there's always someone below you who doesn't have a job. So that was another major culture shock. Coming here and realising that the English way is to do it yourself. If you've got laundry to do or dishes to do you do it yourself.

I had felt safer in South Africa, I'd felt even more safe on the plane and then getting to England made me feel really safe. Having said that, even a few months into my new life in England I still didn't feel completely relaxed. I just thought, "Maybe there's a bullet with my name on it somewhere." I know it's ridiculous saying that now but that was how I felt.

David had arranged for me to play for the Lashings cricket team. He had built up this team of world superstars to play charity matches all over England and beyond as a sort of Harlem Globetrotters of cricket. However, that first summer I didn't play many games because, as arranged, I was commentating on Zimbabwe's tour to England.

Not long after I got to England I was asked to go to a meeting up at the Sunset and Vine offices to meet the rest of the commentary team. We had this brief meeting where everyone got together – Mark Nicholas, Richie Benaud, the whole team – so we could get acquainted with each other and look forward to the summer series. While I was there Gary Francis, the Channel 4 cricket producer, came over and said that the BBC had asked if I'd be willing to do some stuff for them too, meaning I would do a stint for the TV, then run over to the *Test Match Special* studio and do a bit over there. They synchronised the schedule so that I could go from one to the other. They were both very generous with what they paid, which was great because I was broke.

It was great. I had been interviewed by Mark Nicholas when I took 6 for 19 against England in Cape Town in 2000, so I remembered his face but when I turned up at this meeting and I said, "Is your name Mark Nicholas or Mark Nicholls?" I couldn't remember, and he was not impressed. He was really quite put out, and he was like, "You should know who I am." Of course after getting to know him I can vouch for the fact that Mark's a really nice guy, but it was a bit of an odd introduction.

It was great fun to work with these guys who are so good at their jobs. I mean Mark is so slick; he knows the drill. He gave me some great advice, which was, "Don't speak unless you think you can add something to the picture you are seeing." Richie Benaud told me never to say "we" or "us", that you should always be impartial. So as a commentator I always referred to the Zimbabwean team as "they", or "the Zimbabwean team" even though I had been a player in that side barely three months earlier.

During the matches, after doing a bit of TV for Channel 4, I'd shoot over to the *Test Match Special* studio, which really is just a tiny little room crammed full of people. To be honest, I didn't know what an institution *Test Match Special* was, so I really had no idea what a privilege it was to be in this company.

David was very naughty one time when I first started working on the radio. All the Lashings players were being sponsored by Rover. We all got given free cars for the season, and so before I was going up to commentate on the first match he said to me, "Hey, when you're on the BBC, can you mention that you're really happy that Rover are sponsoring the team?"

Now I didn't know anything about the BBC and advertising, and you have to remember that I come from cricket where we do this sort of thing all the time: you've got your cap on with your sponsor on the front and at the end of the match you come up and say, "Hey, we'd just like to thank the sponsors, so and so." We did that all the time. So I'm on *Test Match Special* live with Jonathan Agnew and I just say, "Oh, by the way, I'd like to thank Rover for sponsoring the Lashings cricket team this summer." And Jonathan Agnew's jaw just dropped, there was silence for a few seconds, and then he said, "And we'd like to thank Henry Olonga for that brief commercial break."

There was much pandemonium as the box was full of people in stitches. And then we went to an announcement or something and the producer, Shilpa Patel, came over with a huge grin on her face and said, "You naughty little ****, you're not supposed to say stuff like that on the BBC." I sheepishly said, "What? What did I say?" I realised then that Folby had set me up. He was a real prankster. He once texted me and said to phone a certain number urgently and ask for Liz. I got through to Buckingham Palace.

Another blooper I remember from *Test Match Special* was when Travis Friend, a big, tall fast bowler for Zimbabwe whom I played with a couple of times, was bowling from the far end at Lord's, and he was bowling quick so that the ball thudded heavily into the willow with an almighty thwack. We call this bowling a 'heavy ball', so I said, "As you can see Travis Friend is bowling from the Top End with some heavy balls." I took me a while to figure out why there were a few sniggers and giggles in the background.

It was a great; it was a blast. Obviously there was loads of cake and

Henry Bloefeld is the most eccentric commentator ever, a great guy who has also worked for Lashings. He's just so quintessentially English, talking about the pigeons and double-decker buses. And his clothes, I mean, who wears a cravat in the day? His accent is to die for and I found myself really taking to him.

It was very odd commentating on my former teammates, and of course bumping into my former employers. Having said that there was nothing really said about what had happened. I mean, I'm an easy-going guy on the whole and I don't hold grudges. What saddened me was that we had lost so many players and we got absolutely slaughtered in that series. The Lord's Test was over in three days, it was the same in Durham. But it was great to see my old teammates and there had been no repercussions for them after what had happened so we got on fine. But I suppose that there was inevitably going to be some distance between us as I was a commentator now and at times I had to be a little critical of them. I interviewed a few of them and they got on well with me but unsurprisingly the team management that I bumped into were aloof.

The sense of nostalgia intensifies as one gets older. It's more nowadays that I miss playing and in a funny way I rue all those wasted years when I could have been playing for my country. But I also remember how I was treated and that sobers me up. But I shall never have the wonderful memories of playing eight seasons for my country be soured by the way it all ended. I lived a dream that few ever fulfil.

The first time I remember meeting up with Andy Flower again after the World Cup was when we both received an award at the Cricket Writers' Association dinner. They offered us the year's award for something: I can't remember exactly what it was called but it was because of what we'd done. So I went to this dinner and we said a few words. Andy was there: we sat at the same table and chatted a little. It was good to see him after a couple of months of turmoil, both of us relaxed and out of harm's way.

A few years ago we got invited to a show in the West End called *Breakfast with Mugabe* and we had a dinner beforehand and that was the first time we really had the chance to chat, about what we'd done and the issues surrounding Zimbabwe and Mugabe still being up to his shenanigans.

Andy and I have spent a few get-togethers in England since, chewing the fat and looking back at what we did. We shared something pretty special together after all, and I also have to take my hat off to Andy for everything he has achieved as coach of England. In Zimbabwe we always knew that Andy Flower is world class in all he does and it comes as no surprise that he has transformed England's fortunes. Our lives have taken us in different directions but I have a new-found respect for him. He has grown as a person.

When I first met him at the start of my international career he was a hard taskmaster who set the highest of standards. Nothing wrong with that but if you made a mistake the expletives would fly. I didn't know what to make of him in those days, but I now realise he is a good husband and father, a loyal friend and a genuinely nice man. The only weak link in the chain when I was playing with him would have been his man management, but he has clearly sorted that out with the passage of time and I am sure that he is a fantastic coach. The players must love him.

Andy is a no-nonsense guy. He is capable of giving somebody a kick up the backside but he can now also sit down with a player and put his arm round them. He always talks sense and he does have a larger-than-life aura about him. Remember that he became the world's top-ranked batsman and when you achieve something like that it opens all sorts of doors for you. He was never going to be remembered as the guy who wore the black armband. It has been different for me, though. I did a bit of commentary and TV punditry but it was never really me. I was never going to be remembered for my bowling figures so I was going to have to find something else to do with my life.

Obviously Andy and I had our differences, but we have come out of it being able to look each other in the eye and say, "Hey, we had a common cause; we put our differences aside and worked together." I am so glad we were able to do that. I remain in his corner and still root for him. And it's not just Andy I have those feelings for. Having met many of the former players I played with for Zimbabwe over the years, some of whom I had disagreements with, the overwhelming feeling I have is that it's good to see them and I wish them well. I understand that, in the heat of the moment, people said things they didn't mean to say.

During that first year in England Andy and I were also made honorary life members of the MCC in acknowledgement of what we had done. Normally it takes about 25 years! I am also an honorary member of the

Lord's Taverners, who do a lot of charity work in the UK. So suddenly I found this whole new world opening up to me. I mean you go to these Lord's Taverners dos and you realise there's a Britain and there's a Britain. There's money and there are circles that are exclusive to certain people and suddenly I found myself moving in these. The relationship between power and sport, and cricket in particular, in this country is an intriguing one, and suddenly that's the world I'm mixing in. I discovered that there is a world where people are privileged just because of the family that they were born into: that was foreign to me. The idea that there are people who will not have to do an inch of work in their lives and they'll be all right, I find that weird; the fact that you can have self-made billionaires, not just millionaires.

As a direct consequence of making a protest for human rights in a relatively poor African country, suddenly I was catapulted into the upper echelons of British society. And during that first summer I had a lot of attention. I was invited to the BBC Sports Personality of the Year show and I met Johnny Wilkinson in the year he won it; I saw Roger Federer there; I was invited to the Royal Television Awards.

Rich people like to hang around cool people, and particularly sports people. So as a result of that I've met presidents, I've met prime ministers, I've met Sir Tim Rice, I've met Chris Martin from Coldplay. You know if I wasn't a cricketer I'd never have met these people. So cricket has opened up lots of doors for me, although I'm not sure I've loved every door I've gone through. In Africa, with pretty much everyone you know where you stand – apart from the ones who are trying to nick your stuff. There are no airs and graces, whereas here there are certain ways that you have to behave depending on where you are and what you are doing. In Zimbabwe, we don't bow or curtsey to anyone.

So as far as a career in media went it was all kind of fun but it wasn't for me, to be honest. I'm a quiet, reserved kind of guy, and so I was quite reluctant to be thrust forward. However, I felt in some ways I had an obligation to go to these things and be seen because I knew it would keep people talking about what we had done. I will not close the door on any future opportunities that come my way but my focus will never be on high-level commentating.

Around this time I also started to get invited to dinners and events where I would get up and tell my story. Of course I'd never done any after-dinner speaking, so to start off I was really bland. I was really serious and people must have left those speeches thinking, "Crumbs, the world is an awful place." I was so dire, but that's all I was doing at the time, going on TV and giving a million and one reasons why Mugabe should be deposed. Then I realised that people want to go to these dinners for a good time, so I guess I became slightly more fickle and made them a bit lighter and more entertaining and incorporated some singing. Of course I still talk about Mugabe and what an evil man he is, but I know I can't make it too serious because that's not what people are really there for.

During my second summer in England, I started playing more regularly for Lashings and when I first joined the team it was incredible. There was Junior Murray, he was the keeper, Richie Richardson, Sherwin Campbell, Stuart Williams, Chris Harris, Alvin Kalliteran, Franklyn Rose, Jimmy Adams. I was surrounded by West Indians. I'd played against some of these guys, of course, and they were very, very welcoming. They were great guys. The West Indians are just the most laid-back, easy-going people.

Of course we never practised: we just rocked up and played. I've always said this in jest but it's kind of true: we always pick opposition that we are likely to beat. I am particularly proud of my 75 scored last year against Sutton Valence Prep School!

We played against schools and clubs and we did get beaten every once in a while. But to be honest we went onto the field and it was relaxed and we had great fun. "Hey guys, let's enjoy it; let's have a blast." Once in a while we'd have guys like Curtley Ambrose and Courtney Walsh coming down, and some of the stories these guys would tell were just enthralling. And there was always a bit of banter between the guys from the different islands as well. It was a great atmosphere.

Once in a while people would bring up the subject of what Andy and I had done. I remember having a conversation with Junior Murray and he was like, "Mugabe's a bad man. How can he do that to his own people?" Funnily enough, the black West Indians have no problem believing that Mugabe is a bad guy. They are black themselves and they've had slavery and everything to deal with, but they can see that a black man can be evil. But some black Africans think Mugabe is unquestionably a hero because the white colonialist is always the bigger enemy. The West Indians were like, "This guy's a madman: how can you destroy such a beautiful country?" I think most of them respected what I did.

Of course, when I was playing for Lashings my bowling was rubbish. The saying about the bowler who doesn't know where the ball is going being dangerous because if he doesn't know then the batsman can't know, well, that explains Henry Olonga's bowling to a tee. I've always been erratic but I've always bowled fast. So when I first came here I was bowling flat out, then I realised that I could probably bowl slower and Lashings would still win most of their games. I did and we still kept winning. So then I thought I'd bowl spin, so I did that. And then in 2009 I thought, "You know what, I'm not going to bowl at all."

It was great when I came but Lashings has diversified since. We got Sachin Tendulkar, some Indians and some Pakistanis, and some English players, and as a result of that it's a kind of serious outfit now. So I'm moving more and more into the background. "You know what, you guys play. I'll do some commentary." So now I mainly commentate for the crowd, and I sing for the corporate guys at lunch, and that's it for me.

I still see David regularly. I will for ever be in his debt, and it was fantastic to see him fully recovered after his cancer went into remission in 2009.

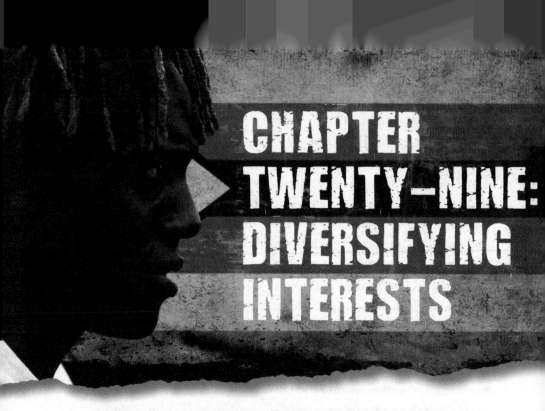

CHAPTER TWENTY-NINE: DIVERSIFYING INTERESTS

Then she appeared and my first words to her were, "You're a lot shorter than I remembered."

My first few months in England were a very reflective time for me, and after all the upheaval in my life I soon came to the realisation I didn't want to live alone and was ready to settle down. I had left a long-term relationship so the question was with whom? And where? And how? Again little did I realise how quickly these questions would be answered.

I remember being shocked when I fired up my laptop for the first time since the World Cup and realised that I had been receiving something like 300 e-mails a day from all around the world. Most of these were from people who wanted to congratulate me on my stance and, as you can imagine, it took a great deal of time to get through them and reply to most of them. I was overwhelmed.

Eventually I came across an e-mail from Tara in Adelaide, asking me how I was. I had her telephone number so I called her and informed her I was in England and safe. It was a nice touch that she sounded so relieved for me. We chatted briefly because yet again I had called her at 5 am in the morning. Tara is definitely not a morning person.

By this time I had received my match fees for appearing in the World Cup so I invited her to England and told her I would pay for her air tickets. We had kept in touch since the first time we had met but I hadn't seen her for eight years.

We aimed to get together in October 2003 but she injured herself playing basketball and had to have her knee reconstructed so couldn't come to England. Bizarrely enough, at the same time as her operation was due to happen, I ended up in hospital as well. I'd had problems with one of my knees and it was troubling me while I was bowling. I had fortuitously met an anaesthetist at Lord's one day while I was doing some TV commentary and asked whether he knew of a surgeon who might be able to help. It turned out that he had a friend who was a knee specialist and before I knew it I was being operated on.

I was on my back for weeks, during which time David Folb was a champion, looking after me and ensuring that my recovery went as planned. There was also a couple in the complex called Phil and Debbie Dickman who were just amazing in making meals for me and being very hospitable.

Because we were both laid up, so to speak, Tara and I spent hours talking to each other on the phone and we discussed her coming to England in December instead. She figured she wasn't going to be able to play tennis that summer, so why not? Plus, she wasn't going to look a gift horse in the mouth if I was buying the tickets. While we were planning her trip over something started to happen that took us both by surprise really. Each day I started to look forward to my chat with Tara.

We discovered we were both single so we talked about what we were both looking for in a lifetime partner. Remember, we had been friends for eight years and felt very comfortable discussing the deeper issues in life with each other. However, up until now we had only had very brief conversations so it was great to be able to talk freely for hours as we had done when we first met.

She found me funny and she always laughed at my corny jokes. I cannot put my finger on the exact time but between October and December of 2003 I had fallen in love with her. So the trip was organised and I couldn't wait to meet this wonderful woman whom I hadn't seen in eight years again. What would she look like after all these years? Any wrinkles yet? Long hair? I had seen the photos but seeing the real thing was going to be great.

My sister Yolande came with me to the airport and, while we were waiting for her arrival, I wasn't sure if I would easily spot her in the crowd at Terminal 3. Then she appeared and my first words to her were, "You're a lot shorter than I remembered." I don't know what it is with me and airports but I always imagine people differently.

We had a great time visiting the usual tourist destinations in London and before long we decided to get married. We flew to Kenya, where I introduced her to my family and told them we planned to get married in April 2004. The wedding plans kicked into full swing and I flew out to Australia two weeks before the wedding to meet Des and Ros, my future in-laws, for the first time. Everything had happened very quickly and most of it over the phone so I hadn't even met the rest of Tara's family yet. I was welcomed with open arms by them all.

Tara has three siblings. Tiffany and Michelene her sisters and a brother called Marcus. Tiffany is married to Grant and they have four children while Marcus is married to Kirsten and they have one daughter.

We had a wonderful wedding in Adelaide and then headed off to Mauritius for our honeymoon, before returning to Kenya in May for another wedding celebration for my side of the family.

We had our reception in the Carnivore Restaurant in Nairobi. It is famous for serving exotic meats, such as crocodile, eland and giraffe, although they gave us beef and rice! It is like going to Paris and not seeing the Eiffel Tower. My mother-in-law Ros had her handbag stolen, which put a dampener on proceedings and we had a bunch of uninvited photographers following us around so it felt like we were being chased by the paparazzi!

All in all, though, we had a great time and a truly amazing African celebration. My dad said a few words, as did Mum, Ma G and Tara's folks.

Tony Brennan, the guy from the Foreign Office who played such a part in helping me to get to England, also came to the wedding, which I found very touching indeed. He is a close friend to this day.

Since getting married, Eliud Masakhalia has kept in touch with me. He is related to me in some way but I am not certain how – I think he's a cousin. Eliud has special needs and he is a fun guy. When we first arrived in Kenya he kept asking me if I would buy him a new camera because his was falling to pieces. It had cost us a lot of money to get to Kenya and then we had to pay for the reception so we didn't have any spare cash and it remains one of my regrets that I wasn't able to replace his camera.

We will help him out at some stage in the future. He still e-mails every other day, asking how we are, telling us about the weather and wondering when we are next going out to see him. He ends every e-mail by asking me to send him some money. It makes me smile. I once sent him a bag full of casual clothes that we had lying around and he said, "Thank you but next time send me office clothes!"

As my new life in England has unfolded, more and more I have found myself drawn away from cricket and leaning towards my music and past interests. When I first arrived in England I had been approached by a group of men who had bought an old recording studio from Sony and said they wanted to work with me. I recorded *You'll Never Walk Alone* for them but nothing came of it. Then I was asked to do a showcase, which means you perform live in front of selected industry people, which was attended by several record company bigwigs. At the end of it, the guy from Universal told me he loved my voice and said he was going to sign me, but nothing came of that either. Through my minimal experience in that world I have come to realise that there are many unscrupulous individuals in the music industry.

But my future career needed to offer some stability if I were to settle down to life after cricket. I was used to being dropped by cricket teams and had learnt to live with disappointments, so I made up my mind that I was going to continue enjoying my music and the way to do it was to record an album myself, on my own terms. Most successful musicians and movie stars have a story to tell of bursting their guts for years before finally getting the break their talent deserved and I thought that if they could do it then so could I.

I got together with Andy Wright, who is a producer and quickly realised that this guy knew what he was doing. I loved what he could do with music. You may know the name Barrington Pheloung – he composed the *Inspector Morse* music and I had also worked with him – and he, too, told me that he thought I had the potential to go far in the music industry.

It was one thing having all these people tell me how far they thought I could go, but nothing was happening for me. I wasn't sure I would ever get round to releasing an album but thanks to a kind gentleman and his generosity I was able to make this dream come true. I was playing in a match for Michael Parkinson, the famous interviewer, at his Maidenhead and Bray Cricket Club's annual day. I sat down for lunch next to a lovely elderly gentleman who introduced himself as Ron. We got chatting, as you do, and he was asking me what I was doing now that I had left international cricket. I told him about my singing and after-dinner speaking and he kindly said that if there was anything he could do to help me, all I had to do was say the word.

He continued to chat with Tara while I took to the field and he reiterated to her that if there was anything he could do to just let him know. She sat there thinking to herself, "What a really sweet guy but unless you are well off there's nothing that you can really do. Henry wants to release an album but we don't have the finances to do it." However, she was too embarrassed to say this out loud.

At some point this man left the table to get another drink, leaving Tara with the other guests. One of them said to her, "Do you know who that is?", to which she of course replied, "Sorry, I have no idea." "That is Sir Ron Brierley, only one of the richest men you will ever meet. If he is offering you help, I'd take it."

When Sir Ron returned he took Tara to one side and asked what I was up to. (He had had a few by now and couldn't remember that he had already asked this question.) She explained that I wanted to record an album so he asked her for her e-mail address and she wrote it down for him. We honestly didn't think we would hear from him again but then, out of the blue several months later, Tara got an e-mail from Sir Ron in which he said, "Hi Tara. I found your e-mail address on a piece of paper and

I've got to be honest and admit that I haven't a clue why you gave it to me. Could you tell me why?"

I was a bit reluctant to ask him for help but Tara said, "What have we got to lose by asking?" She reminded him that I was looking for assistance to make an album and he agreed to give us a contribution of a few thousand pounds. That's one up for the wife!

I had already released a CD in Zimbabwe, and thanks to Sir Ron I now had the opportunity to finally get to work on this album in England. A few more fantastic people chipped in to help pay for the project. Basil Sellers, the wonderful philanthropist and entrepreneur, gave us £5,000 as a gift, Gary Pankhurst, a Lashings sponsor, also gave us £5,000 in return for a family portrait I painted and we raised the rest. We begged and borrowed and eventually got together with Robbie Bronnimann, a record producer who has worked with Howard Jones, among others, and ended up recording the album. It cost me quite a lot to make, but we finished up with a quality album. Technology has now reached the point where it is possible to make an album for a lot less but my problem is that I can't play the instruments, so I will always have to pay for musicians.

We called the album *Aurelia*. It means 'chrysalis' but everyone uses that, not to mention the fact there is a record label with that name. The significance of this was that this album was symbolic of my changing state, my metamorphosis from a cricketer into a singer.

As my new life has taken shape I have decided to go back to the things that I enjoyed at school. I believe that most people are born with unique capabilities that no one else will ever have, no matter how hard they try. Some people are just born without co-ordination and it's not their fault but they will always struggle to run or succeed at any form of athletic pursuit, although with some work they can. There are also people who are born with gifts that they never discover. The only reason I can sing is because I've tried it. I first attempted it at school, was encouraged by teachers and improved. I believe that it is vital that parents, teachers and mentors guide young people in the right direction so that they have the best possible chance to discover whatever gifts they may have.

There is a saying that the grave is the richest place because in the grave you will find unfulfilled potential in many people, and that is true. Everybody has a gift; unfortunately, many people never discover what that gift might be. There are those who try to sing and never sound right – the auditions for *The X Factor* and *Britain's Got Talent* prove that.

I have also been able to turn my hand to public speaking and have found it relatively easy to keep an audience captivated. I know that I have an unusual story to tell but that is only part of it – you need to find a way to get the audience on your side from the second you open your mouth. Often it is being able to tell the right joke. If you can raise a smile, half the battle has already been won. And when you are telling a story as often as I have told mine, you need to find a way to keep it fresh.

As the road to rebuilding has been long for me I have had to learn to not see limitations in life. I just try something and believe that if I work hard enough I will somehow get to know how to do it. One of my regrets is that I have never learned how to play a musical instrument. Maybe if I tried I would succeed but my fingers are so messed up from sport I think I might struggle.

Shortly after arriving in England I bought a Minolta camera which took stills and also allowed me to take video. I hadn't realised just how much I had missed taking pictures and quickly got back into it. I then bought myself a high-end camera that allowed me to do just about anything I wanted. I fell in love with digital photography and discovered the joys of interchangeable lenses, started experimenting and soon realised that I enjoyed film and video-making and that that was another potential way to earn some money.

I also tried to develop my painting. I painted the likes of Richie Benaud and Wasim Akram, but then I discovered that famous cricketers wanted me to pay them if I was going to ask them to sit for me and I couldn't afford that so quickly had to abandon that avenue. Image rights have become a very complicated and lucrative area. I now do the odd commission.

There is one episode in my life that brought it home to me that I was now living in England and what a very odd turn my life had taken. The Lashings World XI had been invited to take part in the De Beers cricket day. De Beers, of course, are the world leaders in diamonds. The cricket was played at Wormsley, a beautiful ground set in the fabulous Buckinghamshire estate of the late John Paul Getty.

DIVERSIFYING INTERESTS

I knew little of De Beers but at the interval from the cricket we joined them for lunch in a marquee packed with rich and powerful people. There was Sol Kerzner, who was involved in putting together the Sun City resort in South Africa and is a fabulously wealthy man, along with his wife, who was wearing a stunning diamond necklace. It was a different world to the one I inhabited – some people even arrived by helicopter.

Sitting across the table was a woman with an American accent who introduced herself to me as Lynn. Now, I have met prime ministers, presidents and the Queen at the 1999 World Cup and I always take people at face value. I have always shown the right amount of decorum but normally I am not enamoured by wealth or power *per se*. With my experiences in Africa I believe good character is far more appealing. However, this was the richest gathering I had ever seen so it got my attention.

Anyway, Lynn turned out to be Lady Lynn Forester de Rothschild. She was an extremely bubbly woman who does a great deal of work for charity. This particular cricket day was in aid of the Africa Foundation which raises money to help poor children in Africa and I was persuaded to get up on stage and sing *Someone for Me* and *Nessum Dorma*. There was also a charity auction and one of the lots was a cricket bat signed by all the Lashings players – in less than a minute it had been sold for £10,000. Wow!

When I got back to the table I was the centre of attention as no one had expected me to get up and sing as I had, including a few of my teammates! Lady de Rothschild asked if I ever sang at parties and when I told her that I did she asked for my e-mail address. As we were about to leave, a striking gentleman took me by the hand and told me that he admired the stance I had taken at the World Cup, handed me his business card and told me to stay in touch. He was Sir Evelyn Robert de Rothschild.

To be honest, I didn't actually know who the de Rothschilds were so when I got home I switched on my computer and did a little bit of research and I was blown away for the second time that day! I realised that cricket can open doors for you, but I did not expect to hear from them again. I was sure they were just being polite.

The cricket season continued and we played several more matches. Then I unexpectedly received an e-mail from Lady de Rothschild, telling me she was putting on a Christmas party and asking whether I would come along and a sing a song for them. Of course I agreed. I sang *Someone for Me* and they asked me to do some more but I had only burnt the music for that one song onto a CD so I couldn't sing anything else. D'oh!

Once again, the room was full of influential people including foreign royalty, Bob Geldof, Peter Mandelson, Cherie Blair and Howard Stringer of Sony. I had an enjoyable conversation with Stringer because I am a Sony nut and love their stuff. At the time, Will Smith was the face of Sony and I made a light-hearted pitch to join him, but Stringer was unimpressed. He did, however, join me and perform as my backing singer when we did the carols at the end of the dinner. Imagine having the CEO of Sony as back-up! It was the biggest gig of my life because of the company I was performing for and the fact that Sting had performed there the previous year.

But I remember the overwhelming feeling I was left with that evening was one that I didn't belong, that I didn't quite make the grade amongst the crème de la crème of the business, political and entertainment worlds. I felt out of place and so much lower class in an odd way, even out of my depth. This was foreign territory for me. I had never felt that as a cricketer, because I felt I held my own because of what I had achieved in the game. But now I had no such credentials. I felt like a nobody.

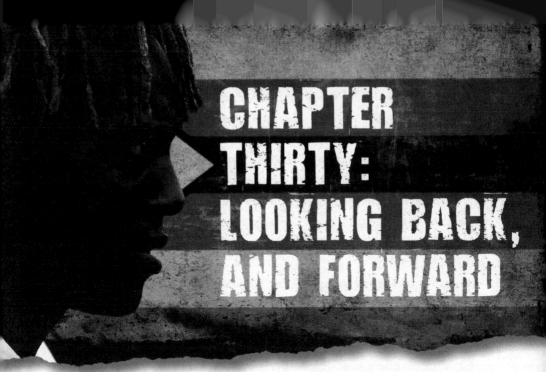

CHAPTER THIRTY: LOOKING BACK, AND FORWARD

I sweated for the country, I bled for it, and now they don't even class me as a citizen. Instead I am a traitor.

From the moment I walked out onto the cricket pitch in Harare in February 2003 wearing a black armband made from insulating tape, the feeling of all this being surreal has never left me. Ever since that moment I have felt like I am in some kind of dream world. But when will I wake up? The only way I can explain it is by saying it's like being in your own movie.

But every word I have written has really happened and I have witnessed it with my own eyes. After that moment everything happened so fast. I can't believe I have been in England more than seven years. I sometimes fail to grasp that I'm not an international cricketer any more. But then suddenly this rollercoaster took off and it hasn't stopped. The way the whole thing has played out, I sometimes find myself metaphorically pinching myself, saying, "Did I really do that?"

In an ironic twist, the team that I played most of my career with was disbanded. Around about May 2004, a clique of 15 white players protested against the sacking of Heath Streak, who was still captain at the time, by refusing to play. Streak had presented a list of demands such as the acknowledgement of alleged malpractices by the ZCU and also a change in the selection panel. As a result of the strike action all the striking players were found to be in breach of contract and unceremoniously fired.

When this happened they issued a brief statement declaring, "Through our years of service and dedication we feel we have been an example of a successful and multiracial team. Despite some perceptions, we have proven time and time again that Zimbabweans of all colours can work together and achieve excellence, as shown in our last two World Cups. As patriotic citizens of the country we love, we still hope a solution will be achieved and that we can soon return to playing for Zimbabwe."

The group then hastily formed a team that would tour the UK to raise money for their legal bills and for a couple of charities. They named themselves the 'Red Lions', a reference to an exclusive bar at the Harare Sports Club frequented by white patrons. It wasn't segregated but you certainly got strange looks if you were not white and you went to drink there so it was an ill-advised name to choose.

The Red Lions played against Lashings at Wimbledon Cricket Club and although it was good to see my old teammates again I couldn't help but think that some of them hadn't changed much from the guys I had experienced friction with. But I realised that I had changed a bit. I wasn't angry with them, nor was I pleased at how they had been treated.

After this, Zimbabwe cricket began the long road back to being competitive again on the international stage. With the recent involvement of former international players, it now appears that it is in good hands, with players like Heath Streak, David Houghton, Alistair Campbell and others returning in administrative and coaching roles.

Many of the young players I worked with at Takashinga have progressed in their careers and have turned into fine cricketers, albeit initially lacking in experience after the rebels were ousted. Their progression has had little to do with my personal involvement but with respect to Stephen Mangongo, irrespective of what I feel about him and his ways, he has been phenomenal in producing international-class players. Prosper Utesya and Taibu have both captained the national side and many other players have come through like Elton Chigumbura, Hamilton Masakadza and Stuart Matsikenyeri. The team was initially all black but over time the integration of young white players like Brendan Taylor, Charles Coventry and others has given the side more balance. They are now a lot more competitive and have continued the Zimbabwean tradition of recording giant-slaying performances, the most famous being the victory over Australia in the 2007 Twenty20 World Cup.

Of course, I sometimes wonder what my life would be like if I had not decided to make the protest, but I don't know that I'd choose that life over what I've got now. As much as this life does at times feel like a dream world, I have never regretted what I did. Seven years on I think I am slightly wiser. I am slightly less rebellious, but I still feel strongly about all the issues, just more mellow in expressing them.

But the consequences of that single day in 2001 are with me all the time in my life. I am very much in limbo as a write this because in 2006 my passport expired which means that I can't travel outside the UK.

When my passport ran out I went to the Zimbabwean embassy to renew it only for them to drop the bombshell that in 2001 a bill had been passed in parliament that declared that anybody who was born or fathered by a person from outside the country – remember I was born in Zambia and my dad was Kenyan – had to renounce any other claims to citizenship that they could possibly hold in order to vote or to get a passport. I think they did it to stop people in the diaspora or people who were British descendents trying to vote against Mugabe, mostly white people who had a claim to external citizenship.

It also meant that many white Zimbabweans did not register to vote because it would mean giving up on any dual citizenship they might have. I mean, you're not going to renounce your British citizenship are you, in case you need to get out or you need help? Anyway, the crazy thing is that I did all this when I decided to play cricket for Zimbabwe. I signed all the paperwork, but many months later I was supposed to have taken that paperwork to the citizenship office and say, "Here's my proof, there you go," and get properly registered. But I didn't. So when I went to the passport office to renew my passport in 2006 they said, "Sorry, Mr Olonga, I'm afraid you don't come up on our database as a citizen."

"But here's my certificate of citizenship," I said. "I renounced all other nationalities, signed the oath of allegiance to Zimbabwe. I represented the country at cricket for a number of years. Why is that not enough?"

"No, no, no, there was a bill passed in Parliament. What you have to do Mr Olonga is you have to go back to Zimbabwe, do this process, and then we will ratify your citizenship."

So basically, at this point in time, in their eyes I am not a citizen of Zimbabwe, and the only way of becoming one is to go back home to regularise it. Not likely.

If I went back to Zimbabwe now I haven't a clue what would happen. I can't second-guess that. I know of people who have been critical of the government who have gone back and had no problems, and I have heard of some people who have had the opposite experience. There was a guy called Roy Bennett who was an MP, a white man, who was imprisoned for about a year for pushing over another MP in Parliament. This guy he pushed was taunting him, saying his ancestors were murderers, so he pushed this guy down in anger and Parliament voted to send him to prison. It was unprecedented. It was not a court – they didn't have the authority to do that – but it's Zimbabwe so they did what they wanted. He went to jail, got released a year or so later, came to England, went to South Africa, and then went back to the country and the last I heard they were framing him for treason. What happens to you probably depends who you have annoyed along the way.

So it's unpredictable what would happen to me. But because of what I did, with Mugabe still being in charge and the youth militia still being in force and constant stories of political abuses going on, I don't think it would be wise for me to go back.

Therefore, I'm not really a citizen of anywhere: I am by their admission stateless. I've been in the UK quite a while now, but I haven't qualified for citizenship yet and that's another complicated story. I came here on a work permit for Lashings, Channel 4 and the BBC, but it was quite restrictive because if your work permit says you can play for Lashings then you cannot play for Yorkshire, not that they ever asked me. I couldn't paint for a living, sing or do public speaking.

I went to see an immigration consultant. I said, "Listen mate, I find this really restricting. How can I do the things I really enjoy doing?" And he said, "You're married to an Australian. If she applies for an ancestry visa and settles here, then if you go on that visa as her dependant you can do what you like." And I said, "Really?"

So we did that, but what we didn't know was that by doing that, any time that I'd spent in the UK prior to us changing my status didn't count any more towards getting citizenship. I'd spent nearly three years here up to that point. But in the eyes of British immigration as soon as I went onto Tara's visa I started from scratch. If I'd stayed on the work permit I could have applied to become a British citizen two years ago. Now it will be another three years before I can apply to be a citizen, in 2013. It would have been nice if someone had told us.

So, not being a citizen of any country, and not being able to travel anywhere outside the UK, only adds to my sense of living this unreal existence. So I have this constant sense of not belonging and all this being rather weird. I am a guy who played cricket for eight years of his life. Cricket is a traveller's game: you are travelling all the time. England is a vast place and there are places I've still to discover, but I've travelled extensively here and now I want to go abroad, I want to be able to go on holiday. I want to go to Kenya and see my family.

So the decision I made at the 2003 World Cup still lives with me every second of every day. I don't let it get to me and I get on with my life, and of course what I did has opened up doors that would never have been opened for me otherwise. I have no argument there. I am not the kind of guy to sit round and mope. I have built a sound studio; I have got into amateur filmmaking; I'm doing a lot of public speaking on the circuit. I'm out there doing my thing.

It has stretched me. It has forced me to consider other things and to change as a person in a good way. It has made me grow up. The change of careers stretched me in a way that was very beneficial, pushing me to my limit and forcing me to find innovative ways to make a living. That's all good, and now I'm 34 I think I have grown up into a man. I was a boy for most of my 20s.

I often think about that poem *If* by Rudyard Kipling and I would say that my moment of realising "now you become a man my son" was probably on the day we walked out onto the field with those armbands. Once that decision was made there was no place for a wuss or a wimp. I had to face the music, not back down or shy away. It was the moment I grew up. My life before was very insular. As a cricketer your world revolves around hotels, getting on the coach, going to the practice ground, going home, thinking about the next game and playing. That's it. And on your off days you go sightseeing. There is a whole big, wide world out there which you are insulated from. Doing what we did enabled me to walk in other people's shoes for the first time, to consider what's happening out there.

I have chosen to never let myself have a victim mentality. I hope that is clear. In most cases I have spoken honestly about things that have happened to me but the buck stops with me. I have always had a choice in how to respond to life's challenges and no one held a gun to my head to do the protest. OK, they did when they carjacked!

If you speak to the majority of cricketers on political issues, issues that are outside of sport, they might have an opinion but generally they are not going to be activists. Once in a while you get the odd Steve Harmison who says, "I don't want to go on this tour because of A, B, C and D". But the majority of them just want to play cricket and their battles revolve around staying in the team, getting wickets or getting runs, staying fit and trying to juggle all that, in short trying to protect that cosy, insulated world they have earned for themselves. And there is absolutely nothing inherently wrong with that. But getting to a place where I was willing to lay it all on the table and see the bigger issues than just wickets and runs was a huge moment of reckoning for me. In a moment in time I recognised and realised that there are deeper issues to life than entertainment, which is essentially what sport is.

Looking at Zimbabwe now, and the fact that the nonsense is still going on, we did the right thing. Zimbabwe has grown worse and worse and challenging this evil dictator who was going to destroy his country, I still believe was the right thing to do. In 2009 the inflation rate in Zimbabwe reached into the millions; the exchange rate to one British pound was into the trillions. The government had gone on to do crazy things since our protest as well, such as bulldozing tens of thousands of people's houses down. If I had the opportunity I would do the protest again because as long as there are wicked things going on in the world there need to be people who are prepared to stand up and confront the perpetrators.

Looking at it seven years on, we were just cricket players who had a platform: we chose to use it for the common good to challenge an evil dictator. Andy and I didn't change the country, we're both honest about that. We didn't change the world. I am certain that we would all like to think that if we saw somebody trapped in a burning car that we would forget all about our own safety and try to save that person, but until we are put in that position none of us know what we would do. Would we put our own lives at risk to try to save a total stranger? I hope I will.

We were always realistic. We knew what we were going to do was not going to solve Zimbabwe's problems overnight. We didn't think we'd end Mugabe's rule, but you have an option in life. You can plough along minding your own business, never criticising, never standing up to things, or you can make an effort. We made an effort. What we did probably had about the same effect as shooting rubber darts at an elephant. You're not going to hurt it, but maybe you'll at least distract him for a few minutes so he stops trampling on the poor guy who is under his feet.

But there is no doubt that there are a lot of people who know more about what is going on in Zimbabwe as a direct result of what we did, and of reading this book. That was a big part of what we hoped to achieve. We got the word out, and maybe as a result people have made donations to victims of Mugabe, or put pressure on their politicians, the UN or whatever. We were hoping it would create some momentum. But even if that didn't happen, it doesn't detract from the fact that we still believe in what we stood for. It was a good cause, it's still a good cause and it still exists: the needs are still there.

What are my hopes for Zimbabwe? I could get all flowery and say I dream of a land with no tyranny where everyone is free. I could do my *Braveheart* thing. But to be honest we can't help but hope we can get away from what we have now and at least go towards a truly democratic and free Zimbabwe. I would love to see a country where the people can vote for the leader they want to have in power. It's not going to happen until Mugabe is gone, I suspect.

People want to live in peace and they want to be able to work and make a good life for themselves. It's not a huge amount to ask. In an ideal world, the people of Zimbabwe would have a leadership that allowed them to enjoy these things. Tyrants such as Robert Mugabe are self-serving. They thrive on power, but their people suffer. In an ideal Zimbabwe you would have good leaders, but that's just for starters. If there were adequate health-care and schooling, enough jobs to go round and a stable economy, most people wouldn't mind if Mugabe were worth millions. He may well be worth far more than that and the country is in turmoil.

Freedom of speech? Newspapers that challenged him had their print-ing presses destroyed and as for television, well, there are a couple of government-run stations. Journalists critical of the regime never seem to last. Even now, most Zimbabweans probably have no idea what I did, or what became of me, although with the Internet people certainly have access to information that was previously hidden.

People ask if I would ever like to get involved in politics, but the answer is a resounding "No". I have a total disdain for Zimbabwean politicians. Many of them are wonderful orators, able to hold the masses in the palms of their hands, but behind closed doors some of these men and women have the most wicked intentions. I was taught in high school that heroes of the liberation were all icons to be exalted without question. We weren't told about the murders, the torture and the vote rigging. Mugabe stands up and tells his people that it is the fault of Great Britain and the USA that they are suffering, and why would the people not believe him? But discern-ing students of history know otherwise.

One of the hopes I have is that the young people of Zimbabwe will have a future. Because one of the things that Mugabe has done is robbed them of that, especially these kids in the youth militia. What do they have? And the damage done to them and the people who are brutalised by them is enormous. They will require counselling for years to come to return to normality.

This is not what Mugabe originally fought for, surely? He fought against the white oppressors that he so loathes and always goes on and on about. But what was he fighting for in the end? His own personal wealth? What is that all about? If that was it then he has betrayed the people of Zimbabwe and the people who call him a hero are misguided and uninformed.

People who fight for liberation are fighting for others. Mugabe fought in a war and is regarded as a hero, but how can he be a hero if he did it for himself and his cronies? That to me is the saddest thing. So my hope for Zimbabwe is that we get selfless leaders, people who genuinely want to serve the country. And when Mugabe goes maybe there will be a chance for that. But unfortunately the African political landscape is littered with people who started with good intentions and then got corrupted. Enough is enough. How many dictators have gone willingly in Africa? Very few. They've either had to be deposed or assassinated. It's the same with Mugabe. It seems like we're just going to have to wait for him to die.

I have met Mugabe twice. The first time it was an honour, but by the time I was shaking his hand for a second time I had done my research and was beginning to realise he was actually pretty dodgy. Thankfully not all politicians are corrupted by power. Of course there are exceptions. David Coltart is such a man, as he got involved in Zimbabwean politics because he wanted to make a difference for the right reasons. Sadly, there aren't too many like him. I have plenty of first-hand experience of politicians because they like to hang around sportsmen, and when you get up close and personal with these people they often let their guard down, even if only for a second or two, and you get to see the real person. Because of my reservations I could never get involved myself.

People tell me that sport and politics should never mix and while I would generally agree with that, I would also say that had I not been in the position I was within the Zimbabwe cricket team then I could never have made my protest in front of such a huge global audience. I have no regrets about that, although I sure did inadvertently annoy a few people with whom I would have liked to have maintained a good relationship.

I wonder about the ways that people could help. Perhaps, instead of spending £50 on a concert at Wembley, wouldn't that money be better spent helping a child in a developing country? I feel that what I am doing with my life now makes more of a difference, and is far more worthwhile, than what I did on any cricket field. Zimbabweans felt pride when we won cricket matches, and so did I, but it never really had an eternal impact.

Since arriving in England I have had the opportunity to tell my story to thousands, perhaps hundreds of thousands of people, and I would hope that some of these people have been sufficiently moved to tell others about what has been going on in Zimbabwe and what is still happening today. I have this naive belief that the more people who know, the greater the chance that something might be done to bring it all to an end. But I know that awareness is just part of the solution. It's really the politicians who ought to make things happen.

I am lucky that I am fulfilled by my faith, my belief in God. Telling people my story, telling them about my faith is important to me. I put my body on the line for Zimbabwe, and I know that many people would kill to play for their country. I never want to give the impression that bowling for my country wasn't fulfilling, but when you set it against speaking up for the widow and the orphan, speaking against the murderous torture of innocent people, speaking against unborn babies being ripped from their mothers' wombs and compare it to taking a red cricket ball and hurtling it at a piece of wood it does put things into perspective.

Having said that, obviously it would have been nice to do this without having to leave the country to save my life. As I get older and get more philosophical I can't deny that I look at the physical cost I have paid, what it has meant for my life

Knowing that you cannot go home is not an easy thing to live with. Zimbabwe is a beautiful country and of course there are times when I miss it, but my life is in England now and if I am going to go anywhere else in the future it is more likely that Tara and I will head to Australia to live. I did what I did because I love Zimbabwe, but now my life has moved on. Maybe Zimbabwe hasn't changed but I have. No longer am I a self-centred cricketer. I felt that I had to stand up and be counted to learn some lessons about myself as well and boy have I learnt them well. Until that happens, you don't really know what sort of person you are.

LOOKING BACK, AND FORWARD

I get asked a lot if I have forgiven Robert Mugabe for what he did to me. The truth is that he didn't do anything directly to me that I should forgive him for. I took my own destiny into my own hands. Yes, the machinery of his state made life difficult for me after I'd made my protest but I am never going to judge him: that is for a greater power than me.

What I see, however, is a man who had the potential to do so much good with his life but failed to do so. Here's a man who could have brought a country together but instead he has divided it, and that is the saddest chapter of the whole story. None of us would have had to protest if only Zimbabwe had had a good leader. I know many will disagree with me. I am not claiming his life has failed to achieve good. The evil has simply overtaken the good.

I despise what he has done with his life and the cruelty he has introduced into the lives of people who were not fighting him. He has committed some dreadful sins and he must pay for them. There must be justice and there will be, in this life or in the next.

Mugabe is an old man, well into his 80s. When you are in the evening of your life, perhaps that is the time to think of a long-term legacy. Surely as the grandfather of the nation the greatest legacy he could have left would have been to teach children to appreciate different people from different backgrounds and cultures; instead, he has done precisely the opposite. His story could have been so very different.

What does the future hold for me? I will continue to develop my videos, films, music, photographs and painting. I will continue to speak to people who would care to invite me to talk to them. Settling down and beginning a family will definitely be on the radar soon.

Despite everything, I am more fulfilled now than I have ever been. The thing that makes me tick is being busy, doing lots of different things. I need variety in my life and like meeting different people and visiting different places.

Do I see myself ever going home? I will never rule it out. I love Zimbabwe. But right now I honestly don't know. I'd love to go back but it's not as simple as that. Never mind the question of whether I could go back: I have a wife now who is Australian; she has family there; we want to start a family. So until I've sorted out my passport I don't know.

BLOOD, SWEAT AND TREASON

I represented Zimbabwe at cricket for eight years. I bled for that country. I had operations to keep playing cricket for Zimbabwe. Blood, sweat and treason. I remember fingernails falling off and continuing to play in agony, grass burns bleeding in the shower. OK, I didn't get shot but I sweated for the country, I bled for it, and now they don't even class me as a citizen. Instead I am a traitor.

In 2006 I wrote a song with my friend Bruce Izzett. It was self-released on the album *Aurelia* and is called *Rise Again*. The words sum up my feelings for Zimbabwe.

> *In your world of jewels, champagne and wine*
> *Your wandering feet have crossed the line*
> *The peace you swore now changed to war*
> *What do you bully these people for?*
>
> *In your mind's delusion you were never wrong*
> *An illusion you gave of being super-strong*
> *But look at the tyrant that you've become*
> *Just fighting people whose strength is gone*
>
> *For one day they will rise again*
> *Above the emptiness and shame*
> *With dignity restored once more*
> *As your oppression is here no more*
>
> *So you sought to kill their biggest dreams*
> *Filling their world with so much misery*
> *But the beach of life will turn this man,*
> *Into a single grain of sand*
>
> *With one heart that's strong the objective's clear*
> *We're casting away this paralysing fear*
> *The clouds will roll on and the sun will shine*
> *We'll find freedom at the break of dawn*

LOOKING BACK, AND FORWARD

For one day they will rise again
Above the emptiness and shame
With dignity restored once more
As your oppression is here no more

I am at peace that I did the right thing. I often wonder what goes through Mugabe's head when he lies in bed at night. Is he tormented by his decisions at all? I know that I don't toss and turn or wonder what is to become of me any more.